# COMPUTING IN THE SOCIAL SCIENCES

## AND HUMANITIES

# Computing

# in the

# Social Sciences

# and Humanities

EDITED BY

ORVILLE VERNON BURTON

**UNIVERSITY OF ILLINOIS PRESS**

Urbana and Chicago

© 2002 by the Board of Trustees
of the University of Illinois
All rights reserved
Manufactured in the United States of America
C 5 4 3 2 1
♾ This book is printed on acid-free paper.

Minimum system requirements for the *Wayfarer* CD-ROM that
accompanies this book: 32 MB available RAM; CD-ROM drive (4x);
256-color monitor and sound capability for some articles and
programs; Macintosh®: System 8.5; Windows®: Intel Pentium®
processor (or equivalent) running Windows® 95 or Windows NT® 4.0

Library of Congress Cataloging-in-Publication Data
Computing in the social sciences and humanities /
edited by Orville Vernon Burton.
p.   cm.
Includes bibliographical references and index.
ISBN 0-252-02685-3
1. Social sciences—Data processing. 2. Humanities—Data processing.
I. Burton, Orville Vernon.
H61.3.C654      2002
300'.285—dc21      2001001491

# Contents

# Acknowledgments

This project grew out of my long association with the National Center for Supercomputing Applications (NCSA) at the University of Illinois at Champaign-Urbana. When Larry Smarr founded NCSA, his vision was broad enough to include the social sciences, humanities, and fine arts. We invited the Social Science Computing Association to meet at NCSA and explore the possibilities for using computers in social science and humanities research. Keith Frazier and Shirley Shore made that conference run smoothly. Melanie Loots has continued to support this project and found Frank Baker to help us with the CD-ROM that accompanies this book. Frank constructed a brilliant design for *Wayfarer: Charting Advances in Social Science and Humanities Computing*. He is simply the best hypermedia communications specialist at NCSA.

Terence Finnegan did a lion's share of the work organizing the successful Conference on Computing in the Social Sciences at NCSA. David Herr has done more than anyone—except maybe Frank—to make *Wayfarer* a reality and has put much effort and time into helping me with this book. I am honored to have had some part in Terence's and David's doctoral work at the University of Illinois and am very proud to be a coeditor of *Wayfarer* with these two historians. Thanks also go to Ian Binnington and Masatomo Ayabe for their excellent help on this project. I also appreciate the support of the University of Illinois Research Board.

I have enjoyed getting to know the splendid people at the University of Illinois Press. David M. Perkins, director of marketing, understands the world of books and the world of business. I also appreciate the excellent work of marketing copywriter Laurie Matheson as well as the superb copyediting of

Carol Peschke. Paul Arroyo, the Press's electronic publisher, provided sound advice on the development of *Wayfarer,* and Theresa L. Sears, the managing editor, moved the book through the production process with efficiency and good humor.

I owe a special debt of gratitude to the legendary Richard L. Wentworth. When we began this project, Dick was director of the University of Illinois Press; he has since retired from that position, but fortunately for his authors he remains active with the Press. His wisdom and guidance throughout this project have been much appreciated. He is a great editor and better friend.

Last but certainly not least, I appreciate the encouragement of Georganne Burton as well as her determination that I eradicate jargon from the book. This book is dedicated with love to our daughter, Morgan, from whom I am always learning about computers.

COMPUTING IN THE SOCIAL SCIENCES

AND HUMANITIES

ORVILLE VERNON BURTON

# Introduction:
# The Renaissance

**Just as the mechanical clock** is the metaphor for the early modern period and the steam engine represents the industrial revolution, the computer is the symbol of our age.[1] Computers affect almost every aspect of our lives, and the social sciences and humanities are no exception. Computers have changed the way scholars research, write, and teach.

The idea for this book began in 1993 at the Conference on Computing in the Social Sciences (CSS93) held at the Beckman Institute for Advanced Science and Technology and sponsored by the National Center for Supercomputing Applications (NCSA) at the University of Illinois at Urbana-Champaign (UIUC). NCSA director Larry Smarr had challenged social scientists to envision new approaches to resolving problems using high-performance computing. Smarr extended the resources of NCSA for Probe projects, which spanned a variety of social science disciplines and used high-performance computing to solve previously intractable problems. The results of thirteen of these high-performance research projects were presented at CSS93.

"Grand Challenges in the Social Sciences" thus became the theme of the conference. To clarify the role of social scientists in defining, shaping, and ultimately overcoming grand challenges, this conference focused on both practical and theoretical aspects of social science computing. The conference highlighted presentations of the most powerful high-performance computing research as well as more common microcomputer use for social scientists and humanists. This volume began as a collection of papers presented at CSS93. However, with the rapid changes in technology, some papers soon became outdated and new issues arose. Thus, only two of these chapters were part of CSS93, and these two papers have been revised and updated. The furious pace of change in the larger computing world juxtaposed with the slower pace of technological adoption and adaptation in the humanities and social sciences redirected our purpose from presenting conference proceedings to providing a usable, meaningful book and multipurpose CD-ROM. This book provides a bridge to those new or uncomfortable with digital media.

Accompanying this book is a CD-ROM titled *Wayfarer: Charting Advances in Social Science and Humanities Computing. Wayfarer* is a new concept. It contains some of the most important ideas, programs, models, and demonstrations in humanities and social science computing and papers more suited to presentation on a CD-ROM than in a printed volume. Current topics in diverse fields are covered. Whereas the nature of the academy and the differing pace of change and innovation in different disciplines tend to keep complementary ideas and approaches apart, this CD-ROM is a concise overview (able to be updated through the Web) of where we have been, where we are, and where we are going. *Wayfarer* is intentionally eclectic, an exhibition that highlights significant perspectives of the computer revolution. The CD-ROM provides something for everyone, from the generalist in the humanities to the social scientist who seeks specialist programs and tools for analysis. Edited by historians, this elaborate CD-ROM was designed for utility by Frank Baker of NCSA. *Wayfarer* contains the papers from this book and many more. *Wayfarer* features an interactive repository, functional demonstrations, and extensive bibliographic materials (some essays from the book have more extensive reference lists than are contained in the Notes in this book.) *Wayfarer* expresses, in ways that scholarly papers alone cannot, the energetic quality of current computer-based and digital media–based experimentation and exploration of the social sciences and humanities.

This book and CD-ROM examine how computers have changed the methods social scientists use and contributed to a reorientation of the craft and how new technology is changing research in the social sciences and humanities. In short, they explore the renaissance in computing in the humanities and social sciences. Scholars have disputed whether such a renaissance has occurred. In May 1990, in an exchange of views in the *Newsletter of the Organization of American Historians,* Walter A. Sutton, professor of history at Lamar College, took exception to early projections of a renaissance in social science computing, writing that "Orville Vernon Burton's view of 'History's Electric Future' seems to be unduly optimistic."[2] Sutton based his opinion on his experience with inadequate computing hardware and software, excessive cost of computing equipment, lack of access among scholars to computing equipment, and imperfections and limitations in existing scanning, optical character recognition, and library system software. Over the last decade, however, as the renaissance has gained momentum, such frustrations have diminished. The cost of computing is shrinking at an astonishing rate, and the capability of computing is increasing even more rapidly. Sutton worried about the excessive cost and "a lack of administrative support for AT-class PCs for people in the liberal arts." Those ATs, which cost $3,000–5,000 in 1990, today are obsolete and cannot even be given away. Capable 650-megahertz Pentium III machines sold for as little as $1,200 new in 2000. In 2001 a 700-MHz system sells for $700 and a 1,000-megahertz to 1.5-gigahertz Pentium 4 for $1,200. In January 1993 storage capacity in a 300-megabyte hard drive cost $2.16 per megabyte; a year later it cost only 88 cents per megabyte, and in 1997 a 1.6-gigabyte hard drive cost 12.5 cents per megabyte. In 2000 a 60-gigabyte hard drive cost just $5.48 per gigabyte, or about 0.5 cents per megabyte. In 2001, hard drives can be bought for around $100 per 30 gigabytes (or 0.33 cents per megabyte) and around $165 for a 60-gigabyte hard drive ($2.75 per gigabyte or 0.3 cent per megabyte). Industry estimates project a $1.00/gigabyte drive by 2003.

Universities and colleges have also addressed the problem of access for all students, including those in the liberal arts. Many schools offer computing labs with high-powered machines, and undergraduates often arrive on campus with their own personal computers. Optical character recognition systems, though still fraught with problems, have come far enough in the last few years to make their use practicable for laptops and notepads. Scholars are now scanning censuses, tax records, and books into machine-readable form. Technology forecasters predict that 1,000-MIPS (millions of instructions per second) desktop machines will soon be affordable. In contrast, large mainframe computers of the mid-1980s could handle only 5–10 MIPS.

Many humanists agree that the computer is valuable as an electronic library, which scholars can peruse at their convenience. The National Science Foundation, recognizing the importance of computers to libraries, made digital libraries one of its grand challenges in 1993. Today we are surprised if a library has not gone digital, and the challenge is to promote creative use by a broader community.[3] Although computers are valuable in cataloguing information, it is the point of this book that computers are vastly more capable than mere information storage devices. As tools for ordering and making sense of information, computers create an environment in which social scientists and humanists can operate.

This renaissance in computing is not utopian. Technological and philosophical problems remain. The technological difficulties will be cured by technological improvements. But what of the problems with the philosophy and culture of computers themselves and within the particular disciplines themselves? These will take longer to work out. Currently, for example, differing philosophical approaches to sociology divide that discipline. Problems parallel those that economics faced in the 1950s and 1960s and that history and political science faced in the late 1960s and 1970s: Are quantitative techniques an appropriate method for understanding society? Should scholars quantify or not? Once upon a time, the debate included whether or not a scholar should even use a computer. Today social scientists and humanists use computers at the office and home to take notes, organize, write, and communicate via e-mail with colleagues and students. Today's debates now center on *how* to use the computer. Scholarly use of computers is no longer limited to number crunching. In 1993 NCSA created Mosaic, a definitive piece of software that turned the arcane realm of the World Wide Web into a point-and-click playground for millions of neophytes, helping build the first mass media outlet in computing. NCSA Mosaic was demonstrated at CSS93 to enthusiastic humanists and social scientists. Derivatives of Mosaic, such as Netscape Communicator and Microsoft Explorer, now provide means of communication through the Internet with other libraries and resources throughout the world. Furthermore, the increasing ease with which computers deal with texts is bringing some social scientists closer to the textual and narrative world of the humanities. Soon Web innovations may offer new operating systems and again narrow the distance between the sciences and the humanities.

History as a discipline has long been divided as to whether it belonged to the humanities or the social sciences. Now, because computers have opened exciting opportunities for historians to work with texts in new and comprehensive ways, the history profession clearly sees itself as part of the humanities. The computer, which some traditional narrative historians despised in the 1960s and 1970s because a group of "New Historians" used it for quantitative analysis, is moving history as a discipline firmly into the humanities and away from the modeling and quantitative techniques generally associated with the social sciences.

C. P. Snow theorized in 1959 that a dichotomy existed between the world of science and the world of humanities. Optimists will acknowledge that those two worlds are converging. Scientists more than ever are interested in the history of their disciplines and the paradigms that inform the way they work and think. Social scientists are likewise interested in the technological revolution, seeking perspective on the larger impact of technology on our society.[4]

The real computing renaissance begins with creative, even speculative thinking. No longer do social scientists have to alter their methods of inquiry to accommodate the computer; computers are now sufficiently flexible to accommodate the social scientist. Computers can cross spatial, chronological, and interdisciplinary boundaries. A social scientist can now incorporate investigations from history, sociology, geography, political science, literature, and any other discipline into one research question. Technology can help answer real questions as social scientists use computers in creative ways to pursue new and previously impossible avenues of inquiry. A social scientist should use the methodological tool appropriate for the particular problem under investigation. Some social scientists, like some historians before them, are now standing firm against quantitative techniques and computer-derived statistical analysis, thinking that statistical analysis limits the profession. But it is limited only by a lack of imagination. The computer allows revelation and discovery, answers to questions previously unanswerable. And increasingly, as the chapters in this volume illustrate, today's hardware and software are suited to all kinds of research, whether qualitative or quantitative. Indeed, the Web and the resources it offers are so much easier to use than they were in the heyday of quantitative techniques that the new technology might revitalize interest in structural questions for humanists and social scientists. Therein lies the renaissance in supercomputing.

The real supercomputer is not a $10-million machine sitting in isolated splendor in a high-tech astronomy or physics laboratory; it is the tens of millions of PCs throughout the world, which more and more are linked with mainframes, LANs, servers, databases, and each other through the Internet. These PCs have the computing power of more than 10,000 Cray-1 supercomputers.[5] When this computing power is combined with the ease of communication among scholars, computers can effect a profound change in scholarly disciplines.

This potential has been realized in specialized forums online. These forums are expanding at an explosive rate. One of the most influential forums is H-Net, the International On-Line Network for the Humanities and Social Sciences. Having begun as a history discussion list on the Internet at the time of CSS93, where Richard Jensen, founder of H-NET, and I, as H-Net treasurer, enlisted supporters, H-Net is now governed by an international council of scholars. It enjoys the support of several institutions, notably Michigan State University, which provides technical infrastructure and administrative staff. Mark Kornbluh, a former chair of H-Net council and professor of history at Michigan State University, has succeeded Jensen as executive director. Under Jensen's and Kornbluh's dynamic leadership, H-Net has expanded to more than 100,000 subscribers internationally with 10 million messages per month. It has pioneered a range of Web-based scholarly publishing ventures such as H-Review, which is now one of the world's largest programs for the review of new monographs in the humanities and social sciences. It has also been a catalyst for innovative use of networked communications for delivering educational resources. In 1997 the American Historical Association awarded H-Net the James Harvey Robinson Prize for the "most outstanding contribution to the teaching and learning of history in any field." Many subscribers are undergraduate teachers with more than a million students every semester.[6]

Scholarly forums such as H-Net are just one example of how scholars are using computers to reshape the workings of the academy. Cooperation between academicians enlarges the scale and narrows the precision of scholarly inquiry; ultimately it will raise thought processes to a higher plane. High-performance computing, in tandem with extremely powerful individual PCs with Web resources, offers enormous opportunities for scholars to organize, analyze, and comprehend information in ways only dreamed about a few years ago.

This volume is a collection of innovative thinking about computing in the humanities and social sciences. Included in this book are some of the practical and theoretical aspects of social science computing. Some of the essays offer insight into accessing the complex and growing archive of social science data and mapping out features of the new social science computing environment. Other articles provide feedback from social science and humanities scholars already working in the new environment. They describe how they have used computers to solve long-standing problems and where current limitations are. Other scholars describe how the new environment of social science and humanities computing and electronic information exchange has changed the way academicians think about their disciplines and communicate with each other and with students.

## PART 1: THE DIGITAL REVOLUTION

The first two chapters take a broad view of the renaissance in social science computing; they get to the very heart of this renaissance, the impact of computers in the classroom. In chapter 1, "Technological Revolutions I Have Known," Edward L. Ayers walks through a gallery of social science technological revolutions. His examples show how each new promise was deflated as yet another innovation replaced what was yesterday's state of the art. Diving into the promise of the Web and the Internet, Ayers calls for using the new media in ways that are challenging intellectually rather than technologically. Rather than worry about the inevitable replacement of current technology, Ayers asks social scientists to take a leading role in shaping research goals. He urges humanists to create the next revolution in computer use with innovative accomplishments.[7]

Randy Bass and Roy Rosenzweig also address the idea of the renaissance and ask whether the new technology is revolutionary in its applicability to learning. In chapter 2, "Rewiring the History and Social Studies Classroom: Needs, Frameworks, Dangers, and Proposals," Bass and Rosenzweig place the digital revolution in historical perspective and address crucial issues for teaching social sciences in the new millennium. Chapter 2 was originally a White Paper prepared for the Department of Education, Forum on Technology in K–12 Education: Envisioning a New Future, December 1, 1999.[8] Although Bass and Rosenzweig focus on K–12 and teaching with information technology, the discussion is applicable to all teaching in the digital age, including the college level. Rosenzweig and Bass draw from their own experiences with workshops sponsored by the American Studies Crossroads Project, the New Media Classroom, and the Library of Congress's American Memory Fellows program and from a nationwide survey of Americans conducted in 1994. Bass, a professor of English, and Rosenzweig, a professor of history, explore three frameworks that promote active learning. Scholars too seldom talk about what goes wrong, but this essay also warns about pitfalls. This essay is a must for anyone who cares about teaching and learning the social sciences and humanities in the twenty-first century.

## PART 2: COMPUTING AND NEW ACCESS TO SOCIAL SCIENCE DATA

The next two chapters illustrate how scholars have developed and are envisioning the information infrastructure so that new approaches will yield faster and more useful results. Much of the power of computing is realized over the Internet. Some research activities can be accomplished at a fraction of their former cost, making research opportunities available to many scholars who would be unable to afford traditional approaches. Other research activities simply could not have been undertaken before the Internet and the Web. These two chapters examine how researchers use computers to analyze data across chronological and geographic boundaries previously impenetrable because of the sheer quantity of data involved. Social scientists are now exploring

content analysis programs and even programs that function on human cognitive models. These essays are not about what social scientists predict for the
future but about how social scientists use computers here and now to make
enormous and unprecedented advances. And because this knowledge is not
limited to one time and place or to one dataset but is transferable, scholars
can build on each other's work. These chapters showcase some of the possibilities that await social scientists willing to use datasets. These authors challenge scholars to expand the scope of their research.

William Sims Bainbridge outlines the general promise of surveys on the
Internet in chapter 3, "Validity of Web-Based Surveys: Explorations with Data
from 2,382 Teenagers." Scholars are beginning to grapple with this new development of Web resources, and Web-based surveys present special problems and opportunities for researchers.[9] Bainbridge addresses a very current
social science problem, and he uses a specific example to draw general conclusions that are applicable to the social science computing community. Too
often academicians, when writing about computing, are theoretical, and here
Bainbridge offers us practical solutions. Bainbridge was centrally involved
with Survey 2000, the extensive Web-based survey carried out in late 1998
by the National Geographic Society. By grounding his study in the reality of
Survey 2000, he is able to answer general problems about all Web-based surveys and provide a detailed application. His study of teenagers' responses and
the gender differences illustrates a sensitive and creative treatment of the
reliability and the dilemmas associated with Web-based surveys. Bainbridge
concludes with a valuable, broad view of how experimental methods and
stringent sampling can be incorporated in future Web-based surveys. In
addition, Bainbridge provides on *Wayfarer* a set of four modules he created
to help with Web-based surveys: "The Year 2100," "Self-Esteem," "Experience," and "Beliefs."

Solidly rooted in the relationship of modern computing and scholarship,
chapter 4, "Computer Environments for Content Analysis: Reconceptualiz-
ing the Roles of Humans and Computers," by William Evans stresses that the
computer is more than a tool; it is an environment for content analysis. In a
thought-provoking essay with implications for all social scientists, Evans
rejects the idea of a computer as a sophisticated adding machine, external
and isolated from the social scientist, and he recommends that social scientists begin to conceptualize the computer as an entity within which the social scientist operates. Computing is not the same thing as conceptualizing
the computation. Evans recommends a computer system design that supports
a wide variety of human coding tasks and says that content analysis should
adopt artificial intelligence techniques.[10]

## PART 3: COMPUTERS, SOCIAL SCIENCE, HUMANITIES, AND THE IMPACT OF THE NEW SOCIAL TERRAIN

The third section in this book contains two chapters that describe how computers provide social scientists and humanists with a working environment. As awesome as computing power is in processing numbers and grappling with large datasets, computing benefits to humanists and social scientists go beyond that power. Computers are flexible, able to store, transmit, use, and create information. The rapid pace of changing technology challenges us to exploit these machines efficiently. Using computers as a tool that stimulates creative thinking should help solve real-world problems.

In chapter 5, "Electronic Texts in the Historical Profession: Perspectives from Across the Scholarly Spectrum," Wendy Plotkin does what no one else has done. In a useful and informative survey of the state of historical publications in the Internet, she discusses the ways in which the Internet has affected historical research and teaching. She looks in particular at the value of electronic primary texts as a historical tool to enhance analysis. Plotkin traces the development of the textual resources available to the historian in electronic form and notes that electronic texts have two principal advantages: they allow broad, easy access to valuable primary materials from remote locations, and they allow systematic searches for words, phrases, or concepts. Plotkin also looks at the disadvantages of electronic texts. Some scholars believe that the physical appearance of the original text is important, some doubt the ability of the computer to improve upon textual analysis, and many question the durability of electronic texts. Plotkin delves into the attitudes of other members of the scholarly community toward electronic texts and the problems electronic texts create for publishers, including cost and copyright issues. Plotkin concludes that these questions may be moot in the near future simply because government and business are shifting rapidly from paper-based communication to electronic communication. Soon electronic texts may comprise much historical evidence, which would increase the incentives for developing text analysis tools. For any person interested in using scholarly resources on the Internet, Plotkin's essay is indispensable.

We now know that one of the dynamic and largely unexpected explosions of computing power has been the rapid exchange of information through computer networks. Attacking a little-considered area—computer-mediated social activism—Daniel J. Myers, in "Social Activism through Computer Networks" (chapter 6), turns the tables on these networks by using them to analyze the people who use networks. Myers examines computer-assisted communication and computer networks in the formation and function of social movements and collective behavior, noting that very little research has been done on the processes by which activists use computers and the results of this use. Myers outlines key characteristics of computer-mediated communication and the ramifications for social movements. He also identifies potentially fruitful areas for research using the activist computer forum.

## PART 4: PHILOSOPHICAL AND ETHICAL CONCERNS OF THE CULTURE OF COMPUTING

This final section addresses some consequences and warnings for the renaissance in social science computing. No renaissance is perfect. Every advance brings inherent problems, usually unforeseen, that must be addressed before the promise of a renaissance can be realized. Bass and Rosenzweig reminded us of the disadvantages minorities and historically black colleges experienced in the technological revolution. Bainbridge discussed how women were lagging behind especially in the sciences, but saw some improvement. In chapter 7, "Creating Cybertrust: Illustrations and Guidelines," H. Jeanie Taylor and Cheris Kramarae discuss an ultimate question about this new technological renaissance: Whom does it benefit? Looking specifically at women's and minority men's roles in defining and using computers, Taylor and Kramarae consider a variety of problems and offer a list of concrete solutions. With so little study of gender and minority participation in the digital age, the issues Taylor and Kramarae address are significant and call out for more research and discussion.

In chapter 8, "Electronic Networks for International Research Collaboration: Implications for Intellectual Property Protection in the Early Twenty-first Century," Carole Ganz-Brown cautions that traditional concepts of ownership of information are being challenged, if not overrun, by the rapid growth of electronic networks. In this informative and provocative essay, Ganz-Brown points out that electronic networks have exposed an inherent contradiction in the doctrine of intellectual property: Intellectual property systems aim to promote public disclosure of intellectual works while conferring on the creators the exclusive rights to distribute their works. With a lucid explanation of the legal issues surrounding intellectual property protection, Ganz-Brown raises an issue that scholars must confront as they embark upon the renaissance in social science computing.

It is possible that the humanities and social sciences, because they have not traditionally made heavy use of computing power, will use computers more creatively than other disciplines. Social scientists will bring fresh perspectives and ask, rightly so, what the computer can do for social science rather than what the social scientist can do for the computer. Although knowledge of computer operation and programming language is valuable to social scientists, the principal goal of social science is the acquisition of relevant knowledge. Previously, social scientists and humanists had difficulties using computers creatively because they first had to set their projects aside and gain detailed knowledge of computers. Just as automobiles were of limited use when it was necessary to be a roadside mechanic as well as a driver, the promise held out by computers was ephemeral as long as scholars and teachers also had to be computer scientists. As computing technology has evolved, these barriers have fallen. Computers are now accessible to every social science and humanities scholar. Despite all the monumental gains in computers as discussed in this book of essays, the technology will never again be as primitive as it is right now; technology will only continue to improve. These essays illustrate the hopes and the frustrations of computing. This is the brink of a new age, and the future of the social sciences and humanities calls for optimism. The renaissance is upon us.

## "WAYFARER"

The accompanying CD-ROM, *Wayfarer,* includes multimedia entries such as the Global Jukebox, by folklorist Alan Lomax, interesting to read about but alive, vibrant, and spirited on the CD-ROM. This interactive system maps the universe of human expressive behavior with an illustrated geography of song and dance that illuminates the worldview of historians of culture. Even in its prototype stage, the Global Jukebox allows a user to explore the main regions of human song (with excerpts available from about 130 songs and 50 dances) to explore their distinctive characteristics and acquire an appreciative overview of music and dance in their global cultural settings.

Brian Orland's essay, "Visualizing Wildlife Population Dynamics: The Powerful Owl," demonstrates the efficacy of the World Wide Web and CD-ROM in exhibiting papers. Orland uses the capability of online publishing to express complex problems with interactive visual displays. He created bird population models to exemplify interactions between the vegetative and wildlife components of forest ecology. Concrete examples bring clarity to simple correlations as well as more complex log or U-shaped relationships, and computer interface tools and interactive representations display these processes. Orland describes his creation of a museum exhibit where a user can manipulate variables relating to an owl population and view the effects in various graphic forms. This project taps into the new power of interactive multimedia, with significant benefits for teaching and learning.

Other treats on the CD-ROM include anthropologist and former Social Science Computing Association president Doug White's PGRAPH, a kinship network analysis program that studies and analyzes marriage and family structures within a given community. Sociologists Gillian Stevens and Tim Futing Liao present programs useful to demographers. Political scientists Michael McBurnett and Thad A. Brown present their paper, "The Emergence of Elites through Adaptive Interaction and the Consequences for Stability in Political Science," along with simulation models investigating the role of elites in the American political order. Using a series of dynamic lattice computer models, McBurnett and Brown explore how they believe interdependent elite hierarchies develop and influence our political system.

Another exciting entry in the *Wayfarer* collection is RiverWeb, a multimedia interactive archive of information on the Mississippi River that is particularly well suited for use in distance education. This interdisciplinary collaboration, which I directed and which is managed and maintained by David Herr and Ian Binnington, graduate students in history at UIUC, brings together resources, information, and technology to explore the history, culture, and science of the Mighty Mississippi in a unique and significant milieu. The CD-ROM includes one portion of a "landing site" along the Mississippi River, East St. Louis. This East St. Louis site incorporates the history of the city, the musical scene including the blues, the development of steamboats on the Mississippi, and contemporary East St. Louis with its community and neighborhood projects. Together with the East St. Louis Action Research Project (ESLARP), an endeavor of the University of Illinois Department of Landscape Architecture, RiverWeb brings a missing past to residents of both the city and the world, providing information from yesteryear that people can use today.

Harnessing the potential of the Internet and the World Wide Web has become a primary concern among humanists. In "The 'Pictures of Health' Project," Paul Turnbull, elected the first president of H-Net in 2000, reflects on using the Web in teaching the history of the social sciences, truly part of the current renaissance. Turnbull's article deals with networked digital information systems and the ways in which computing is increasingly being used in the social sciences and humanities and the challenges we consequently face. Turnbull is asking the most relevant question about computer technology: How is it connected to the changes now affecting scholarly culture? He offers us a case study in which the technology was used creatively to address disturbing assumptions about the relationships between technology and social change. He discusses the motivation, aims, and outcomes of integrating a series of online interactive learning exercises, tutorials, and consultation facilities within an advanced undergraduate course at James Cook University. Essentially, he set students to explore how statistical techniques and new technologies such as photography were used by several leading nineteenth-century social scientists. Students were encouraged to see how anxieties about population increase, industrialization, and the growth of cities found expression in the knowledge these scientists produced. In the process, students were invited to reflect on how their own understanding and uses of new technologies might be subject to the influences of wider economic and cultural forces. Turnbull's essay highlights the ways in which virtual teaching and learning is developing in similar cultural contexts. Turnbull discusses Web-based teaching and offers practical experience from an extensive project by one of the leading scholars in these technologies. Moreover, the same type of procedure Turnbull discusses is necessary today for anyone wanting to teach history in an Internet-based environment. The international context of Turnbull's essay is especially important because U.S. scholars need to be aware of the different problems faced in different educational contexts, and this essay gives an American audience some insight into the particular problems and opportunities of computers in a different cultural context. *Wayfarer* users will be able to explore Turnbull's Web site.

In "Representing Metadata with Intelligent Agents: An Initial Prototype," Albert F. Anderson, 1996 president of the Social Science Computing Association, and co-authors Edward Brent and G. Alan Thompson deal with the problems of large datasets such as the U.S. Bureau of the Census Public Use Microdata Sample (PUMS), Integrated Public Use Microdata Series (IPUMS), and Supersample. This paper and these scholars' work are visionary as they describe two prototype modules and their PDQ-Explore system, which works as an active agent. This paper addresses what the Web offers scholars in the way of data sources and suggests better ways to access large stores of information. Where might computers take social scientists, or are these paths unpredictable? What can social scientists do with computers, and what computing tools and skills do social scientists need? Social scientists have used the computer as a machine for statistical analysis or storing large (and often unwieldy) quantities of information, but this paper focuses instead on information management and manipulation. Users of *Wayfarer* may use this prototype readily to generate tables from millions of records in a matter of seconds. The PDQ-Explore system represents a realization of the promise of high-performance information and computing technology to work with large, complex datasets, without the previous penalties of excessive time, cost, and technical prowess.[11]

William deB. Mills, in "Forests or Trees: Clear Thinking about Social Science Systems," discusses how to use computers creatively. He presents a set of generic dimensions along which all biological systems can be compared. Mills argues that this focus on system performance in generic dimensions allows insight into the underlying causes of policy problems, insights that might otherwise be obscured by overemphasis on superficial descriptive details. On *Wayfarer,* Mills includes his software System 101, which readers may use to implement his carefully described approach.[12]

In addition to such state-of-the-art essays, *Wayfarer* provides a summary of the major trends and issues of the computing revolution for social science of the last decade. Selected revised papers from CSS93, as well as updated papers from later CSS conferences and solicited other papers, are on *Wayfarer.* Some of the essays are placed in their historical context; for example, a historical snapshot of where social scientists believed they were and where they predicted computing was going in 1995 is found in Bruce Tonn, "Using the National Information Infrastructure for Social Science, Education, and Informed Decision Making: A White Paper." Tonn, former president of the Social Science Computing Association, held a round-table discussion at CSS93 of "Grand Challenges for the Social Sciences" where participants debated issues in social science computing. From that discussion, Tonn began a White Paper elucidating the challenges for social science computing and computing needs for the next generation.

The preceding examples are just a sampling of the programs available on the CD-ROM. Other authors in the written volume have also included programs on the CD-ROM. These programs make visible and concrete what the chapters in this printed volume portend. Videos, graphs, color pictures, and illustrations of geographic information systems (GIS illustrations) accompany the essays. Applications and datasets give readers the first-hand excitement of the research as the authors and research teams share their experiences.

*Wayfarer* also has connections to many World Wide Web sites, including a link to a Web site devoted to the CD-ROM itself. In addition, it contains a collection of sites in itself; for those working remotely with no Internet access and those with a slow Internet connection, these offline Web sites make it possible to appreciate fully the nature of the material. For those with Internet access, *Wayfarer*'s Web links move seamlessly from the CD-ROM to the Web, enabling the reader to experience the full power of the medium.

*Wayfarer* is intended to benefit those interested in assessing how to harness effectively the Internet and computers for teaching and research. All in all, wonders await the readers willing to try *Wayfarer,* readers willing to enter into the renaissance in social science and humanities computing.

## NOTES

1. J. David Bolter, *Turing's Man: Western Culture in the Computer Age* (Chapel Hill: University of North Carolina Press, 1984).

2. Orville Vernon Burton, "History's Electric Future," in *OAH Newsletter* 17:4 (November 1989): 12–13, replied to by Walter A. Sutton, "Another View: History's Electric Future," *OAH Newsletter* 18:2 (May 1990): 6.

3. Another challenge is convincing the latest generation of college students that not all information is online. Students often are surprised that libraries have holdings and archives that are not available in digital format.

4. C. P. Snow, *The Two Cultures: And a Second Look* (Cambridge, England: Cambridge University Press, 1965). Part 1, the Rede Lecture, was published in 1959. See also the critique by F. R. Leavis and Michael Yudkin, *Two Cultures?: The Significance of C. P. Snow and an Essay on Sir Charles Snow's Rede Lecture* (New York: Pantheon, 1963).

5. Larry L. Smarr, "The Computational Science Revolution: Technology, Methodology, and Sociology," in *High-Speed Computing: Scientific Applications and Algorithm Design,* ed. Robert B. Wilhelmson (Urbana: University of Illinois Press, 1988); William J. Kaufmann III and Larry L. Smarr, *Supercomputing and the Transformation of Science* (New York: Scientific American Library/W. H. Freeman, 1993).

6. See Mark Lawrence Kornbluh, "Envisioning the Future: Arts and Letters in the Digital Age," on *Wayfarer.*

7. See Ayers's own technological revolution, "The Valley of the Shadow," an award-winning multimedia study of the Civil War as experienced in two communities, Northern Chambersburg, Pennsylvania and Southern Staunton, Virginia, on *Wayfarer.*

8. An earlier version of this essay first appeared in *The Journal of Education* 181:3 (1999): 41–61.

9. See the special issue of *Social Science Computer Review* 18:4 (Winter 2000) on "Survey and Statistical Computing in the New Millennium.

10. See also Lyn Richards, "Qualitative Software Meets Qualitative Method: QSR's NUD*IST 4 and NVivo as Results," and the accompanying content analysis programs, QSR NUD*IST 4.0 and NVivo, on *Wayfarer.* Qualitative Solutions and Research's NUD*IST 4.0 program (originally programmed by Tom Richards and designed by Lyn Richards) and NVivo are multifunctional software systems for developing, supporting, and managing qualitative data analysis projects. With NUD*IST 4.0 and NVivo, scholars can analyze unstructured data, such as text from interviews, historical or legal documents, or nontextual documentary material such as videotapes.

11. See also "Interactive Access to Large Census Data Sets," by Albert F. Anderson and his son, Paul H. Anderson, and try the PDQ EXPLORE application on *Wayfarer.*

12. For further exploration of Mills's argument that we should understand computers as tools to enhance creativity rather than devices to improve our efficiency, see "Working Smarter: Computers as Stimulants for Human Creativity" and his other applications on *Wayfarer.*

# PART 1

# The

# Digital

# Revolution

# 1 / Technological Revolutions I Have Known

**Historians are trained** to see things in the context of change, but even a historian might find it hard to gain a sense of perspective on the technological changes sweeping over us these days. The machinery itself is evolving with astonishing speed, and the larger culture seems obsessed with the evolution. Articles on the latest high-tech stock miracle fill the business pages while advertisements for automobiles and sport leagues bear their World Wide Web addresses like badges of honor. Books and magazines for and against the new media pepper the bestseller lists, and how-to books on computing dominate new sections of bookstores.

The effects of the new technology in the classroom receive their share of attention as well. While the computer companies and politicians fall over one another with promises and proposals to equip classrooms with as many machines as possible, ominous voices warn that we are ushering in the end of real education with such innovations. Teachers will be replaced with machines, they warn, human interaction supplanted by keyboards and screens. Teachers view the changes warily, eager for the stimulation and excitement computers can bring yet leery of inflated expectations and skewed funding. Higher education is, if anything, even more confused and ambivalent than its primary and secondary counterparts. There, some scholars and teachers are eagerly innovating with the newest media while others hold it in open contempt.

Educators at every level have been burned before, when gadgets ranging from filmstrips to overhead projectors to televisions have been ballyhooed as the saviors of the American classroom. The computers that have occupied corners of classrooms for the last decade have made some impact on matters involving rote learning but have not lived up to their earlier billing. Our classrooms still mainly involve the scraping of one rock against another, chalk on blackboard. Has the time finally arrived when the big changes will be felt? Have we achieved critical mass? Are we on the verge of a fundamental change in the boundaries and possibilities of the classroom? If so, what role might those of us in research universities play?

Many academics who came of professional age some time between the late 1960s and early 1980s have already experienced what felt like—at the time, at least—three electronic revolutions. As a historian attracted to the potential of computing since the 1970s, I have seen these changes at close range. Like others of my generation, I confronted mainframe computers before personal computers. I remember how impressive it felt at the computer center: the heavy metal machinery, the hard math done automatically, the promise of being freed from uncertainty and imprecision. True, I had to copy records from dusty originals to coding sheets and then to brittle punchcards, but the excitement when all the cards were ready for batch processing was worth it. One made a ritualistic sacrifice of the cards to the priestly attendant behind the glass wall, then waited in a room where it always seemed to be a fluorescent-lit 3 A.M. Eventually reams of paper began to pour out, perhaps the findings on which so much depended. After proudly bearing the impressively large stack of paper through the rows of computer science graduate students, the humanist eagerly opened the stack to see what revolution in historical understanding might be revealed in the columns and numbers. Unfortunately, seeing the entire stack of paper filled with one message repeated 2,789 times—error number 17—was not as edifying as one had hoped. Eventually, though, I figured out the machinery enough to get some reasonable-looking numbers for a dissertation.

Looking back, the incongruity in this first computer revolution is obvious. The same dissertation that drew on a computer the size of a 747 for its data manipulation had to be translated into English with a used Adler Satellite portable electric typewriter. It was a tactile experience, with the grinding little motor and belts, the keys interlocking tenaciously, the pockmarked surface where wet correction fluid had been typed over. And it was intellectually challenging as well, for it was not always easy to find another nine-letter word for, say, "lassitude" when, against all odds, "lassitude" appeared in consecutive paragraphs. Despite such obstacles, I managed to write enough of a dissertation with such a machine to get a job.

That particular kind of challenge came to an end with the word-processing revolution. In 1981 the machines took over what had been our little faculty lounge. My department decided that dedicated Wang word processors were the wave of the future, and it certainly seemed so in the evenings, when professors could gain access to the two machines in what quickly became known as the Wang Room. There, we simply could not get over the fact that we could delete words we had written many pages back. We could delete "lassitude" every time it appeared, even replacing it with a *five-letter* word if we chose! It was miracle, even better than number-crunching, because these were the humanists' familiar and beloved words that could be manipulated so easily.

Nothing was perfect, of course. A flicker of lightning in the next county often triggered a complete breakdown of the machines; the daisy wheel printer ate ribbons and daisy wheels the way the computer in graduate school ate paper; the disks, the size of small pizzas, seemed to erase themselves in the filing cabinet drawer; the cutting-edge Wang format soon proved to be a dead end in word-processing evolution. Nevertheless, once one had processed words, there was no going back.

In 1985, thanks to the beneficence of my university, I got my very own machine at home and became a part of the Internet revolution. To my delight and the envy of my friends, it had a color monitor rather than the murky green of the Wang, its own actual hard drive able to hold 10 entire megabytes, and—shades of the future—a 2,400-baud modem. Trying to live up to such a machine, I learned to use yet another mainframe computer interactively, punchcards having been thrown on the computing trash heap along with the Wang. I taught myself multiple regression analysis and other things contrary to my character and abilities. But the real excitement came in the discovery of electronic mail. The combination of written language, informality, efficiency, and, in the mid-1980s, the feeling of being among the information technology elite proved surprisingly satisfying. And when the university's card catalog came online I thought we had approached the limits of technological progress.

By then, the first two computer revolutions had been completely domesticated. The computer had become an appliance, about as exciting—and as essential—as the coffee maker that made my day as productive as possible. That was all the contact I wanted with electronic machinery. I had had enough of number crunching and SPSS runs. I was planning a new, non-electronic project, a project that would take me back to ground level, a local study in which I knew the names of people. It seemed clear to me that my mild interest in computers made me something of a dinosaur in the age after the linguistic turn. I wanted to do the sort of highly inflected, nuanced, individualized history that had attracted me to social history in the first place. I wanted to write a narrative of human scale. And I could see no place for computing in that.

But the machines, like so many cyborgs, tracked me down one more time. Trying to achieve a token balance on the committee that oversees computing at my university, they appointed me—a humanist—to occupy some space on a committee dominated by scientists, physicians, and engineers. At first I was befuddled by the lingo, but something interesting soon came up: IBM was interested in helping computing at the university and wanted our committee to suggest something. We batted it around for a while until I timorously noted that many of us in the humanities and social sciences had no computers on our desks at all. There was some good-natured joshing among the physicists and medical imaging specialists about aid to the third world of computing, but what could we do for such backward people who showed so little interest in helping themselves? Almost all my humanist colleagues seemed content with what little computing they had. No clamor of discontent arose from the quiet offices where pens still scratched on paper.

Slowly, though, some forward-thinking people in computer science began to think that maybe computing in the humanities might be the most exciting frontier of all. What if we really could use computers to help make sense of the great store of human knowledge and striving locked away in archives and books? What if computers were just getting good enough for humanists to use, now that they could deal with images as easily as they could with linear numbers and letters, now that they were networked, now that they had enough storage space to hold the vast and messy stuff historians habitually collected?

With this premise, IBM agreed to donate a number of RISC workstations, a server, and a technical advisor to create something we decided, after much debate, to call the Institute for Advanced Technology in the Humanities. Almost against my will, I was posted on the electronic frontier, armed with networking, digitization, JPEGs, and SGML even before Mosaic and the World Wide Web became household words. For the last several years I have been overseeing a project based in that institute. I converted my small-scale, intimate, handmade community study into a large archive on the World Wide Web and on CD-ROM. It is now known as the Valley of the Shadow Project and it has involved more than twenty people working to fill up several gigabytes of electronic storage with historical data.

Once again I'm a true believer, eyes burning with fervor, brimming with enthusiasm, just as I was for the big mainframe of 1978, the sleek Wangs of 1981, and the interconnected IBM clone of 1985. We look back on those machines with a mixture of contempt and nostalgia; we will never be so innocent again as we were before. We know from painful experience that today's miracles will be tomorrow's embarrassments or, if they succeed, mundane paper clips. We have learned from those earlier revolutions that revolutions do not always happen at the speed people predict or want. From one point of view, we have seen blistering speed; from the other, things have moved slowly. Computing power and storage have increased dramatically, and universities have been wired. Word processing and e-mail and have become staples of life for many professors and students. But the failures are pretty obvious, too.

Skepticism and even resistance to all things electronic by many humanists and even social scientists endures and even grows; a sort of passive aggression flourishes. There has been too much hype, too many commercials showing dolphins leaping out of computer screens. It is unfortunate that what computers, including networked computers, can do best is not particularly valued or necessary right now: providing more information, more specialized knowledge. If you want *stuff*, the Web has it. But the Web gives everything equal weight and authority, from conspiracy theorists to the federal government. Fortunately, the Web is too slow to be very satisfying over a modem, negating some of the appeal to the impatient young. The intellectual changes widely predicted to have accompanied widespread computing have not. The quantitative techniques so widely predicted as the wave of the future in the 1960s are now almost invisible within the historical profession; they have been replaced with a fascination with even closer attention to, of all things, words and texts. Students still turn to books for authority, still strive to write linear prose, and still print out much of what they discover online. Only a fraction of professors have integrated any form of electronic enhancements into their classes.

So should humanists get out of the way? Should historians and literary scholars, anthropologists and poets put our energies toward what we already know how to do in traditional media, valuing that work as a humane counterweight to the arcadelike values of this new technology? Some of us should. There is no compelling reason for most teachers and scholars to throw themselves into the gears of the new machine. Search tools and e-mail can be helpful to almost everyone, to be sure, and few writers of nonfiction long for the days before word processors, but hours devoted to integrating things electronic do not always pay off. Thus far, so-called electronic classrooms have offered only limited returns; most multimedia lectures often are not worth the investment of money and time they demand.

Some people have asked whether the Internet and the Web are like the citizens' band radio craze of the 1970s, except that you have to type rather than talk with a countrified accent. But today's technology more closely resembles what began as another technological fad: high fidelity. In the early

1950s one had to be a real nerd to care about woofers and tweeters; the records stamped "HiFi" were designed to show off what full stereo could do. Trains roared through your living room or birds called in the distance. But now high-quality sound reproduction is everywhere, from our cars to our homes to our offices to our malls to our televisions to our pockets. More than likely, that is how computers—or whatever we call them a few years from now—will evolve. Soon, they will be everywhere, taken for granted, boring.

That is just what we need. As long as the machine itself is a fetish item, it will repel as much as attract, engendering fear as much as affection. As long as the machine is a separate box needing elaborate maintenance and full attention, it will be hard to integrate effectively into teaching. As long as the machine is held up as an alternative to traditional learning, it will be seen as a challenge and an affront to proven ways to sharing knowledge. It is not until we find ways to integrate electronic teaching into our established rhythms, strategies, and purposes that the very real potential of the new media will begin to be realized.

Perhaps the first step is to dispense with the idea that the new forms of learning will necessarily displace others. Each kind of interaction between student and teacher accomplishes something unique. It might be useful to think of each form of learning located on a grid, with group and individual learning at the ends of one axis, active and passive learning at the poles of the other. Americans take as a matter of faith that learning that is both individual and active is best, and that which is group and passive is worst. But even passive learning can be effective. The most passive and isolating mechanism of all, television, has taught millions of people many things, some of them useful. Despite the criticism so often heaped on live lectures, they accomplish important and valuable purposes. The lecturer dramatizes, embodies the intellectual content and excitement of the material. The lecturer acts out the appeal and importance of the information, which could otherwise be presented more effectively in print. Generations of students at every college in the country eagerly compete to get into the best lectures, knowing that they are something more than television and more satisfying than many smaller classes with discussion.

If lectures are at one end of the group versus individual axis, reading is at the other. Reading is the most individualized, active, and reflective intellectual activity and as such is the measure for intellectual work in general. Reading can also be passive and boring, with the reader trapped in language, pacing, and organization that hold little appeal and convey little useful information. When critics decry computers' displacement of reading, they tend to judge it against the best that reading can be rather than the average. In fact, a computer is more like reading than a lecture. A person using digital information, like a reader, tends to be alone and actively engaged in the information before him or her. The major difference between reading and using a computer is that computers do not seem to be friendly to reflection. The computer, unlike a text, is built for action; it sits there humming, waiting, demanding that you punch some key or click some button. It is distracting, perpetually promising something more interesting than your own unfocused thoughts or the words currently before you on the screen.

In its demand for interactivity, in fact, the computer bears greater resemblance to a discussion group than it does to reading. Although a discussion, like a lecture, benefits from the physical presence of other people, from body language, it does not necessarily depend on them. Some of the most successful uses of information technology for teaching have been group discussions based on typing into a computer. Students and teachers claim that such discussions bring in a higher proportion of participants than traditional classrooms, that shy students will speak up in ways they would not otherwise, that the discussion tends to be less focused on the professor. Anyone with even a slow modem and a monochrome screen can participate in sequential discussions of themes of common interest. Unlike the World Wide Web, this text-based technology is inexpensive in time and in machinery, both to produce and to consume. It is an incremental technology, partaking of the benefits of reading and writing as well as the benefits of interconnectivity. It involves active, group learning disguised as individual effort.

Another incremental technology is the CD-ROM. Just a couple of years ago, CD-ROMs were being written off by the cognoscenti as the eight-track tapes of information technology. Unlike information on the Internet, CD-ROMs are physical commodities, bound in plastic, static. On the other hand, unlike information on the Internet, they are fast, fluid, and local. Given the current state of the Internet, CD-ROMs' positive qualities often outweigh their negative ones. Anyone who wants to present large images, to create a unique and compelling visual environment, use sound intensively, or use customized search tools is driven toward CD-ROM. Even those engaged in producing CD-ROMs recognize that they are a transitional technology, but the transition may take longer than anyone had expected. Until the networks and the machines at the receiving end can transmit enormous files as easily as television currently does, there will be a place for CD-ROMs. They are currently on the individual and active parts of the learning grid, but recent advances permit users to marry those benefits with those of the World Wide Web: connection, conversation, collaboration, and expandability. That marriage permits students to toggle between individual and group learning, reflection and activity.

That toggling may be the major advantage of the new media. They are protean, able to behave like a lecture or a book, able to foster individual or group activity. The new media should not be thought of as alternatives, rebukes, to traditional learning, but rather as ways to bridge some of the distances between those time-proven ways of teaching.

The new media are simultaneously in their infancy and in their old age. No one has created a CD-ROM or Web site yet that can hold its own against a really good book or film. The World Wide Web, the most heavily discussed manifestation of the new technology, bears a family resemblance to the original Volkswagen Beetle. It runs, and it can even be spruced up so that it is fun to drive and look at, but it remains a Beetle, wheezing to get up hills, possessing little storage capacity, and threatening serious damage in a crash. Veterans of the computer revolutions of the last fifteen years cannot help but see the Web with the eyes of someone five years from now, simultaneously impressed with Java and embarrassed by being impressed, knowing that soon it will seem as primitive as Pong. To those of us who remember batch jobs, daisy wheels, and monochrome, it still seems a slight miracle that pictures, sound, and video can come over our phone lines. But even that novelty wears off.

So how do we handle this new medium, so tempting and so ruthless, so postmodern in its simultaneous newness and obsolescence? There are some obvious truths: Use standard image formats, remain flexible, and look around. But there are other problems and issues. Perhaps these new media necessitate a compensatory style of writing, bending to the problems of nonuniform page sizes, page breaks, and short attention spans, maybe by presenting itself in shorter pieces, maybe by taking on the nonlinearity of hypertext. Or maybe new media writing should emphasize its traditional strengths of coherence and continuity. Maybe the computer screen should not be considered a place for serious, sustained writing at all until it is more portable and wirelessly interconnected.

We need to give users the information and the techniques they need to handle the complexity of large databases, but such information threatens to swell to the size of DOS user's guides. The basic metaphor for the current networks is "surfing," but deep projects require breaking the surface and diving instead of skimming across the top. We need to give people a place to gather what they have learned, a place to assemble their new knowledge into larger and more durable constructs than lists of bookmarks. We need to use machines of great efficiency to generate creative inefficiency. Historians, for example, provide information that is inevitably dirty, contradictory, incor-

rect, and incomplete in a medium that prides itself on quickness, capacious-
ness, and attractiveness. Historical evidence was not created for the computer,
so it is often an awkward fit between tidy machinery and smeared newspaper type, blurred handwriting, torn photographs, and thousands of sources,
none of which were designed to fit together by their original creators.

To academics who have internalized the conventions of the various forms
of scholarly discourse—the article, the review, the monograph, the lecture—
the new media can be confusing and even threatening. We know a good book
when we read one. Do the new media call for new standards? The intellectual standards seem to be the same: originality, thorough grounding in the
field, clarity of expression. But the standards of presentation in the new media
are certainly different, whether we want them to be or not. We cannot judge
a Web site by its cover—or its heft, its publisher's imprint, or the blurbs it
wears.

Whatever a project's scale and level of complexity, new media should meet
several standards to justify the extra effort they take to create, disseminate,
and use. We might as well admit that they are not as good as established media
for some purposes. They cannot present a linear argument or narrative nearly
as well as a book; indeed, they are generally not good for presenting substantial bodies of text. And they cannot convey reactive, personal energy as a good
lecture or discussion group can.

However, the new media can do things that traditional media cannot, and
that is what should be emphasized in their creation. New media should be
challenging intellectually but not technologically; if you need a user's manual, they are too difficult to use. New media should do things one cannot do
with print pages; hypertext links, personal annotation, and effective searching tools are a bare minimum. They should be flexible; if a new media project
merely poses a few problems and a few solutions, students cannot be expected
to find it very appealing for very long. New media should permit points of
accomplishment along the way; a project should not take hours of investment
before it pays a dividend. New media should offer opportunities for collaboration; one of the great strengths of network-based projects is that they are
open-ended, able to benefit from joint effort and imagination. New media
should be cumulative; users can enrich the project, leaving behind a new
insight, discovery, or criticism on which others can build. If a new media
project can provide these benefits, then the form in which it is currently transmitted will soon cease to be such an issue.

The lessons of the several minor revolutions we have witnessed over the
last two decades is this: The technology will rapidly evolve no matter what
we do. We have to decide what purposes we want to accomplish with the

current state of the art and plunge in, with the full knowledge that we are chasing something we can never catch. To compensate for that inevitable frustration, we can take pleasure and satisfaction from knowing that we are participating, in however minor a role, in some of the more interesting changes of our time.

RANDY BASS

AND ROY ROSENZWEIG

## 2 / Rewiring the History and Social Studies Classroom: Needs, Frameworks, Dangers, and Proposals

**Within five years** of Alexander Graham Bell's first display of his telephone at the 1876 Centennial Exposition, *Scientific American* promised that the new device would bring a greater "kinship of humanity" and "nothing less than a new organization of society." Others were less sanguine, worrying that telephones would spread germs through the wires, destroy local accents, and give authoritarian governments a listening box in the homes of their subjects. The Knights of Columbus fretted that phones might wreck home life, stop people from visiting friends, and create a nation of slugs who would not stir from their desks.[1]

Extravagant predictions of utopia or doom have accompanied most new communication technologies, and the same rhetoric of celebration and denunciation has enveloped the Internet. For *Wired* magazine publisher Louis Rossetto, the digital revolution promises "social changes so profound that their only parallel is probably the discovery of fire." According to Iraq's official government newspaper, *Al-Jumhuriya*, the Internet spells "the end of civilizations, cultures, interests, and ethics."[2]

The same excessive rhetoric has surrounded specific discussions of computers and education. "Thirty years from now the big university campuses will be relics," proclaims Peter Drucker in *Forbes.* "It took more than 200 years (1440 to the late 1600s) for the printed book to create the modern school. It won't take nearly that long for the [next] big change." One advertisement on the Web captures the mixture of opportunity and anxiety occasioned by the new technology. Three little red schoolhouses stand together in a field. A pulsing green line or wire lights up one of the schools with a pulse of energy and excitement, casting the others into shadow. "Intraschool is Coming to a District Near You," a sign flashes. "Don't Be Left Behind!" And the other side has similarly mobilized exaggerated forecasts of doom. Sven Birkerts, for example, laments new media as a dire threat to essential habits of wisdom, "the struggle for which has for millennia been central to the very idea of culture."[3]

There are some encouraging recent signs that the exaggerated prophecies of utopia or dystopia are fading and we are beginning the more sober process of assessing where computers, networks, and digital media (our working definition of "technology") are and aren't useful. Rather than apocalyptic transformation, we seem to be heading toward what Phil Agre calls the "digestion model." "As a new technology arises," he observes, "various organized groups of participants in an existing institutional field selectively appropriate the technology in order to do more of what they are already doing—assimilating new technology to old roles, old practices, and old ways of thinking. And yet once this appropriation takes place, the selective amplification of particular functions disrupts the equilibrium of the existing order, giving rise to dynamics internal to the institution and the eventual emergence of a new, perhaps qualitatively different equilibrium."[4]

In social studies education, we have already begun the process of "selective appropriation" of technology. But before we can move to a new and better equilibrium, we need to ask some difficult questions. First, and most important, what are we trying to accomplish? Second, what approaches will work best? Third, are there dangers that we need to avoid as we selectively appropriate new technology into the social studies classroom? Fourth, how can we encourage and support the adoption and development of the best practices?

## WHY USE TECHNOLOGY IN SOCIAL STUDIES EDUCATION?

Over the past five years of running technology workshops with thousands of college and precollege teachers, we have usually begun by asking them, "What are you doing now in your teaching that you would like to do better? What do you wish your students did more often or differently? What pedagogical problems are you looking to solve?" Most commonly, they say they want their students to be more engaged with learning; they want students to construct new and better relationships to knowledge, not just represent it on tests; and they want students to acquire deeper, more lasting understanding of essential concepts.

Such responses run counter to another public discourse about history and social science education: the worry, often alarm, about student knowledge of a body of factual material. "Surely a grade of 33 in 100 on the simplest and most obvious facts of American history is not a record in which any high school can take pride," goes a lament that anyone who follows social studies education will find familiar. It should be familiar: This particular quote comes from a study published in the *Journal of Educational Psychology* in 1917. As educational psychologist Sam Wineburg points out, "Considering the differences between the elite stratum of society attending high school in 1917 and the near universal enrollments of today, the stability of this ignorance inspires incredulity. Nearly everything has changed between 1917 and today except for one thing: kids don't know any history."[5] Also unchanged is the persistent worry by school boards and public officials about that seeming ignorance.

And yet based on our own experience, this is not the problem that most concerns those teaching in our classrooms (except insofar as curriculum standards and exams constrain innovation and flexibility); neither is the problem that most concerns those who have studied in those classrooms. In 1994, we undertook a nationwide study of a representative cross-section of 808 Americans (as well as additional special samples of 600 African Americans, Mexican Americans, and Sioux Indians) that sought to uncover how Americans use and understand the past. We asked a portion of our sample "to pick one word or phrase to describe your experiences with history classes in elementary or high school." Negative descriptions significantly outweighed positive ones. "Boring" was the single most common word offered. In the entire study, the words "boring" or "boredom" almost never appeared in descriptions of activities connected with the pursuit of the past, with the significant exception of respondents' comments about studying history in school, where it comes up repeatedly.[6]

The same point came across even more clearly when we asked respondents to identify how connected with the past they felt in seven different situations: gathering with their families, celebrating holidays, reading books, watching films, visiting museums or historic sites, and studying history in school. Respondents ranked classrooms dead last, with an average score of 5.7 on a 10-point scale (as compared with 7.9 when they gathered with their families). Whereas one-fifth of respondents reported feeling very connected with the past in school (by giving those experiences a rank of 8 or higher), more than two-thirds felt very connected with the past when they gathered with their families. Of course, the comparison we posed is not an entirely fair one. Schools are the only compulsory activity we asked about; the others are largely voluntary (although some might disagree about family gatherings). Still, our survey finds people most detached from the past in the place that they most systematically encountered it: the schools.

To be sure, these negative comments about classroom-based history were not always reflected in remarks about specific teachers. Respondents applauded teachers for engaging students in the study of the past through active learning. A North Carolina man in his mid-twenties, for example, praised a teacher who "got us very involved" because she "took us on various trips and we got hands-on" history. A Bronx woman similarly talked enthusiastically about the "realism" of a class project's engagement with an incident in Puerto Rican history: "Everybody had different information about it, and everyone was giving different things about the same thing, so it made it very exciting."

Although teachers could make history classrooms resemble the settings in which respondents liked to engage the past, most Americans reported that history classrooms more often seemed to include a content that was removed from their interests and to feature memorization and regurgitation of senseless details. Respondents recalled with great vehemence how teachers had required them to memorize and regurgitate names, dates, and details that had no connection to them. They often added that they forgot the details as soon as the exam had ended. Such complaints could be captured in the words of a thirty-six-year-old financial analyst from Palo Alto, California: "It was just a giant data dump that we were supposed to memorize . . . just numbers and names and to this day I still can't remember them."

Not everyone would agree with these complaints. Others argue that the real problem of the schools is historical and civic illiteracy: a lack of knowledge of the basic facts about history, politics, and society. Our own view (and that of the teachers with whom we have worked) is that such factual knowledge emerges out of active engagement with learning rather than out of textbook- and test-driven curriculum. Given that these are contentious issues, we think that it is important to acknowledge our bias up front. The problem we seek to address is the one that preoccupies the teachers with whom we have worked and the survey respondents with whom we talked: How can the history classroom become a site of active learning and critical thinking? Can technology foster those goals?

## WHAT WORKS? THREE FRAMEWORKS FOR USING TECHNOLOGY TO PROMOTE ACTIVE LEARNING

The encouraging, albeit anecdotal news from the field is that technology has served those goals for a number of teachers and students across the country and that an emerging body of experience suggests some of the most promising approaches. Our own framework for categorizing and discussing these approaches grows out of our observation of scores of teachers in workshops sponsored by the American Studies Crossroads Project, the New Media Classroom, and the Library of Congress's American Memory Fellows program.[7] Based on these interactions, we have concluded that the most successful educational uses of digital technology fall into three broad categories:

> *Inquiry-based learning* using primary sources available on CD-ROMs and the World Wide Web and including the exploration of multimedia environments with potentially fluid combinations of text, image, sound, and moving images in presentational and inquiry activities, involving different senses and forms of expression and addressing different learning styles

> *Bridging reading and writing through online interaction,* extending the time and space for dialogue and learning, and joining literacy with disciplinary and interdisciplinary inquiry

> *Making student work public in new media formats,* encouraging constructivist pedagogies through the creation and exchange of knowledge representations and creating opportunities for review by broader professional and public audiences

Each type of activity takes advantage of particular qualities of the new media. And each type of activity is also linked to particular pedagogical strategies and goals.

## Inquiry Activities: The Novice in the Archive

Probably the most important influence of the availability of digital materials and computer networks has been on the development of inquiry-based exercises rooted in retrieving and analyzing primary social and cultural documents. These range from simple Web exercises in which students must find a photo that tells something about work in the late nineteenth century to elaborate assignments in which students carefully consider how different photographers, artists, and writers historically have treated the subject of poverty. Indeed, teachers report that inquiry activities with digital materials have been effective at all levels of the K–12 curriculum. In Hillsborough, California, for example, middle school students simulate the work of historians by closely analyzing images of children at the turn of the century that can be found online. They build from that to a semester-long project that asks students to construct an understanding of the major themes of the period and how they might affect a child born in 1900. To do that, they must assemble a physical and digital scrapbook of letters, images, oral histories, artifacts, and diary entries and think critically about those sources.[8] Similarly, fourth graders in New York use the Works Progress Administration (WPA) life histories on line at the Library of Congress to reconstruct the worlds of immigrants and then use photographs from online archives to illustrate these narratives in poster presentations. And high school juniors in Kansas City scrutinize the "Registers of Free Blacks" at the *Valley of the Shadow* Civil War Web site not only to learn about the lives of free African Americans in the Shenandoah Valley before the Civil War but also to reflect on the uses and limitations of different kinds of digital and primary materials to achieve an understanding of the past.[9]

The analysis of primary sources and the structured inquiry learning process often used in such examinations are widely recognized as essential steps in building student interest in history and culture and helping them understand the ways in which scholars engage in research, study, and interpretation. Primary documents give students a sense of the reality and the complexity of the past; they represent an opportunity to go beyond the predigested, seamless quality of most textbooks to engage with real people and problems. The fragmentary and contradictory nature of primary sources can be challenging and frustrating but also intriguing and ultimately rewarding, helping students understand the problematic nature of evidence and the constructed quality of historical and social interpretations. Almost all versions of the national standards for social studies and history published in the 1990s have (in this regard, at least) followed the lead of the 1994 *National Standards for United States History,* which declared that "perhaps no aspect of historical thinking is as exciting to students or as productive of their growth as historical thinkers as 'doing history'" by directly encountering "historical documents, eyewitness accounts, letters, diaries, artifacts, [and] photos."[10]

Of course, the use of primary sources and inquiry methods does not require digital tools. Teachers have long used documentary anthologies and source books (often taking advantage of a somewhat less recent technological advance, the Xerox machine). But the rise of new media and new computer technology has fostered and improved inquiry-based teaching for three key reasons.

First and most obviously is the greatly enhanced access to primary sources that CD-ROMs and the Internet have made possible. Almost overnight, teachers, school librarians, and students who previously had scant access to the primary materials from which scholars construct interpretations of society and culture gained access to vast depositories of primary cultural and historical materials. A single Internet connection gives teachers at inner-city urban schools access to more primary source materials than the best-funded private or suburban high school in the United States. Just the ninety different collections (containing about 5 million different primary documents) that the Library of Congress has made available since the mid-1990s constitute a revolution in the resources available to those who teach about American history, society, or culture. And almost weekly, major additional archives are coming online. These include such diverse collections as the U.S. Supreme Court Multimedia Database, at Northwestern University (with its huge archive of written and audio decisions and arguments before to the Court), the U.S. Holocaust Memorial Museum (with its searchable database of 50,000 images), and Exploring the French Revolution, at George Mason University (with its comprehensive archive of images and documents).[11]

For the history and social studies teacher and the school librarian, even the most frequently criticized feature of the Web—the unfiltered presence of large amounts of junk—can be an opportunity, albeit one that must be approached with care. Biased Web sites in the hands of the creative teacher are fascinating and revealing primary sources. In effect, many skills traditionally taught by social studies teacher—for example, the critical evaluation of sources—have become even more important in the online world. The Web offers an exciting and authentic arena in which students can learn to become critical consumers of information. Equally important, the Web presents the student with social knowledge used in a "real" context. A student studying Marcus Garvey or Franklin Roosevelt through Web-based sources learns not only what Garvey or Roosevelt did in the 1920s and 1930s but also what these historical figures mean to people in the present.

A second appealing feature of this new distributed cultural archive is its multimedia character. The teacher with the Xerox machine is limited to written texts and static (and perhaps poorly copied) images. Now, teachers can engage their students with analyzing the hundreds of early motion pictures placed online by the Library of Congress, the speeches and oral histories available at the National Gallery of Recorded Sound that Michigan State is beginning to assemble, and hundreds of thousands of historical photographs.[12]

Third, the digitization of documents allows students to examine them with supple electronic tools, conducting searches that facilitate and transform the inquiry process. For example, the American Memory Collection provides search engines that operate within and across collections; if one is researching sharecropping in the thousands of interview transcripts held in the Federal Writers' Project archive, a search can quickly find (and take you to) every mention of sharecropping in every transcript. Similarly, searches for key words such as *race* or *ethnicity* turn up interesting patterns and unexpected insights into the language and assumptions of the day. In other words, the search engines not only help students to find what they are looking for, they also allow them to examine patterns of word usage and language formation within and across documents.

These kinds of activities—searching, examining patterns, discovering connections between artifacts—are all germane to the authentic thinking processes of historians and scholars of society and culture. Digital media not only give flexible access to these resources but also make visible the often invisible archival contexts from which interpretive meaning is derived. "Everyone knows the past was wonderfully complex," notes historian Ed Ayres. "In conventional practice, historians obscure choices and compromises as we winnow evidence through finer and finer grids of note-taking, narrative, and analysis, as the abstracted patterns take on a fixity of their own. A digital archive, on the other hand, reminds us every time we look at it of the connections we are not making, of the complications of the past."[13]

The combination of increased access with the development of powerful digital searching tools has the potential to transform the nature and the scale of students' relationship to the material itself. For the first time, perhaps, it allows the novice learner to get into the archives and engage in the kinds of archival activities that only expert learners used to be able to do.[14] Of course, the nature of their encounter with primary materials and primary processes is still as novice learners. The unique opportunity with electronic, simulated archives is to create open but guided experiences for students that would be difficult or impractical to recreate in most research library environments. It also frees students and teachers from their traditional dependence on place for first-hand social, political, or historical research. Or, perhaps more importantly, it means that students can more readily compare their own community with others, more distant.

The task of creating these open but guided experiences is demanding. Teachers must not only learn how to use the new technology but also spend time exploring the digital archives (perhaps in partnership with school librarians) to learn what they hold and consider what students can learn from them. Constructing effective inquiry activities demands knowledge of the topic, the documents, the archive, and the craft of introducing students to the inquiry process. Implementing inquiry approaches in the classroom takes class time that teachers sometimes are reluctant to give. And the inquiry process is by definition not easy to control; students are likely to come up with unanticipated answers. At their best, however, new media technologies can help make the intermediate processes of historical cognition visible and accessible to learners, in part by helping students approach problem solving and knowledge making as open, revisable processes and in part by providing tools to give teachers—as expert learners—a window into student thinking processes.[15]

## Bridging Reading and Writing through Online Interaction

One very significant dimension of "making thinking visible" is the bridging of reading and writing through online writing and electronic dialogue. The benefits of writing and dialogue for student learning were well established before the emergence of computers and the Internet. Over the last several decades, educators in many disciplines and at every level of education have come to believe that meaningful education involves students not merely as passive recipients of knowledge dispensed by the instructor but as active contributors to the learning process. One of the key elements in this pedagogy is the importance of student discussion and interaction with the instructor and with each other, which provides opportunities for students to articulate, exchange, and deepen their learning. Educators in a wide range of settings practice variations of this process.

But the emergence of digital media, tools, and networks has multiplied the possibilities. Electronic mail, electronic discussion lists, and Web bulletin boards can support and enhance such pedagogies by creating new spaces for group conversations.[16] One of the greatest advantages to using electronic interaction involves the writing process, which can facilitate complex thinking and learning and build related skills. These advantages can combine with the potential for electronic discussion to draw out students who remain silent in face-to-face discussion. Online interaction has also proven to be effective in helping to build connections between subject-based learning and literacy skills (reading and writing), which too often are treated separately.

Online discussion tools also foster community and dialogue. Active, guided dialogue helps involve students in the processes of making knowledge, testing and rehearsing interpretations, and communicating their ideas to others in public ways. Another advantage to online dialogue tools is in helping students make connections beyond the classroom, whether it is enhancing the study of regional and national history through connections with a classroom elsewhere in the United States or enhancing global social studies curricula through e-mail "pen pal" programs with students elsewhere in the world. Postcard Geography is a simple project, organized through the Internet, in which hundreds of classes (particularly elementary school classes) learn geography by exchanging postcards (real and virtual, purchased and computer generated) with each other. An Alabama elementary school teacher notes the galvanizing effect of the project on her rural students who "don't get out of their city, let alone their state or country!"[17] At North Hagerstown High School in Maryland, high school students mount online discussions of issues such as the crisis in Kosovo, engaging in dialogue among themselves and with more far-flung contributors, from Brooklyn to Belgrade.[18]

## Designing Constructive Public Spaces for Learning

Closely connected to both online writing and inquiry activities is the third dimension of our framework: the use of constructive virtual spaces as environments for students to synthesize their reading and writing through public products. As with the other uses of new technology, the advantages of public presentations of student work are well known. But, here again, the new technology—particularly the emergence of the Web as a public space that is accessible to all—has greatly leveraged an existing practice. Virtual environments offer many layers of public space that help make thinking visible and lead students to develop a stronger sense of public accountability for their ideas. The creation of public, constructed projects is another manifestation of these public pedagogies, one that engages students significantly in the design and building of knowledge products as a critical part of the learning process.

In the use of new media technologies in culture and history fields, constructivist and constructionist approaches provide ways for students to make their work public in new media spaces as part of the learning process, ranging from the individual construction of Web pages to participation in large, ongoing collaborative resource projects that involve many students and faculty over many years development.[19] For example, at an elementary school in Virginia, fifth graders studying world cultures build a different wing of a virtual museum each year, researching and annotating cultural artifacts and then mounting them online; similarly, at a middle school in Philadelphia sixth graders worked closely with a local museum to create a CD-ROM exhibit on Mesopotamia, using images and resources from the museum's collections.[20] Seventh graders in Arlington, Virginia published an online "Civil War Newspaper" with Matthew Brady photographs from the Library of Congress as well as their own analyses of the photos.[21] More ambitious student-constructed projects can evolve over several years and connect students more closely to their communities as in St. Ignatius, Montana, where high school students have helped to create online community archives.[22]

The power of the digital environment for these kinds of projects comes not merely from their public nature but also from the capabilities of electronic tools for representing knowledge in nonlinear ways and through multiple media and multiple voices. Digital tools can represent complex connections and relationships and make large amounts of information available and manipulable. There is great potential, which we have only begun to understand, in using digital tools for constructionist learning approaches that help students acquire and express the complexity of culture and history knowledge. Student constructionist projects offer a potentially very rich synthesis of resources and expressive capabilities; they combine archival and database resources with conversational, collaborative, and dialogic tools, in digital contexts characterized by hypertext and other modes for discovering and representing relationships between knowledge objects.

## WHAT TO AVOID?:
## HAZARDS ALONG THE ELECTRONIC FRONTIERS

These are all appealing goals, and there is some encouraging but preliminary experience to suggest that technology can help us achieve them. But it would be foolish, if not dangerous, to suggest that technology is a panacea for the problems of history education or that any of these approaches is easy to implement. Indeed, the most serious danger of introducing technology into the classroom is the mistaken assumption that it, alone, can transform education. The single-minded application of technological solutions to teaching will as surely be as much of a disaster as the application of single-minded solutions to agriculture or forest management. As the first generation of scientific foresters learned, any change in a complex environment must be thought about ecologically.[23] New technologically enhanced approaches, whether inquiry-based learning or student constructionist exercises, must be carefully introduced within the context of existing teaching approaches and existing courses and assignments. What assignments are already working well? How will a new assignment alter the overall balance of a course? How do new approaches manifest themselves throughout a curriculum or a school?

By asking these questions, we should be also reminding ourselves to use technology only where it makes a clear contribution to classroom learning. Some teaching strategies work better with traditional materials. A teacher who has students post rules of historical significance on butcher paper around the classroom may find that their visual presence is stronger on the classroom walls than on the class Web site. More generally, technology generally is better used to provide a deeper understanding of some pivotal issues through inquiry and constructionist assignments rather than being pressed into service to respond to standards-based pressures for coverage.

By always thinking about whether new technologies respond to the goals with which we began, we can also be alert to the situations in which technology might operate in the opposite direction from which we intend. Here, it is important to acknowledge that although there are plenty of positive experiences with technology to draw upon, there is also a large body of negative examples that we need to learn from. The most obvious set of examples can be found in a large body of educational software that promotes passivity rather than the much-promised "interactivity." One of the great advantages of digital media—the ability to incorporate sound and film with text and images— is also one of its greatest problems because of the temptation to turn history into TV commercials in which the media glitz overwhelms sustained contact with difficult ideas. This has been the case with some multi-million-dollar multimedia extravaganzas that offer multiple interpretations of topics without giving the user any sense of which interpretations are more plausible than others or without any real level of interactivity that encourages active and critical thinking.

Some of these same tendencies were also embodied in the worst of the CD-ROMs that appeared on the market in the early and mid-1990s. In many, the notion of multimedia was a voice reading words that already appeared on the screen. One CD-ROM (which sold for $395) turned out to be a recycled filmstrip—and a twenty-five-year-old one at that.[24] Such uses of digital media promote the same deadening memorization of facts that generations of students have complained about and waste scarce school funds on the products of sleazy educational hucksters.

The pressure of commercial vendors leads to a related pitfall: the possibility that school systems will invest in equipment, software, and narrowly defined technological training at the expense of funding professional development to use new technology wisely. Computers are expensive, delicate machines that break down often and need maintenance. The rapid development of the field means that computer labs quickly become outdated. Wiring classrooms for Internet access is expensive and sometimes difficult, particularly in older school buildings. Software can also be costly, and the constant updates necessary to stay in step with new resources increase the demand for instructional technology staff. Providing effective staff development for teachers throughout the educational system would add significantly to the cost of purchasing hardware. The combined expense of installing, maintaining, and supporting the effective use of operative computer labs can be overwhelming. And, as Diane Ravitch rightly points out, "the billions spent on technology represent money not spent on music, art, libraries, maintenance and other essential functions."[25]

Such costs weigh unevenly on different schools, school systems, and communities, another key threat that new technology poses. Underresourced schools and colleges have a particularly difficult time finding the funds to buy new technology. Although federal, state, and corporate grant programs are helpful, they are not sufficient, and they usually pay only for hardware, not for maintenance or staff development. As a result, the schools and colleges serving poor and working-class communities lag behind in the effective implementation of technology. And their students—disproportionately African American or Latino—suffer most. According to a 1999 report from the National Center for Education Statistics, 51 percent of public school classrooms nationwide have Internet access. But for schools with large numbers of poor or minority students, the number drops to less than 40 percent. This disparity shapes colleges and universities as well. Whereas 80.1 percent of all students entering elite private colleges report that they use computers regularly, only 41.1 percent of students entering historically black colleges report similar usage. In many colleges, students who come from underresourced school systems will find technology to be one more item on an already daunting list of educational and social challenges. There is a real and growing threat that new technology will add to the already immense nationwide stratification of educational opportunity. Indeed, a 1999 national report on the digital divide indicates that technology use continues to split along lines of class and race.[26] And the problem is even worse when considered internationally.

Finally, there is the larger danger that educators, parents, and school boards will come to see technology as an end in itself rather than a means to achieving better student learning. Technology can be a powerful narcotic that lulls us into believing that we are teaching students to think simply by putting machines into classrooms. The hardest intellectual and pedagogical problems—teaching students to judge the quality of information, deal with conflicting evidence, and develop analytical frameworks—are present in both the print and digital environments.

## WHAT NEXT? TOWARD STUDENT LEARNING

Not surprisingly, our recommendations for the future grow out of our experience with this decade-long history of digital technology in the social studies classroom.

First, we urge a renewed national commitment to ensuring that the benefits of new technology are shared equally. Many others have made the same point, and there is little need to belabor it here.

Second (and while we are still tilting at windmills), we argue that assessment must be revised to accurately measure learning in the new media environment. Right now, standards and assessment tend to hinder the integration of technology into teaching. When assessment entails pre-twentieth-century technology (i.e., pen and paper) and is focused on content and factual knowledge, as in most states, teachers are understandably reluctant to adopt strategies that take advantage of the potential of technology to promote deeper understanding. But if the assessment were designed to reflect deeper understanding of reading, interpreting, and arguing processes and other things students need to know in the twenty-first century—including how to use the Internet and computers to research, analyze, and present information—then the integration of technology into the social studies and other academic curricula would be greatly fostered.

Third, teachers need more tools and supports that will enable them to use electronic resources actively and critically. Teachers value gateway sites because they provide reliable starting points, filtering mechanisms, and sample curricula for using the Web.[27] In addition, because many teachers are novices in the archives, they need guides to evaluating and analyzing primary source materials. They also need the kinds of software tools that allow their students to collaborate electronically with ease. And they need access to software and hardware that make student constructionist projects feasible in multiple settings. Such software environments must be open and flexible, not one-size-fits-all templates that presuppose certain teaching styles or approaches.

Fourth, teachers need robust professional development programs that will allow them to retool for the electronic future. The billions of dollars invested in preparing schools for the twenty-first century have gone (and continue to go) overwhelmingly to hardware and wiring. Where teachers lack necessary training and support, computer labs often wind up gathering dust or being used as glorified typing labs. If meaningful progress is to occur in this field, funding for professional development must be given equal priority with funding for hardware. But it is not simply a matter of the quantity of available faculty development; it is also a question of quality. Typically, professional development in technology focuses narrowly on building technology skills or familiarizing teachers with particular software applications. The most common faculty development structure is a two- to four-hour workshop led by technology support staff who are skilled in technical issues but distant from the latest thinking about disciplinary content and teaching methodology. Our experience and feedback from our colleagues suggests the importance of developing a different approach.

In particular, we encourage leaders in the field to create, nurture, and support professional development approaches that are deeply rooted in the issues and experiences of everyday classroom practice, build directly on teacher's expertise teaching in nontechnological settings, and help teachers adapt their skills to a new context. They need to speak to real classroom needs, helping teachers find ways to use technology to solve long-standing problems, do their work better, and more effectively reach their goals for their courses and their students. And they must point teachers toward classroom implementation, testing, and experimentation with real students in real classroom situations. In addition, professional development must involve a sustained and recursive process. Instead of one-shot workshops, effective professional development with technology must unfold over time and provide multiple opportunities for teachers to move back and forth between initial training workshops, classroom testing, and reflective seminars where they can articulate and collectively analyze their experiments using new technology resources.

Such approaches will benefit from the effective uses of technology. One of the most exciting things the Internet has brought to teachers has been the erosion of the isolation that traditionally afflicts the classroom teacher. The teachers with whom we have worked in Crossroads, the New Media Classroom, and the American Memory Fellows program have acquired a much broader set of colleagues than was possible before. They consult with each other on how to teach a particular subject or organize a particular assignment. Other teachers have developed mutually supportive relationships with teachers across the country whom they have never met but with whom they converse through lists such as H-High, H-Teach, the "Talking History" forums sponsored by *History Matters*, or "Highroads" sponsored by Crossroads. In some of these settings, the high school teacher in Kansas City can get advice on the latest developments in women's history from a leading scholar such as Gerda Lerner or find out about successful assignments from an award-winning high school teacher from Virginia. The often chaotic environment of the Web also encourages teachers to forge partnerships with school librarians, who can bring particular skills in information evaluation to the table.

Fifth, given the difficulty of altering entrenched patterns of professional development, it makes sense to focus efforts on preservice education as well as in-service. Such efforts, as manifest in education curricula and state certification requirements, must go far beyond courses on new media and teaching methods. Future teachers most need discipline-based courses in which technology is integrated into the course content. Such courses can enable teachers to understand the archive-at-a-mouse-click not as some new way to bring the library to the doorstep but as a fundamental shift in how society handles knowledge, its accessibility, and what one can do with it. Moreover, teachers will never make effective use of the vast archives now accessible to them unless they understand, for example, the nature of historical evidence and argumentation or other disciplinary contexts for using new media.[28] More generally, educating teachers to use technology effectively must go far beyond simple training in software or techniques for implementation to include an initiation into habits of reflective practice that will allow them to adapt and innovate in new learning environments throughout their careers, even as specific technologies and applications change.

Sixth, we need to acknowledge that we are still at the starting point of the selective appropriation of new technology and that we need serious classroom research into what does and doesn't work. Some of this research must come from professional educational researchers. But we also believe that research can be combined with professional development where the teacher becomes the researcher. The approaches that have begun to emerge on the college level under the rubric of the scholarship of teaching are beginning to be explored on the precollege level as well.[29]

But whatever approaches we take, we need to return continually to first principles and ask, What are we trying to accomplish in the classroom? Can technology help make that possible? One way to do this is to recall the old joke about a man who works in a factory and leaves there every evening with a wheelbarrow full of straw. Every night as he exits the factory and passes through the gate, the guard looks through the straw, certain that the man is stealing something. At the end of twenty years employment, the man is departing with his wheelbarrow full of straw, as always. The guard turns to the man and says,

> "For twenty years you have been leaving every night with a wheelbarrow full of straw. For twenty years, every night, I look through the straw and find nothing. I know you have been stealing something. This is your last night. For my own curiosity, you have to tell me: what have you been stealing all these years?"
> The man replied, "Wheelbarrows."

If that joke were taken as an analogy, then technology is the straw. It is merely the prop by which we are getting something more valuable (the wheelbarrow) out the door. And what are the more valuable things we're trying to get out the door? They are the enhancement of learning through interaction and dialogue; an increasingly expansive, inclusive, and socially conscientious approach to the study of history, society, and culture; and the elevation of our standards for what passes as student learning.

## NOTES

This chapter was originally written for the U.S. Department of Education's "Forum on Technology in Education: Envisioning the Future," held in Washington, D.C., in December 1999. An earlier version was published in the *Journal of Education* 181:3 (1999) and is reprinted with their permission. Some of the material in this chapter was drawn from "Teaching Culture, Learning Culture, and New Media Technologies," by Randy Bass and Bret Eynon, an introductory essay for the volume "Intentional Media: The Crossroads Conversations on Learning and Technology in the American Culture and History Classroom," *Works & Days* (Spring/Fall 1998). The authors are indebted to Bret Eynon, deputy director of the American Social History Project/Center for Media and Learning, both for his contributions to the earlier text and, more significantly, to the ideas behind this chapter, which are in many ways the product of his collaborations. We also want to thank the following for helpful comments on and suggestions for this chapter: Debbie Abilock, Mike Alcoff, Marta Brooks, Leni Donlan, John Elfrank-Dana, Kathy Isaacs, Frances Jacobson, Dawn Jaeger, Ron Stoloff, Carl Schulkin, Peter Seixas, Bill Tally, Eileen Walsh, and Sam Wineburg.

1. Quotes from 1880 and 1881 *Scientific American* in Steven Lubar, *InfoCulture: The Smithsonian Book of Information Age Inventions* (Boston: Houghton Mifflin, 1993), 130, and Claude S. Fischer, *America Calling: A Social History of the Telephone to 1940* (Berkeley: University of California Press, 1992), 2 (see also pp. 1 and 26). Carolyn Marvin, *When Old Technologies Were New: Thinking about Electrical Communication in the Late Nineteenth Century* (New York: Oxford University Press, 1988) and Graham Rayman, "Hello, Utopia Calling?" in *Word* (no date) at <http://www.word.com/machine/jacobs/phone/index.html>.

2. Rossetto quoted in David Hudson, *Rewired: A Brief and Opinionated Net History* (Indianapolis: Macmillan Technical, 1997), 7; *Al-Jumhuriya* in R. J. Lambrose, "The Abusable Past," *Radical History Review* 70 (1998): 184.

3. Robert Lenzner and Stephen S. Johnson, "Seeing Things as They Really Are," *Forbes* (March 10, 1997), available online at <http://www.forbes.com/forbes/97/0310/5905122a. htm>; Birkerts in "The Electronic Hive: Two Views," "Refuse It" (Sven Birkerts), and "Embrace It" (Kevin Kelly), *Harper's Magazine* (May 1994), 17–21, 24–25. See also Sven Birkerts, *The Gutenberg Elegies: The Fate of Reading in an Electronic Age* (Boston: Faber & Faber, 1994); Todd Oppenheimer, "The Computer Delusion," *Atlantic Monthly* (July 1997), 45–62.

4. Philip E. Agre, "Communities and Institutions: The Internet and the Structuring of Human Relationships," circulated through Red Rock Eater's News Service, copy available at <http://www.egroups.com/group/rre/804.html>.

5. Sam Wineburg, "Making Historical Sense," in *History Education in a National and International Context,* ed. Peter Stearns, Sam Wineburg, and Peter Seixas (New York: New York University Press, 2000). On the question of factual knowledge, the most influential study of recent years has been Diane Ravitch and Chester Finn Jr., *What Do Our 17-Year-Olds Know? A Report on the First National Assessment of History and Literature* (New York: Harper & Row, 1987). There is a large literature debating the work of Ravitch and Finn.

See William Ayers, "What Do 17-Year-Olds Know? A Critique of Recent Research," *Education Digest* 53 (April 1988): 37–39; Dale Whittington, "What Have 17-Year-Olds Known in the Past?" *American Educational Research Journal* 28 (Winter 1991): 759–80; Deborah Meier and Florence Miller, "The Book of Lists," *Nation,* 245 (January 9, 1988): 25–27; and Terry Teachout, "Why Johnny Is Ignorant," *Commentary* 85 (March 1988): 69–71. There have been two more recent studies by the National Assessment of Education Progress (NAEP). For brief reports on these, see Michael Mehle, "History Basics Stump U.S. Kids, Study Finds," *Bergen Record,* April 3, 1990, A1; Carol Innerst, "History Test Results Aren't Encouraging; US Teens Flop on 'Basic' Quiz," *Washington Times,* November 2, 1995, A2.

6. Roy Rosenzweig and David Thelen, *The Presence of the Past: Popular Uses of History in American Life* (New York: Columbia University Press, 1998); see also <http://chnm.gmu.edu/survey>.

7. For Crossroads, see <http://www.georgetown.edu/crossroads/>; for New Media Classroom, which is cosponsored by American Social History Project/Center for Media & Learning (ASHP/CML) in collaboration with the American Studies Association's Crossroads Project, see <http://www.ashp.cuny.edu/index new.html>; for American Memory Fellows, see <http://memory.loc.gov/ammem/ndlpedu/amfp/intro.html>.

8. See <http://www.nueva.pvt.k12.ca.us/debbie/library/cur/20c/turn.html>.

9. For WPA life histories, see <http://lcweb2.loc.gov/ammem/ndlpedu/lesson97/firsthand/main.html>; for use of free black registers, see <http://historymatters.gmu.edu/text/3freeblacks-shulkin.html>.

10. National Center for History in the Schools, *National Standards for United States History: Exploring the American Experience* (Los Angeles: The Center, 1994), 29. The new American Association of School Librarians standards for student learning similarly focus on information literacy, the ability to find, select, analyze, and interpret primary sources. See "Information Power: The Nine Information Literacy Standards for Student Learning" at <http://www.ala.org/aasl/ip nine.html>.

11. The Oyez Project, Northwestern University, *U.S. Supreme Court Multimedia Database* at <http://oyez.nwu.edu/>; the *U.S. Holocaust Memorial Museum* at <http://www.ushmm.org>. *Liberty, Equality, Fraternity: Exploring the French Revolution,* developed by the Center for History and New Media at GMU and the American Social History Project at CUNY, is available at <http://chnm.gmu.edu/revolution>. For discussions of history Web sites, see Mike O'Malley and Roy Rosenzweig, "Brave New World or Blind Alley? American History on the World Wide Web," *Journal of American History* 84 (June 1997): 132–55; and Roy Rosenzweig, "The Road to Zanadu: Public and Private Pathways on the History Web," *Journal of American History* (Spring 2001).

12. Library of Congress, *Inventing Entertainment: The Early Motion Pictures and Sound Recordings of the Edison Companies* at <http://memory.loc.gov/ammem/edhtml/edhome.html>. For plans for National Gallery of Recorded Sound, see <http://www. h-net.msu.edu/about/press/ngsw.html>.

13. Ed Ayres, "The Futures of Digital History," paper delivered at the Organization of American Historians meeting, Toronto, April 1999 (copy in possession of authors).

14. On the novice in the archive, see Randy Bass, "Engines of Inquiry: Teaching, Technology, and Learner-Centered Approaches to Culture and History," in *Engines of Inquiry: A Practical Guide for Using Technology in Teaching American Culture* (Washington, D.C.:

American Studies Crossroads Project Publication, 1997), 1–35, which can be ordered from <http://www.georgetown.edu/crossroads>.

15. Sam Wineburg, "The Cognitive Representation of Historical Texts," in *Teaching and Learning in History,* ed. G. Leinhardt, I. L. Beck, and C. Stanton (Hillsdale, N.J.: Erlbaum, 1994), 85. See also Allan Collins, John Seeley Brown, and Ann Holum, "Cognitive Apprenticeship: Making Thinking Visible," *American Educator* 15 (Winter 1991): 6–11, 38–46.

16. At the collegiate level, one of the greatest advantages to using electronic interaction is that it increases the amount of time students are focused on and interacting about the subject. Another advantage is the opportunity for asynchronous discussion: Students can engage in the conversation on their own schedule rather than only when the instructor and other students are available.

17. See <http://www.internet-catalyst.org/projects/PCG/postcard.html>.

18. See <http://www.fred.net/nhhs/html/newspage.html>.

19. Constructivism is a theory of learning that emphasizes the active creation of knowledge by the learner rather than the imparting of information and knowledge by the instructor. A second meaning for constructivism, sometimes also called constructionism, is the extension of constructivist approaches that stresses the building of knowledge objects. "Constructionism," as defined by Yasmin Kafai and Mitchel Resnick, "suggests that learners are particularly likely to make new ideas when they are actively engaged in making some type of external artifact . . . which they can reflect upon and share with others" (Kafai and Resnick, *Constructionism in Practice: Designing, Thinking, and Learning in a Digital World* [Mahwah, N.J.: Erlbaum, 1996], 1).

20. See <http://www.fcps.k12.va.us/VirginiaRunES/museum/museum.htm>; Daniel Sipe, presentation at New Media Classroom, New York, July 1997.

21. See <http://www.wms-arl.org/amf1/student.htm>.

22. See <http://206.252.235.34/projects/local.htm>. For a taxonomy of student constructive projects, with links to school and college-based examples, see <http://www.georgetown. edu/crossroads/constructive.html>.

23. On the problems of scientific forestry, see James Scott, *Thinking Like a State: How Certain Schemes to Improve the Human Condition Have Failed* (New Haven, Conn.: Yale University Press, 1998), 11–22.

24. On history CD-ROMs, see Roy Rosenzweig, "So, What's Next for Clio?: CD-ROM and Historians," *Journal of American History* 81 (March 1995): 1621–40.

25. Diane Ravitch, "The Great Technology Mania," *Forbes* (March 23, 1998), available online at <http://www.forbes.com/forbes/98/0323/6106134a.htm>.

26. U.S. Department of Education, National Center for Education Statistics, "Internet Access in Public Schools and Classrooms: 1994–98," February 1999, available online at <http://nces.ed.gov/pubs99/1999017.html>. See also National Telecommunications and Information Administration, U.S. Department of Commerce, *Falling through the Net: Defining the Digital Divide* (July 1999), available at <http://www.ntia.doc.gov/ntiahome/digitaldivide/>; and Paul Attewell and Juan Battle, "Home Computers and School Performance," *The Information Society* 15:1 (1999): 1–10, which finds that students with computers at home have higher test scores even after controlling for family income but that children from high socioeconomic (and white) homes show larger educational gains with home computers than do minority children and those of lower socioeconomic status.

27. For two examples of gateways see *American Studies Electronic Crossroads* <http://www.georgetown.edu/crossroads/> and *History Matters: The U.S. Survey Course on the Web* <http://historymatters.gmu.edu>.

28. See Sam Wineburg, "Historical Thinking and Other Unnatural Acts," *Phi Delta Kappan* 80 (March 1999): 488–99.

29. An extensive national project on applying the scholarship of teaching to history and the humanities is the Visible Knowledge Project, based in the Center for New Designs in Learning and Scholarship at Georgetown University, Washington, D.C. See <http://crossroads.georgetown.edu/vkp/>. For more information on broad, cross-disciplinary approaches to the scholarship of teaching in higher education and K–12 education, see the Carnegie Foundation for the Advancement of Teaching at <http://www. carnegiefoundation.org/>.

# PART 2

# Computing and New Access to Social Science Data: Innovations in Applications

# 3 / Validity of Web-Based Surveys: Explorations with Data from 2,382 Teenagers

**The World Wide Web** offers many advantages for administering questionnaire surveys, yet survey researchers are reluctant to use it because of concerns about the quality of respondent samples.[1] This chapter considers the value of Web-based surveys and questions that must be addressed about their reliability and validity, anchoring the discussion in data from 2,382 children aged thirteen through fifteen obtained in late 1998 as part of the *Survey 2000* project.[2] Our analytical method is to compare responses from two very different subsets of respondents. To illustrate the substantive value of Web-based survey data, we focus on an empirical question of widespread scientific and public interest: the differences in attitudes and interests between girls and boys. In addition, the design of this study reveals much about the differences between children who actively use the Web and those who do not.

On November 2, 1999, *The Washington Post* reported that women slightly outnumber men among AOL subscribers and that they are approaching parity among American users of the Internet more generally.[3] It seems likely that AOL's subscriber list is unrepresentative, but a number of different indicators seem to show that women are increasing their representation in a number of previously male domains. For example, from 1966 to 1995, the proportion of American doctorates in science and engineering going to women rose from 8.0 percent to 31.2 percent.[4] A survey of a narrow age group done at a single point in time cannot chart changes over the years. But it can examine the connections between gender and a number of other variables, explore the connections between those variables, and identify indicators and measurement scales that can be used in a series of studies over time to see how the transformations are progressing. Our goals here are primarily methodological, but we use the issue of gender differences to illustrate the problems and advantages of Web-based questionnaires.

*Survey 2000* was an extensive, pioneering Internet survey sponsored by the National Geographic Society and created by a team headed by sociologist James Witte. There were several versions of the survey for people of different ages and nationalities. About 50,000 adults completed the survey, mostly Americans and Canadians but with at least 100 from each of thirty-three other nations. The chief focus of the survey was migration, regional culture, and community involvement. For U.S. and Canadian respondents over age fifteen, the computer individually tailored sections of the questionnaire about food and literature preferences in accordance with the respondent's region of birth and current region of residence. Some of the numerous questions about musical preferences played sound clips over the respondent's computer, asking him or her to evaluate them.

Children aged thirteen through fifteen answered a long but straightforward questionnaire containing major sections of questions about their favorite activities, musical preferences, friends' values, and attitudes toward science. A total of 2,942 completed the survey at one of five locations: at home (51.3 percent), at school (40.6 percent), at a parent's workplace (1.7 percent), at a community center or library (1.3 percent), or at some other location such as a friend's house (3.3 percent). Most of those who responded at school did so as part of a class assignment in connection with Geography Awareness Week, and National Geographic recruited teachers in all U.S. states and Canadian provinces to have their students participate. Thus, school respondents are more like a random sample than are the teenagers who responded at home, attracted by advertisements in National Geographic publications and on the society's popular Web site.[5]

## CONCERNS ABOUT WEB-BASED SURVEYS

Sociology, political science, cultural anthropology, and perhaps several related fields are not merely sciences but also include aspects of the humanities, social criticism, and political action. In addition, their topic areas are highly complex, and even the best scientific methods have limited power. Thus, there is a constant danger that other tendencies will overwhelm the scientific orientation of these fields, and researchers dedicated to systematic methods are understandably nervous about relaxing their standards of rigor. Ultimately, they may fear that the dam of rationality may burst, and antiscientific elements will take over these vulnerable fields. In this context, Web-based surveys may seem dangerous, even reckless.

This is not the place to critique traditional survey methods or to criticize particular existing surveys. But it should be noted that expensive national samples fall somewhat short of being true random samples, and the complexity of their sampling frames often makes it difficult to determine the exact degree to which this is the case. Furthermore, the high cost of this approach typically limits the number of items that can be included. Much of the sophisticated multiple-indicator methodology developed a quarter century ago has been abandoned in a heroic attempt to maximize the representativeness of the sample. Some political scientists give a high priority to predicting election outcomes, and for them the sample of respondents should match actual voters as closely as possible.[6] Research that attempts to track social indicators over time, such as the structure of the American family or the personal well-being of citizens, needs stable sampling methods throughout the years. Studies of social class stratification certainly need data about all social classes, and random samples may be the best way to obtain them.

On the other hand, other research areas such as culture, ideology, personality, and economic preferences may need data about a very large number of variables, some of which may be meaningful only to small subgroups in the general population. Some of my own work falls in this area, notably studies I did using informal purposive samples of people who had thoughts and opinions about space flight and science fiction, topics of little interest to most citizens. In each case, a battery of more than 100 questionnaire items were to be rated on a consistent scale, and the data were subjected to an exploratory factor analysis or cluster analysis to identify dimensions of variation or groups of items that fit together in respondents' minds. The aim is to identify underlying cultural schemas, folk categorization systems, or other mental constructs that guide people with respect to the topic in question. As in the development of personality tests in psychology, nonrandom samples produced the initial data for identifying clusters of cultural elements and developing measurement scales. Subsequent research can determine whether the findings generalize to other populations.

The reliability and validity of Web-based surveys are a subject for research and debate, not assumption, and may depend very much on the scientific goals. Surveys can be targeted to specific populations and even to selected lists of individuals over Internet and need not be a convenience sample of visitors to a Web site.[7] However, the difficulty of motivating targeted individuals and the fact that many people still cannot be reached via Internet mean that Web-based surveys may often be far less representative than conventional surveys, even though the latter fall short of being true random samples of the population. Thus we need to develop means to compensate for these limitations, to the extent possible, which requires us to explore the nature of these limitations empirically.

Young teens who responded at home to *Survey 2000* probably differ from at-school respondents in several ways. There ought to be social class differences because computers with Internet access are still much more common in affluent households. Most at-home respondents found the survey from advertisements in the National Geographic Society's magazines or Web site, so they are probably more intellectual and culturally cosmopolitan than the average child their age. On the other hand, they are probably less busy with other things that would prevent them from surfing the Web, such as social gatherings and outdoor activities.

The following analysis examines gender differences in four groups of *Survey 2000* items: favorite activities, attitudes toward science, musical preferences, and peer values. For each group of items, we compare the two groups of respondents in terms of the proportions who respond in a particular way and in the correlations linking the items to being female. We are particularly interested in cases in which one group exhibits a significant correlation but the other does not. All items in this study are dichotomous, and items that were recoded were handled in such a way that there are no missing data. This allows us to use simple quantitative methods of analysis, but the data will be made available by National Geographic to interested scholars who want to try different or more complex statistical techniques.

## FAVORITE ACTIVITIES

The largest section of the youth survey was headed "What Do You Like?" Three pages containing fifty-three items were offered with these instructions: "Look through the following list of activities and interests. Which are your favorites? (Check as many as apply.)." For example, the first page had six rows of three items each, and the first row was "❏ Acting/drama  ❏ Archaeology  ❏ Arts/crafts." The box to the left of each item was an HTML checkbox that allows the respondent to select as many of the items as desired. The first two columns of table 3.1 report how many children in each of the two groups checked each of the fifty-three boxes. For example, 42.7 percent of the children who answered at home checked the box for "acting/drama," compared with 34.3 percent of those who responded at school.

The fifty-three items are listed in alphabetical order, but it may make more sense to consider them in groups, based on how children responded to them. For example, there were twenty items for which there was a difference of more than ten percentage points in the proportions of the two groups who say the

*Table 3.1.* Children's Favorite Activities

| Favorite Interest or Activity | Percentage | | Correlation with Female | |
| --- | --- | --- | --- | --- |
| | Home | School | Home | School |
| 1. Acting/drama | 42.7 | 34.3 | .22** | .30** |
| 2. Archaeology | 25.4 | 10.4 | .05 | .00 |
| 3. Arts/crafts | 46.2 | 41.6 | .31** | .30** |
| 4. Astronomy | 35.8 | 15.6 | −.07 | .02 |
| 5. Baseball/cricket | 25.9 | 38.4 | −.14** | −.10* |
| 6. Basketball | 33.8 | 52.5 | −.02 | −.06 |
| 7. Bicycling | 49.1 | 49.3 | −.10* | −.09 |
| 8. Boating | 24.0 | 32.2 | −.01 | −.11** |
| 9. Bowling | 22.3 | 34.5 | −.02 | −.06 |
| 10. Camping | 43.7 | 46.8 | .01 | −.04 |
| 11. Cheerleading | 6.5 | 13.4 | .23** | .33** |
| 12. Collecting | 35.3 | 29.0 | −.03 | −.02 |
| 13. Computers | 71.5 | 54.0 | −.25** | −.19** |
| 14. Cooking | 31.2 | 37.3 | .19** | .27** |
| 15. Dancing | 26.1 | 32.7 | .35** | .42** |
| 16. Diving | 15.6 | 23.6 | .05 | .06 |
| 17. Dolls | 6.0 | 4.2 | .22** | .11* |
| 18. Environment | 38.0 | 21.2 | .07 | .07 |
| 19. Fishing | 25.0 | 42.9 | −.17** | −.29** |
| 20. Football (U.S.) | 22.3 | 45.8 | −.21** | −.41** |
| 21. Geography | 37.4 | 17.3 | −.15** | −.14** |
| 22. Gymnastics | 11.9 | 20.0 | .21** | .36** |
| 23. Hiking | 33.6 | 32.6 | .02 | −.05 |
| 24. History | 44.2 | 19.6 | −.05 | −.02 |
| 25. Horseback riding | 25.1 | 30.4 | .27** | .23** |
| 26. Ice hockey | 13.4 | 23.5 | −.09 | −.18** |
| 27. Ice skating | 21.3 | 29.6 | .19** | .21** |
| 28. Jump/skip rope | 8.3 | 12.9 | .17** | .21** |
| 29. Lacrosse | 3.5 | 7.1 | .03 | −.07 |
| 30. Martial arts | 11.3 | 15.8 | −.06 | −.12** |
| 31. Mathematics | 34.4 | 24.0 | −.09 | −.04 |
| 32. Music listening | 82.0 | 73.6 | .21** | .30** |
| 33. Music/play instrument | 46.0 | 32.1 | .12** | .06 |
| 34. Music/singing | 35.5 | 35.9 | .30** | .41** |
| 35. Pets/animals | 65.9 | 66.8 | .10* | .20** |
| 36. Photography | 43.7 | 33.4 | .20** | .28** |
| 37. Reading | 73.5 | 42.2 | .12** | .25** |
| 38. Rock climbing | 24.5 | 28.5 | −.07 | −.13** |
| 39. Roller skating | 29.1 | 47.6 | .15** | .14** |
| 40. Running | 33.3 | 40.9 | .01 | .00 |
| 41. Sailing | 15.5 | 17.0 | .05 | .01 |
| 42. Science | 49.5 | 26.4 | −.12** | −.06 |
| 43. Scouts/guides | 11.1 | 8.6 | −.06 | −.09 |
| 44. Sewing | 11.8 | 14.0 | .27** | .27** |
| 45. Skateboarding | 11.0 | 23.8 | −.04 | −.19** |
| 46. Skiing | 29.2 | 32.9 | −.03 | .02 |
| 47. Soccer (football) | 37.5 | 47.6 | −.13** | −.15** |

*Table 3.1.* (Cont.)

| Favorite Interest or Activity | Percentage | | Correlation with Female | |
|---|---|---|---|---|
| | Home | School | Home | School |
| 48. Stamps | 13.1 | 7.7 | .02 | .03 |
| 49. Swimming | 60.0 | 66.8 | .18** | .17** |
| 50. Tennis | 21.8 | 24.3 | .01 | .10* |
| 51. Traveling | 55.8 | 50.0 | .12** | .11** |
| 52. Video games | 47.7 | 64.2 | −.38** | −.40** |
| 53. Watching television | 68.8 | 77.9 | −.08 | −.02 |

*Statistically significant beyond the .001 level.
**Statistically significant beyond the .0001 level.

activity is one of their favorites. The at-home respondents were markedly more enthusiastic about archaeology, astronomy, computers, environment, geography, history, mathematics, music (playing an instrument), photography, reading, and science. Most of these distinguish readers of *National Geographic Magazine* who enjoy using a computer, qualities that would have motivated the child to take the survey in the first place. The at-school respondents showed significantly more interest in baseball, basketball, bowling, fishing, football, ice hockey, roller skating, skateboarding, soccer, and video games. None of these are intellectual activities, most require physical activity, and even video games and fishing generally require manual rather than mental dexterity.

The third and fourth columns in table 3.1 give the correlations (tau-b) between being female and having the activity for a favorite. Positive correlations, such as those for cheerleading, sewing, music/singing, and cooking, mark the activity as one that girls are more likely to favor than boys. Negative correlations, notably for football and video games, identify things that boys tend to like more than girls do. It is interesting to note that among today's young teens, a number of activities are equally popular, having correlations insignificantly different from zero. A few activities, such as stamp collecting, are so unpopular that the response distributions are highly skewed, and there is not much room in the data for boys and girls to differ.

The important thing to note for our present purposes is that most items have very similar correlations in the two samples, at-home and at-school. We would not expect the numbers to be identical because there is random variation in both sets of respondents. But the average difference between the correlations is only .06. For thirty-five of these activities, at least one dataset shows a statistically significant correlation with gender, and for twenty-six of these both datasets do. But there are nine instances in which one dataset has a significant correlation whereas the other does not. These deserve a close look.

In five of the nine cases (bicycling, playing a musical instrument, martial arts, rock climbing, and science), the two coefficients differ by no more than .06, which is the average difference across all fifty-three pairs. In the case of bicycling, the correlation at home is −.10, and at school it is −.09, a difference of just .01. Clearly the correlation at home is barely above the threshold of statistical significance, and the correlation at school is slightly below it. Even if both sets of respondents were perfect random samples of the population, one would expect many differences of this insignificant size.

To assess the statistical significance of differences between the correlations, I wrote a bootstrapping computer program that worked as follows. It took the data, divided into two comparison groups of 1,191 who responded at home or at school, and recalculated the correlations for a selected activity. Call these correlations A (home respondents) and B (school respondents). At each step of the simulation it derived a random sample of 1,191 from each group of respondents, with replacement. That means that some respondents might be represented several times in the sample and others not at all, but the simulated samples would have characteristics similar to those of the original data. Finally, it calculated new correlations, A' and B', and compared them. For each significance test, the program iterated this calculation-intensive procedure 1,000,000 times. From these simulation trials, the program derived the probable distribution of correlations from samples. If the correlations in the data are such that $A < B$, then the statistical significance of the difference in correlations is the fraction of the simulation iterations in which $B' \geq A'$.

These tests show that the differences for five of these variables are not statistically significant: bicycling (probability estimated to be .34), playing a musical instrument (.09), martial arts (.1), rock climbing (.09), and science (.07). Three others are moderately significant: boating (.005), tennis (.02), and ice hockey (.01). The statistical significance of the .15 difference for skateboarding (−.04 at home and −.19 at school) is highly significant (.00003). It is worth noting that the response distribution concerning skateboarding is highly skewed for the at-home respondents. Only 12.1 percent of boys responding at home claim to engage in skateboarding, compared with 10.1 percent of girls.

The bootstrapping method of assessing statistical significance takes care of the statistical difficulties involved with highly skewed data and is a robust estimator technique based on the actual distributions of values for the variables rather than on some abstraction such as the statistical normal curve, but it does not deal with a more fundamental measurement issue aggravated when the distribution is skewed. An unknown fraction of the respondents are claiming to skateboard when they may have tried the sport only once or twice or merely mean that they might want to try it in the future. In other words, there is always some level of meaningless noise in the data, and when a distribution is highly skewed the noise may dominate the correlations. Thus it could be that the insignificant negative correlation between skateboarding and being female among the students responding at home results from the fact that none of these Web-surfing readers of National Geographic actually skateboard—or perhaps only 2 percent of the boys—and something like 10 percent of the respondents are emitting noise that is uncorrelated with sex.

Another highly skewed example is cheerleading, which has a correlation with being female of .23 among the at-home respondents and .33 among the at-school respondents. The difference between the gender and cheerleading patterns in the two samples is highly significant (.0002). But this may merely reflect the fact that hardly any of the at-home respondents claim to do cheerleading, 6.5 percent at home compared with 13.4 percent at school. Even when the distribution of one variable is highly skewed, given a large number of cases a real relationship may be detectable despite the noise.

## ATTITUDES TOWARD SCIENCE

The early-teen version of *Survey 2000* included several agree-or-disagree items specifically to advance my research on attitudes toward science and technology, and they are listed in table 3.2. Four response categories were offered: "strongly agree," "agree," "disagree," and "strongly disagree." The online survey used a radio button method for responding that prevented a respondent from selecting more than one response but did permit no response. About 1 to 4 percent of the respondents failed to answer a given question in this group of twelve. For purposes of this study, I dichotomized the variables, coding "1" for agree and strongly agree and "0" for disagreement and nonresponses. This is substantively meaningful because it clearly distinguishes those who expressed agreement with each statement from those who did not. By dichotomizing responses to these twelve items, I made them comparable to the fifty-three items in table 3.1, allowing us to use a uniform approach. Naturally, other studies will use the data in their original form.

We might expect the at-home respondents to differ significantly from those who responded at school in their levels of agreement with the science and technology items, chiefly because they are probably *National Geographic* readers and this magazine sensitizes readers to several scientific issues, notably those concerning the environment. In addition, it is possible that habitual

*Table 3.2.* Attitudes toward Science and Technology

| | Percentage | | Correlation with Female | |
|---|---|---|---|---|
| Respondent Agrees That . . . | Home | School | Home | School |
| Science will do more good than harm in the next century. | 76.1 | 70.9 | −.05 | −.03 |
| Intelligent life probably does not exist on any planet but our own. | 26.7 | 37.4 | .01 | −.04 |
| Space exploration should be delayed until we have solved more of our problems here on earth. | 32.2 | 43.0 | .02 | .01 |
| Funding for the space program should be increased. | 52.7 | 46.4 | −.16** | −.11* |
| If I were asked to go along on the first rocket trip to Mars, I would go. | 63.8 | 58.0 | −.12** | −.16** |
| All nuclear power plants should be shut down or converted to safer fuels. | 61.4 | 62.0 | .18** | .13** |
| Development of nuclear power should continue, because the benefits strongly outweigh the harmful results. | 41.4 | 45.8 | −.20** | −.19** |
| There should be a law against cloning human beings. | 70.9 | 57.1 | .13** | .10* |
| Research on human cloning should be encouraged, because it will have great benefits for science and medicine. | 38.8 | 49.5 | −.18** | −.19** |
| We should not worry much about environmental problems, because modern science will solve them with little change to our way of life. | 5.4 | 21.2 | −.07 | −.15** |
| We should accept cuts in our standard of living in order to protect the environment. | 73.9 | 65.4 | .07 | .09 |
| All in all, the world's population will be better off in the next 100 years. | 38.0 | 41.2 | −.15** | −.09 |

*Statistically significant beyond the .001 level.
**Statistically significant beyond the .0001 level.

Web surfers have a different and possibly more favorable orientation toward technology because they are willing computer users.

Some social scientists might argue that one virtue of a random sample is that it will reflect greater variation on most variables, whereas a convenience sample is likely to exhibit truncation on several variables and thus be inferior at detecting relationships and measuring them accurately. This may well be the case for many of the activities listed in table 3.1. However, the opposite could be argued for many of the science and technology attitudes listed in table 3.2. Perhaps these issues have been rendered more salient for at-home respondents by the fact that they read *National Geographic* and similar publications. Indeed, one of the traditional critiques of survey research has been that many respondents may not have meaningful responses to many questions.[8]

The data cannot entirely resolve this issue, but they do illuminate it. The average percentage who agree across the twelve items is quite similar in the two groups of respondents: 48.4 percent at home and 49.8 percent at school. But the proportions range more widely across items at home. The average difference from the mean is 18.0 percentage points at home, compared with only 10.7 percentage points at school. The average absolute value of the correlations is .11 both at home and at school (or .117 and .108, respectively). And the correlations range only slightly more widely at home, an average of .06 versus .05. We can interpret this pattern as follows.

At-home respondents read more than do at-school respondents, on average, and they are much more likely to be *National Geographic* readers. Thus many of the science and technology issues are more salient to them, and they have better-informed opinions. Because of the particular items chosen, especially the fact that the list contains both protechnology and antitechnology items, this fact does not greatly affect the average level of agreement across the twelve items. However, it does produce a wider range of responses. There is little net impact on the correlations between these items on gender because the effect of gender is not mediated by a deep intellectual understanding of the issues. The intellectual issues may be far more salient for the at-home respondents, and they may provide superior data for many scientific purposes.

This last observation is supported by an examination of the correlations linking logically related attitudinal items. Eight of the twelve statements were written in pairs, one member of each pair being favorable to a particular aspect of science and technology and the other unfavorable. Consider this pair of statements: "Space exploration should be delayed until we have solved more of our problems here on earth" and "Funding for the space program should be increased." Although these items are not exact mirror images of each other, a person who agreed with the first might be expected to disagree with the second. Indeed, the correlation between them in the at-home group of respondents is −.33. But among the at-school group the negative relationship is much weaker, only −.14. This very large difference supports the hypothesis that the science and technology items are more salient to the at-home group and receive more thoughtful responses from them.

The three other pairs show the same effect. Among at-home respondents, there is a very strong correlation of −.52 between "All nuclear power plants should be shut down or converted to safer fuels" and "Development of nuclear power should continue, because the benefits strongly outweigh the harmful results." But the negative association is only −.18 in the at-school group. Similarly, at home there is a correlation of −.51 between "There should be a law against cloning human beings" and "Research on human cloning should be encouraged, because it will have great benefits for science and medicine." Again, the correlation is weaker at school, −.31. Finally, among at-home respondents there is only a very small but statistically significant correlation of −.16 between "We should not worry much about environmental problems, because modern science will solve them with little change to our way of life" and "We should accept cuts in our standard of living in order to protect the environment." At school, this relationship actually goes the other side of zero, +.06, statistically significant at the .05 level. Perhaps the at-school respondents merely responded to the word "environment" in both statements, treating them as similar instead of opposite, possibly not even appreciating fully what the sentences meant.

## MUSICAL PREFERENCES

The chief focus of the adult survey was popular culture, and twenty items about musical preferences were carried over into the youth survey. These items were preceded by the instruction, "Please indicate your feelings about each type of music." The response categories were "like it very much," "like it," "have mixed feelings about it," "dislike it," "dislike it very much," and "don't know much about it." For purposes of this chapter I dichotomized response data, distinguishing respondents who said they liked the particular kind of music from all other respondents. Table 3.3 lists the twenty kinds of music.

Interestingly, there are very clear and powerful differences in musical tastes between the at-home and at-school respondents. I speculate that they reflect social class differences because presumably at-home respondents live in much more affluent homes that already had Internet connections in late 1998, but I do not have the data to test that hypothesis.[9] Only four musical styles are liked more often by the at-school respondents: country and western; rap or hip-hop, dance music, and heavy metal. On average, 42.8 percent of at-school respondents like these four types of music, compared with 32.5 percent of at-home respondents. In contrast, on average just 29.5 percent of at-school respondents like the other sixteen types, compared with 39.9 percent of at-home respondents. In table 3.1 we see that at-school respondents have a slightly greater tendency to like dancing, 32.7 percent compared with 26.1

*Table 3.3.* Music Preferences

| Like or Like Very Much | Percentage | | Correlation with Female | |
|---|---|---|---|---|
| | Home | School | Home | School |
| Classic, symphony, and chamber music | 51.7 | 23.4 | .08 | .02 |
| Opera | 14.4 | 7.8 | .12** | .00 |
| Broadway musicals/show tunes | 46.5 | 29.1 | .29** | .20** |
| Jazz | 45.8 | 33.1 | .00 | −.04 |
| Big band/swing | 50.0 | 42.7 | .09 | .03 |
| Mood/easy listening | 37.6 | 26.5 | .09 | .09 |
| Country and western | 17.6 | 18.4 | .11** | .06 |
| Bluegrass | 10.3 | 9.5 | .05 | −.11** |
| Hymns/gospel | 26.1 | 20.1 | .12** | .08 |
| Rhythm and blues | 41.3 | 33.8 | −.01 | −.02 |
| Rap/hip-hop | 41.3 | 61.4 | .07 | −.01 |
| Dance music (e.g., electronica) | 45.8 | 54.2 | .16** | .24** |
| Caribbean (e.g., reggae, soca, calypso) 38.7 | 31.1 | −.02 | −.03 | |
| Latin (e.g., mariachi, salsa) | 23.2 | 17.0 | .06 | .06 |
| Music of ethnic/national tradition | 38.2 | 27.9 | .07 | .07 |
| Modern folk/singer-songwriter | 28.2 | 16.3 | .17** | .07 |
| Contemporary pop/rock | 67.1 | 53.7 | .07 | .15** |
| Alternative rock | 65.2 | 61.7 | .06 | .01 |
| Oldies/classic rock | 54.5 | 38.2 | .12** | .09 |
| Heavy metal | 25.2 | 37.2 | −.08 | −.18** |

*Statistically significant beyond the .001 level.
**Statistically significant beyond the .0001 level.

percent, and about the same tendency to like singing, 35.9 percent versus 35.5. But the proportion of at-school respondents who played an instrument was much lower, 31.1 percent versus 46.0, although respondents' definition of what it meant to play an instrument must have been liberal. There is even a difference on listening to music, with 73.6 percent of at-school respondents marking this as a favorite activity compared with 82.0 percent of at-home respondents.

Again, the two groups of respondents have similar patterns of correlations between musical tastes and gender, with a few notable exceptions. The statistically significant difference on opera, .12 at home versus .00 at school, is easy to explain in terms of the extremely skewed distributions, notably the fact that only 7.8 percent of at-school respondents claim to like this specialized and costly art form. The significant difference on bluegrass, −.11 at school and +.05 at home also involves a highly skewed variable, but the distributions are about the same in the two groups, so an explanation would have to be somewhat subtle. Other correlation differences are minor but occasionally statistically significant.

## PEER VALUES

The final group of items we will consider offered respondents a list of things such as "attend classes regularly" and "be popular," asking, "Among the friends you hang out with, how important is it to. . . ." Three radio button responses were offered: "not important," "somewhat important," and "very important." I dichotomized the data to contrast "very important" with all other categories (including no response), because this produced the most balanced distribution across the ten items, which are listed in table 3.4.

Several of the peer values concern school, and these show an interesting pattern of differences between the two groups of respondents. Essentially identical percentages of both groups say their friends consider getting good grades to be important. Overwhelming majorities of both groups consider finishing high school to be important, but even a bigger majority of those answering at home, 93.1 percent versus 86.9. The difference on going to college is small, just 3 percentage points in favor of the at-home respondents. These three items all concern goals, but the two items about means to these goals show larger differences, around 10 percentage points. More of the at-home respondents say their friends value attending classes regularly and studying.

At-school respondents are much more likely to say that their friends value three items having to do with peer-group social activities: playing sports, being popular, and having a boyfriend or girlfriend. Those who responded at school are also slightly more likely to report that their friends value religious activities, which may again reflect a social class difference.

*Table 3.4.* Peer Values

| Friends Consider It Very Important to . . . | Percentage | | Correlation with Female | |
|---|---|---|---|---|
| | Home | School | Home | School |
| Attend classes regularly | 79.9 | 68.3 | .07 | .09 |
| Study | 53.5 | 43.8 | .10* | .12** |
| Play sports | 34.3 | 51.3 | −.15** | −.19** |
| Get good grades | 69.6 | 69.7 | .03 | .07 |
| Be popular | 19.7 | 32.3 | −.16** | −.23** |
| Finish high school | 93.1 | 86.9 | .05 | .13** |
| Have a steady boyfriend or girlfriend | 12.2 | 32.8 | −.17** | −.21** |
| Go to college | 76.2 | 73.0 | .05 | .06 |
| Participate in religious activities | 18.3 | 24.8 | .04 | −.01 |
| Do community work or volunteer | 12.3 | 13.1 | .10* | .03 |

*Statistically significant beyond the .001 level.
**Statistically significant beyond the .0001 level.

The pattern of correlations is similar across the two groups, and the exceptions are two highly skewed variables. With 93.1 percent of the at-home respondents saying finishing high school is a peer value, there really is not much room for a correlation connecting this variable with gender. The statistical significance of the difference between the tau correlations in the two groups of respondents is .03, figured by the bootstrap method. The item about doing community or volunteer work is also highly skewed, but about equally so in both groups of respondents, and the difference in the correlations is only .07.

## CONCLUSION

Our discussion highlights the differences between the at-home and at-school respondents, but in many respects the responses of the two groups are very similar. The tables compared percentages and correlations for 95 variables, a number large enough to consider using statistical analysis to compare the two subsamples. At home, the average proportion giving the "yes" or "agree" response was 37.4 percent, compared with 36.8 percent at school. The average correlation at home was .03, compared with .02. Because the correlations are a mixture of positive and negative values, a better measure of the strengths of the relationships is the absolute value of correlations, ignoring the minus signs. The average absolute value of correlations is .11 at home and .13 at school. The correlation (Pearson's $r$) between the 95 percentages at home versus in school is .83. This is a strong association, but the correlation between the correlations in the two groups is higher, .92, very close to unity. All these analyses indicate that the pattern of results is similar across the two different groups, especially the correlations.

The at-school group is more like a random sample than the at-home group, but of course it is far from a random sample of American and Canadian schoolchildren. But we must keep in mind that random samples are only one of several methods for rendering results generalizable. An alternative method is experimentation, with random assignment of research subjects to treatment and control groups. *Survey 2000* demonstrated the techniques needed for online experimentation because it administered different questions to different adult respondents, but it did not do so following a theory-based random manipulation plan. One approach that could easily incorporate the experimental method into online surveys is the vignette method. The respondent is given a little story to read and then is asked a number of questions about the people or events described therein. The experimental manipulation is that the contents of the story are altered at random for different respondents (for example, independently varying the race, age, and sex of a character in the story to see whether people judge him or her differently).

We have just carried out a nonexperimental form of analysis that can compensate for many of the defects of nonrandom samples. This is repeated replication of the same study with different groups believed to differ significantly in terms of relevant parameters. Because our at-home and at-school groups differed greatly on a number of important variables, any finding that is fundamentally the same in both datasets is of interest. Future major online surveys could target a number of very different groups and use sophisticated variants of meta-analysis to determine how the phenomenon of interest varies across the population.[10] It is very important to note that multiple replication on different groups within a single study not only gives greater confidence to the more consistent results but also can help us understand what makes some measures and correlations vary across different social contexts.

If we know what sample selection factors affect the variables of interest in a particular research study, we can compensate to some extent with statistical weighting procedures. Especially in the adult versions, *Survey 2000* was designed to include variables that would permit such weighting, and future studies will report the results. Of course, if inexpensive Web-based surveys produce a really interesting finding with some regularity, then a good argument can be made for including the best measures in an expensive survey carried out by more traditional means.

The present study finds that Web-based volunteer survey samples may indeed diverge significantly from the data that would have been obtained from a pure random sample, but it is possible to identify and to some extent protect against their biases. For example, we have seen that it is risky to rely on variables with highly skewed distributions and correlations that are only marginally significant. General patterns of correlation may be more robust than the frequency distribution of a single variable. By using two or more distinctly different samples, one can judge the generalizability of findings.

Were this a substantive study of gender differences among children rather than a methodological exploration, we would have examined some of the empirical findings of this study closely. The differences between the genders with respect to interest in mathematics and several of the sciences are very small or nonexistent, although girls have less favorable attitudes toward space flight, nuclear power, and human cloning. Given all the public interest in gender fairness in school sports, it is interesting to see that in both groups of children, of the athletic activities preferred by girls only gymnastics is widely offered at schools, basketball is gender-neutral in popularity, and schools that want to support healthy physical activity for girls might want to consider adding dancing to the competitive team sports preferred by boys. Recognizing that the two groups of respondents differ in *National Geographic* readership as well as Web usage, those responding at home seem far more intellectual and far less active socially. If these particular findings seem unsurprising, then at least they reinforce our confidence that Web-based surveys are capable of achieving valid results.

## NOTES

1. Colleen M. Kehoe and James E. Pitkow, "Surveying the Territory: GVU's Five WWW User Surveys," *The World Wide Web Journal* 1:3 (1996): 77–84, available at <http://www.cc.gatech.edu/gvu/user_surveys/papers/w3j.html>; Christine B. Smith, "Casting the Net: Surveying an Internet Population," *Journal of Computer-Mediated Communication* 3:1 (1997), available at <http://www.ascusc.org/jcmc/vol3/issue1/smith.html>.

2. James C. Witte, Lisa M. Amoroso, and Philip E. N. Howard, "Method and Representation in Internet-Based Survey Tools: Mobility, Community, and Cultural Identity in Survey 2000," *Social Science Computer Review* 18 (2000): 179–95.

3. S. Stoughton and L. Walker, "Shopping for Presence Online," *Washington Post* (online edition), November 2, 1999 (p. A1 in the print version).

4. National Science Foundation, *Women, Minorities, and Persons with Disabilities in Science and Engineering: 1998* (Arlington, Va.: National Science Foundation, 1999), 255.

5. National Geographic Society Web site at <http://www.nationalgeographic.com>.

6. James E. Campbell and James C. Garand, *Before the Vote: Forecasting American National Elections* (Thousand Oaks, Calif.: Sage, 2000).

7. David Schaefer and Don A. Dillman, "Development of a Standard E-mail Methodology," *Public Opinion Quarterly* 62 (1998): 378–97.

8. Howard Schuman and Stanley Presser, "Public Opinion and Public Ignorance: The Fine Line between Attitudes and Nonattitudes," *American Journal of Sociology* 85 (1980): 1214–25.

9. Department of Commerce, *Falling through the Net: Defining the Digital Divide* (Washington, D.C.: Department of Commerce, 2000) available at <http://www.ntia.doc.gov/ntiahome/fttn99/contents.html>.

10. B. T. Johnson, "Insights about Attitudes: Meta-Analytic Perspectives," *Personality and Social Psychology Bulletin* 17 (1991): 289–99.

# 4 / Computer Environments for Content Analysis: Reconceptualizing the Roles of Humans and Computers

## DICTIONARY-BASED PROGRAMS: THE LEGACY OF THE GENERAL INQUIRER

The General Inquirer was among the first computer programs for content analysis. As recently as the mid-1990s the General Inquirer remained the most often discussed computer program in the communication literature, dominating discussions of computer-assisted content analysis in methodology textbooks and monographs. Developed and refined by Stone and associates in the early 1960s, by 1966 the General Inquirer had already been applied to a wide variety of texts.[1] However, the General Inquirer has been used only by a small number of researchers. It fell into disuse not because better programs became available but because content analysts failed to embrace computer-assisted methods. In fact, computer techniques remain the exception rather than the rule in published content analyses. Because the General Inquirer gave birth to, and continues to shape, researchers' conceptions of computational content analysis, it is worth reviewing some limitations of the General Inquirer, limitations that are too often seen as limitations of computational content analysis in general rather than merely as limitations of a specific computer program.

The General Inquirer is a dictionary-based program in that it assigns words to various researcher-defined categories. For example, the word *money* is assigned by one of the General Inquirer dictionaries (the Lasswell Value Dictionary) to the category "wealth." An occurrence of the word *money* in a text is an indicator of a concern with wealth, along with words such as *resource, industry,* and *economy,* which are also assigned to the "wealth" category.[2] The

General Inquirer has been described as a theme-based program[3] or, somewhat less kindly but no less accurately, a "single-word-out-of-context" program.[4] The General Inquirer removes words from their linguistic context and treats them as indicators of the themes, concerns, or values that the dictionary was designed to assess. The General Inquirer washes out grammatical features of language to assess strictly lexical features, and it cannot readily assess relationships between words across sentences and paragraphs. In short, it is linguistically unsophisticated, and it limits users to the use of words (or phrases) as the unit of analysis.

Of course, dictionary-based programs are appropriate for many research questions. Unfortunately, the General Inquirer leaves a great deal to be desired in terms of letting users create their own dictionaries or customize existing dictionaries. The General Inquirer is customizable in principle, but in practice most users apply one of the two dictionaries—the Lasswell Value Dictionary or the Harvard IV Psychosocial Dictionary—currently packaged with General Inquirer. The General Inquirer is difficult to use because it retains many vestiges of its origins on early IBM mainframe computers. And the developers of the General Inquirer have in recent years seemed more interested in demonstrating the validity of the dictionaries across a variety of texts than in improving the program itself.

Despite these limitations, it is important to note the many important accomplishments of General Inquirer developers and users. The rigor with which many General Inquirer users have pursued their research programs remains underappreciated and all too rarely matched by other content analysts. For example, the last two books published by General Inquirer users, although now more than ten years old, are exemplars of analytical clarity and methodological sophistication.[5] General Inquirer users were among the first to demonstrate that computers do not necessarily discourage careful scholarship in textual analyses (although some skeptics of quantitative approaches may remain unconvinced). Unfortunately, the rigor evident in much General Inquirer research is in the service of dictionary-based procedures, which are appropriate only for a subset of content analytic research questions.

A better dictionary-based program has not come along to replace the General Inquirer. Indeed, there seems to be no market for one. The limitations of dictionary-based programs and the inability or unwillingness of researchers to think beyond these limitations left a legacy of disuse and misunderstanding of computer techniques for content analysis. Dictionary-based computer procedures contribute to the somewhat accurate belief that content analysts are obsessed with counting rather than understanding texts, that they are fascinated with texts but perversely uninterested in language per se. Computer techniques typically receive limited and cursory treatment in textbook discussions of content analysis. Computers are seen as adjuncts to content analysis proper; in fact, computational content analysis often is seen as an entirely separable subspecialty of sorts. Certainly, computers are not yet integrated into mainstream content analysis research programs.

## CONTENT IN CONTEXT: THE LINGUISTIC TURN IN COMPUTATIONAL CONTENT ANALYSIS

In recent years there has been a growing movement to devise content analytic computer programs that are sensitive to issues of language and meaning and that permit researchers to more readily adapt the program to specific research questions and text genres. These two developments in content analytic computing—linguistic sophistication and program flexibility—are closely related. They represent a movement toward seeing computers not as surrogate researchers but rather as tools for gleaning information from texts without sacrificing context. They address a litany of complaints about the difficulty of constructing content analytic research designs that capture linguistic and relational aspects of texts.[6] Recent advances in computer programs for qualitative data analysis and, especially, clause-based content analysis suggest that researchers need no longer sacrifice context to exploit the power of computers in content analysis.

There is a growing use of and literature on computer tools for qualitative research. Programs such as NUDIST NVivo and HyperRESEARCH enable researchers to code texts online and to create, display, and explore relationships between segments of coded text.[7] Although these programs are not designed for content analysis per se, they impressively demonstrate the computer's ability to support context-sensitive text analysis.

Roberts and Popping review programs that facilitate what they call clause-based text analyses. As Roberts and Popping note, theme-based programs such as the General Inquirer capture only one relevant type of text variable—frequency of occurrence of various themes—whereas clause-based programs allow researchers to examine the relationships between themes in texts. This is accomplished by using the computer to help generate and analyze relationally encoded texts.[8]

Computer-Assisted Evaluative Text Analysis (CETA) is an innovative clause-based program that facilitates the implementation of Osgood's evaluative assertion analysis as slightly reformulated by CETA developers.[9] CETA facilitates the parsing of texts into nuclear sentences that predicate something positive or negative about meaning objects (e.g., people, institutions, concepts, events) or about the relationship between meaning objects. The goal is not only to count how frequently various meaning objects are mentioned but also to determine the qualities (positive and negative) and other meaning objects with which a meaning object is associated (explicitly and implicitly) across the entire text under study. The Map Extraction, Comparison and Analysis (MECA) program also facilitates the discovery and analysis of relationships between words and phrases across entire texts.[10] Unlike theme-based programs, CETA and MECA capture rather than filter out relationships between text elements.

Another promising clause-based program, Program for Linguistic Content Analysis (PLCA), facilitates Roberts's method of Linguistic Content Analysis by helping researchers discover and code basic linguistic patterns underlying the surface features of a text.[11] PLCA uses a dictionary-based approach in that frequently occurring verbs and nouns are assigned numerical codes, but it preserves the grammatical context of the coded words. Eltinge and Roberts used PLCA to determine the extent to which science is portrayed as a process of inquiry (as opposed to an accumulation of facts) in high school biology textbooks. They assigned words to various categories such that the textbook sentence "The diagram in Fig. 48-4 shows the results of a cross involving two characteristics" was rewritten in PLCA as "THE FIGURE REVEALS/SHOWS an EVENT's RESULT," where the words in uppercase were from the PLCA dictionary created by the researchers.[12] The rewritten sentence was meant to show a somewhat deeper, more basic linguistic structure. Thus, PLCA can be used to determine, say, how often a person (e.g., a student or scientist) rather than a disembodied noun (e.g., figure, laboratory, science) functions as an agent in textbook sentences.

Franzosi has developed a computer program to facilitate text coding using the principles of semantic text grammar.[13] Unlike the PLCA approach, Franzosi's approach does not aim to rewrite sentences as more basic sentences per se but to filter out linguistic complexity deemed irrelevant for the research purpose at hand. The program helps coders identify and record basic linguistic information—subjects, actions, objects, and modifiers—that is retained in its grammatical context. The coded text is then entered into a relational database management system for analysis. Shapiro and Markoff use a similar computer-supported approach in an extraordinarily detailed study of public documents from eighteenth-century France.[14]

These programs for qualitative and content analytic research have in common a responsiveness to issues of language and meaning and a flexibility that permits researchers to readily tailor the program to their specific needs (although these programs impose significant limitations, discussed later in this chapter). These programs also have in common features designed to support human coders, and in this respect they differ markedly from most dictionary-based programs.

## FROM COMPUTERIZED TO COMPUTER-SUPPORTED CONTENT ANALYSIS

Many new programs for content analysis, including most of those discussed in the preceding section, provide online support for human coders. CETA prompts coders in three early stages of analysis: defining scoring options, parsing text, and assigning numeric values to text features. MECA also offers interactive guidance to help coders choose coding options and assign numeric values. PLCA gives coders feedback by displaying reconstructed clauses immediately after their component parts are coded. The coder can choose to recode the clause if the reconstruction is inadequate. Deffner describes a simple but helpful program that prompts coders to assign numeric scores to text passages.[15]

In providing online support for human coders, these programs do much to redress another unfortunate legacy of dictionary-based programs such as the General Inquirer: the notion that computers can or should somehow automate content analysis. Adopting the terminology and enthusiasm of early research in artificial intelligence, developers of some early computer programs for content analysis spoke of automating the process, and some more recent authors continue to speak of "computerized content analysis," an unfortunate phrase that overstates the possibilities of computational content analysis and cultivates the misleading but nonetheless commonly asserted distinction between computational and manual content analysis. The phrases "computer-assisted" and "computer-aided content analysis" are preferable and have achieved limited usage. At the risk of being deemed overly sensitive to semantic niceties, I recommend the label "computer-*supported* content analysis"[16] because a focus on computer support or scaffolding for various tasks has proven quite useful in designing systems for human-computer interaction. Perhaps the most important feature of many of the recently developed programs for content analysis is their ability to support human coding. The developers of these programs recognize that for the foreseeable future humans will have to code texts if the coding is to be sensitive to the complexities of language and meaning. Programs such as CETA, MECA, and PLCA are designed to support rather than supplant human coders and therefore may help integrate computer techniques with mainstream content analysis.

Despite the conceptual and technological improvements manifested in these programs, they have two important limitations. First, although they are more readily customizable than their forebears, these programs remain appropriate only for certain kinds of analysis, such as linguistic content analysis (PLCA) or evaluative assertion analysis (CETA). These areas of analysis are rich, and these programs can accommodate a fairly diverse range of research questions and materials, but these programs remain most useful to researchers who share the developers' theoretical perspectives. Second, these programs are limited to basic coding units no larger than sentences. They allow analysis of relationships across sentences, but coding must occur at the level of sentence, clause, or word. It is possible to aggregate sentence-, clause-, or word-level data, but for the researcher who wants to collect data only on larger coding units (e.g., paragraphs or entire texts), the coding of smaller units as an intermediary step will add unnecessary costs and complexity to the project.

On one hand, content analysis programs designed to advance a particular theoretical approach—and that, as a result, necessarily support only a subset of all potentially useful coding tasks—are welcome in that they facilitate theoretical content analyses and in doing so address the long-standing (and largely justifiable) complaint that content analysis is too often atheoretical. Certainly, it is heartening to see content analysts use computer tools to develop more sophisticated content analytic research programs. On the other hand, the pluralistic nature of communication research and theory militates against the widespread adoption of any program tailored to a single theory. Indeed, the clause-based computer programs discussed in this chapter have not been widely adopted by content analysts, few of whom share the developers' particular theoretical commitments. Moreover, it is unreasonable to expect researchers to develop theory-specific programs in adequate numbers because many researchers lack the computer skills and resources needed to develop such programs.

## COMPUTER ENVIRONMENTS FOR CONTENT ANALYSIS

There is a need, then, for a computer tool that can facilitate a wide range of human coding tasks and thereby permit computers to be brought to bear from a wide range of theoretical frameworks on a wide range of materials, both textual and visual. Programs such as CETA, MECA, and PLCA suggest that computers show great promise in supporting human coding tasks.[17] Deffner was perhaps the first to show how researchers might exploit the interactive capabilities of computers to facilitate human coding protocols.[18] Franzosi claims that many human coding tasks are best done online, and he outlines the desirable features and likely benefits of a system for computer-supported coding: The system should display the material to be coded, prompt coders to enter data (numeric or textual) in specific fields, provide an online code book and help function, and allow coders some choice in how to proceed through the coding protocol.[19] Franzosi claims that such a system would provide data that are richer, more reliable, and less costly to collect than the data collected in traditional manual coding procedures. More specifically, data errors would be reduced by eliminating the paper shuffling typical of manual procedures, providing online checks to confirm that entered values fall within a specified range and are logically consistent with values entered in other coding fields, and eliminating the need to keypunch data from paper forms (because coders enter the data directly into the computer). Data errors and other coding problems could also be detected more quickly because researchers will have immediate access to the data. Immediate access also offers researchers more flexibility to change coding protocols as unforeseen problems (and opportunities) arise and makes it possible to analyze and publish research results more quickly. Costs would be lower because online coding can be completed more quickly than manual coding.

In short, Franzosi recommends that content analysts adopt a computer system similar to those used in computer-assisted telephone interviewing (CATI). CATI systems enjoy widespread use in survey research data collection because of their ability to facilitate reliable and cost-effective data collection. Franzosi suggests that similar benefits regarding data quality and research costs can be realized by content analysts who go online. Franzosi claims that his procedure of coding texts according to the principles of semantic text grammars is particularly (and perhaps uniquely) appropriate for implementation on a computer, but there is no reason why a computer system could not accommodate a wide variety of coding tasks (although such a system admittedly seems unnecessary for dictionary-based coding because most dictionary-based procedures can be readily handled by computer programs that need little or no human coding). There seems to be much to recommend a computer system that would permit researchers to create coding protocols (or select from a variety of customizable coding templates) to be completed online by coders who have access to online support. Such a system would provide the data collection and project management benefits typical of CATI systems to many content analysts, not just to those with extensive computer skills and resources, or to those whose theoretical preferences are already manifested in theory-specific software such as CETA or PLCA. A more general system for computer-supported content analysis would recognize and encourage the pluralism inherent in communication research.

In addition, such a system could be implemented on a network, thereby facilitating research projects that involve research collaborators and coders at distant sites.

Finally, such a system would facilitate the content analytic study of images, from drawings to photographs to television footage. Content analysts have in recent years moved away from an exclusive focus on texts to the role of images in our symbolic environment, but to date little attention has been paid to the need for a computer tool to facilitate the study of images. Evans reviews the rapidly growing field of video information retrieval, suggesting how social scientists can exploit the many new systems that aim to index and retrieve video content.[20] These systems have been designed primarily to help corporations manage digital video repositories, but as Evans notes, these systems hold great promise in supporting content analysis of film and television.

The computer tool suggested here would be applicable to linguistic as well as nonlinguistic phenomena. Indeed, it could provide interactive support for assigning numeric values to artifacts from almost any communicative act.

Such a tool would be worthwhile simply because it provides for content analysts the data quality and cost-effectiveness benefits typical of CATI systems. But it can also be argued that computer-supported content analysis can increase the sophistication of content analytic research design and play an important role in advancing content analytic theory. Franzosi suggests that the computer is an ideal environment in which to implement sophisticated content analytic research designs,[21] but to date there is little empirical evidence that shows under what conditions, or even whether, computer-supported coding is more effective than traditional paper-and-pencil methods (indeed, there is a paucity of research on the effectiveness of content analytic procedures in general). We need to know more about what coding tasks are best accomplished in a computer environment and why. Still, it seems likely that a computer system to support human coding can facilitate research designs that are more sophisticated than those possible using paper-and-pencil methods.

The CATI-like system recommended here is not necessarily preferable to theory-specific content analysis programs. In fact, theory-specific programs seem more desirable in that they more readily support and implement theory-driven research designs. The system recommended here is meant only to provide a way for many researchers, with disparate research interests, to move quickly into a computer environment. As discussed later in this chapter, this general system may even encourage the development of more sophisticated, theory-specific programs.

## MAGIC IN COMPUTER-SUPPORTED CONTENT ANALYSIS: ARTIFICIAL INTELLIGENCE

Almost 50 years ago, Berelson, a seminal figure in content analysis, warned, "Content analysis, as a method, has no magical qualities—you rarely get out of it more than you put in, and sometimes you get less. In the last analysis there is no substitute for a good idea."[22] This warning, or something like it, is often echoed in treatises on content analysis and is especially common in textbook discussions of computer-supported content analysis. In his influential 1969 textbook, Holsti quotes Berelson approvingly and adds, "Development of computer content analysis programs detracts nothing from the wisdom of [Berelson's] assertion."[23]

In contrast, I argue that the time has come to expect some computer magic in content analysis. Though certainly valid as a warning about unsophisticated research designs, sentiments like Berelson's also promote a misleading separation between our theories and research designs and the tools with which they are implemented, especially when these sentiments are ritually repeated in contemporary textbook discussions of computer-supported content analysis. It is no longer tenable to presume that computers cannot help content analysts discover important patterns in their data, patterns that researchers neither intended to investigate nor would have discovered without computer tools. Given recent advances in artificial intelligence, it is no longer tenable to presume that productive insights must be the exclusive province of the content analyst rather than his or her computer.

Social scientists interested in computer modeling and simulation have adopted artificial intelligence techniques with promising results, and artificial intelligence techniques have already led to several promising advances in computer programs for content analysis. Both CETA and MECA feature inference engines that can identify implicit relationships between text elements. For example, if one clause of a newspaper editorial notes that "Politician X supports Senate bill Y" and a later clause (even many paragraphs away) opines that "Senate bill Y may result in increased unemployment," CETA will make the logical inference that the source of the statements (in this case the editorial writer) implies that "Politician X may cause an increase in unemployment." Furthermore, because CETA implements basic principles of evaluative assertion analysis, it probably will "know" (or certainly be told by coders) that the word *unemployment* is evaluated negatively by most people. Thus, CETA can also generate the inference that the source suggests that "Politician X may cause something bad to happen."[24]

Developers of programs for qualitative data analysis recently have adopted several promising artificial intelligence techniques. HyperRESEARCH
supports the use of production rules similar to those typical of expert system software to help researchers discover and create relationships between
coded text segments and to formulate and test hypotheses about these relationships.[25] Analysis of Qualitative Data (AQUAD) also supports users in
formulating and testing hypotheses about textual data. AQUAD is written
in the logic programming language Prolog and allows users to select from
several Prolog procedures for hypothesis testing or to create customized procedures.[26] Although programs for qualitative data analysis typically provide
only minimal support for quantitative analysis, content analysts are well
advised to look into these programs to get a sense of how artificial intelligence techniques are already being brought to bear, albeit in a limited way,
on problems of text analysis.

As promising as artificial intelligence is for content analysis, it probably
will be many years before a system is developed that can fully automate a
clause-based content analytic procedure of even minimal sophistication. Even
the most advanced programs for natural language processing of new stories,
for example, are effective only in a narrow range of tasks within a restricted
range of texts. Fan found no viable artificial intelligence applications that
would reliably identify and code passages in wire service texts that suggested a positive, negative, or neutral stance toward specific political issues such
as the presence of U.S. troops in Lebanon.[27] Fan devised a "successive filtration" method using iterative computer procedures, customized for each top-
ical issue and revised after each iteration, that successively remove irrelevant
text, eventually leaving only the material crucial to the coding task, which is
then accomplished in the last iteration. In doing so, Fan cleverly mimics a
sophisticated natural language parsing routine, with impressive results. Fan's
method illustrates the power of combining natural language text processing
with human coding.[28] This combination exploits the computer's ability to
parse large amounts of text and the researcher's ability to devise and apply
meaning-sensitive coding protocols. As Fan's dilemma and solution suggest,
both artificial and human intelligence are desirable in content analysis.

Fan's work also illustrates the usefulness of developing intelligent computer
applications tailored to specific content analytic problems and theories. Indeed, problem- and theory-specific programs may be all that are viable, at least
for the foreseeable future. Like the field of communication, artificial intelligence is a diverse field that offers several (sometimes incompatible) approaches to text analysis. Given the constraints of current artificial intelligence techniques, any intelligent program for content analysis probably will use only a

handful of available techniques, be applicable only to a restricted range of texts, and support only a subset of content analytic research designs. This reality conflicts with traditional views (and hopes) about the role of computers in content analysis. The developers and users of the General Inquirer have long suggested that the General Inquirer can handle all or most of the computer needs of content analysts. The limitations of the General Inquirer often are noted with admirable insight,[29] but it is seldom suggested that alternative computer approaches are desirable or even viable. Even the name of the program, the *General Inquirer,* boasts of its allegedly wide applicability. Thus, the notion that there must be numerous computer approaches to accommodate the wide variety of content analytic concerns is perhaps puzzling to researchers who are accustomed to routine popular news accounts of great advances in computing.

The idea that content analysts may have to develop the computer techniques most appropriate for their research may even be distressing to many. Certainly, only a handful of content analysts have developed computer tools to support their work. Forty years ago, the resources and skills needed to develop computer tools for content analysis were immense; the General Inquirer was an heroic achievement given the limitations of computers in the early 1960s. Fortunately, in recent years there has been rapid growth in the availability of software to support the development of intelligent systems. The success of commercial expert systems development tools is but one example of this trend. Thus, content analysts need not necessarily be programmers to exploit intelligent systems, but of course programming skills will be helpful (as will interdisciplinary initiatives with computer scientists; there have been far too few such initiatives). Although they may have to acquire a new set of skills, content analysts need not wait for others to provide sophisticated computer tools for content analysis.

In fact, it is crucial that researchers *not* wait for others to develop intelligent computer tools for content analysis. Researchers should begin to develop computer tools that embody and extend specific aspects of their own expertise in understanding texts and images. They might develop techniques to automate some—although probably not all—of the coding tasks relevant to certain problems. Even some of the more sophisticated coding tasks can be automated or at least supported by artificial intelligence techniques. Just as research in artificial intelligence has advanced our understanding of human cognition, content analysts who attempt to build their expertise into intelligent systems may in doing so learn much about the processes and possibilities of content analysis.

It should be noted that the recommendation made in the preceding section to develop a single computer system to support a wide variety of human coding tasks may seem incompatible with a call to develop theory- and problem-specific programs and to automate as much of the coding process as possible. However, a general system may provide an environment in which to implement intelligent functions, either to support human coders or to automate a part of the coding protocol. In this sense, the general system recommended earlier is designed to take full advantage of, and in fact encourage, developments in artificial intelligence that may ultimately, albeit slowly, lead to fully automated content analyses. In the long term, it seems plausible—indeed, likely—that even very sophisticated content analytic projects can be automated. A general computer environment for human coding is recommended here as an interim step between predominantly manual and predominantly computerized coding.

Ultimately, we can expect a system that will monitor, process, and code texts and images with little human intervention. This system may be able to retrieve and manage great quantities of material and may actively identify opportunities for content analysis, devise and test content analytic hypotheses, and even learn as it does so. In other words, it is now feasible to begin working toward a kind of magic in content analysis. Furthermore, this magic is appropriate and even necessary if content analysts are to take full advantage of opportunities afforded by the emerging era of electronic databases and interactive media.

## CONTENT ANALYSIS IN THE ERA OF ELECTRONIC MEDIA

Communication researchers must strive to exploit for scholarly purposes the torrent of electronic information flowing from news outlets and other sources worldwide. They must also learn to mine more effectively the increasing number of online databases. The abundance of electronic texts from a wide variety of sources, created for a wide variety of audiences, makes it easier than ever before to test content analytic hypotheses. Computers enable content analysts to more effectively locate, manage, and process texts, of course, but computers may also help improve content analytic practice and theory by facilitating less costly and more sophisticated research designs.

The growth of digital image repositories and the increasing sophistication of systems for storing and retrieving these images provide an opportunity for content analysts to turn their attention to image analysis. Despite the fact that images have long been said to fall within the purview of content analysis and despite the increasing salience of images in contemporary media, content analysts have done little to document and explain the role of images in our symbolic environment. Computer tools for assigning numeric values to image features are now feasible. As noted earlier, a general computer system for content analysis could support human coding of images. In addition, it is already possible to automate some basic image analysis tasks. Emerging in the commercial marketplace are systems that automate the detection of objects in images, automatically parse video into its constituent shots and scenes, and use face and speech recognition techniques to automatically identify people in video sequences.[30] Even the seemingly intractable problems of automating moving image analysis are being solved quickly.

The nature of media content itself will change in the emerging era of electronic and interactive media, and content analysts must develop new theories and technologies to understand this change. We are entering an era in which content metadata will be common. Bauer and Scharl demonstrate how social scientists can exploit HTML tags to facilitate analysis of Web page content (a trick used by most Internet search engines as well).[31] Looking beyond HTML, we can expect that online texts will soon be implemented in XML, with which Web developers can create markup tags that provide rich data about the structure and content of a text. Emerging standards for digital video, such as MPEG-7, will enable video producers to append content descriptions and other data to video files. In other words, many of the texts and images distributed and consumed around the world will soon feature content metadata. Content analysts should work to become ready to exploit these metadata.

The flexible, interactive structure of hypertext and hypermedia require that content analysts develop new conceptions of media content (e.g., where is the "content" of a hypermedia document that may offer tens of thousands of paths through the material?). A discussion of content analytic frameworks for interactive media is beyond the scope of this chapter,[32] but it seems clear that new computer tools will be needed if content analysts are to devise and implement sophisticated procedures for assessing interactive media.

## CONCLUSION

Currently, many content analysts use information retrieval and database management programs to help locate and manage material to be coded, and many exploit the increasingly sophisticated data analysis and display features of statistical packages to assist in exploring and understanding the data that result from coding. But computers are still seen as adjuncts, at best, in the research process. Most content analysts seem unaware of the possibility of computers serving as full partners in formulating research hypotheses, creating and implementing coding protocols, and analyzing and modeling data. In fact, many continue to doubt the ability of computers to support these tasks, as evidenced by the wariness often expressed in textbooks regarding what is seen as undue reliance on computers in content analysis. This wariness was justifiable in the era of dictionary-based programs, and it reflects an admirable concern that content analysts continue to strive for sophistication. But it also poses a danger that content analysts will overlook relevant innovations in the fields of information retrieval, human-computer interaction, and artificial intelligence and therefore fail to develop tools to encourage sophisticated content analytic research in the emerging information era.

In this chapter I have assiduously avoided arguments about the usefulness of content analysis, computer supported or otherwise, as a method of understanding communication processes. I have asserted only that computers can make content analysis more sophisticated. I leave the reader to judge the sophistication of current content analytic approaches. I am more concerned with challenging the notion that computers have little to offer content analysts or may even hinder the content analyst who relies on them. It seems clear that computers can help in many ways, from reducing research costs to improving data quality. Certainly, we need no longer worry that computers are too stupid to help, that they are merely calculating machines that cultivate naive reductionism among content analysts who use them. Computers are getting smarter at a rate far exceeding any improvements in human thinking skills. Much of the expertise content analysts bring to bear on research problems can be built into computer systems, enabling content analysts to refine, enhance, and extend their thinking.

It should be noted that the emerging approaches to computer-supported content analysis reviewed in this chapter are not panaceas. All the computer programs discussed here remain so limited as to have found only a handful of users. These programs must be further refined, and new, more sophisticated programs must be created. Still, despite their limitations, the programs discussed here suggest a new and invaluable conceptual framework in which computers are seen not as adjuncts to content analytic research but as tools that can be integrated with human expertise throughout the research process.[33] In the near future, it may be unnecessary to demarcate computer-supported and noncomputational content analysis. We might once again speak simply of "content analysis"; computers will be both ubiquitous and transparent in the research process. We will seldom be concerned in our methodology textbooks (or rather in whatever hypermedia products replace methodology textbooks) with reifying what is already a somewhat arbitrary distinction between computers and humans. This new conceptual framework can be expected to encourage—and is in fact a necessary condition for—content analysis research programs that are responsive to the complexities of language and meaning and capable of assessing twenty-first century communication media and practices.

## NOTES

1. Philip J. Stone, Dexter C. Dunphy, Marshall S. Smith, and Daniel M. Ogilvie, *The General Inquirer: A Computer Approach to Content Analysis* (Cambridge, Mass.: MIT Press, 1966).

2. To be more specific, the words *money, resource, industry,* and *economy* are assigned to the category "wealth-other," which is one of three wealth-related categories (along with "wealth-participant" and "wealth-transaction"). The three categories can be collapsed into a single "wealth" category, designated "wealth-total." See Robert Philip Weber, *Basic Content Analysis,* 2d ed. (Newbury Park, Calif.: Sage, 1990).

3. Roel Popping, *Computer-Assisted Text Analysis* (Thousand Oaks, Calif.: Sage, 2000).

4. Klaus Krippendorff, *Content Analysis: An Introduction to Its Methodology* (Beverly Hills, Calif.: Sage, 1980), 126.

5. J. Zvi Namenwirth and Robert Philip Weber, *Dynamics of Culture* (Boston: Allen & Unwin, 1987); Weber, *Basic Content Analysis.*

6. See Hans Mathias Kepplinger, "Content Analysis and Reception Analysis," *American Behavioral Scientist* 33 (November/December 1989): 175–82; Carl W. Roberts, "Other Than Counting Words: A Linguistic Approach to Content Analysis," *Social Forces* 68 (September 1989): 147–77; Krippendorff, *Content Analysis.*

7. Sharlene Hesse-Biber, Paul Dupuis, and T. Scott Kinder, "HyperRESEARCH: A Computer Program for the Analysis of Qualitative Data with an Emphasis on Hypothesis Testing and Multimedia Analysis," *Qualitative Sociology* 14 (Winter 1991): 289–306; Lyn Richards, *Using NVivo in Qualitative Research* (Thousand Oaks, Calif.: Sage, 1999). For overviews of software for qualitative data analysis, see Melina Alexa and Cornelia Zuell, *A Review of Software for Text Analysis* (Mannheim, Germany: Zentrum für Umfragen, Methoden und Analysen, 1999); Nigel G. Fielding and Raymond M. Lee, *Computer Analysis and Qualitative Research* (Thousand Oaks, Calif.: Sage, 1998).

8. Carl W. Roberts and Roel Popping, "Computer-Supported Content Analysis: Some Recent Developments," *Social Science Computing Review* 11 (Fall 1993): 283–91, quote on 284.

9. Jan J. Cuilenberg, Jan Kleinnijenhuis, and Jan A. de Ridder, "Artificial Intelligence and Content Analysis: Problems of and Strategies for Computer Text Analysis," *Quality and Quantity* 22 (Spring 1988): 65–97.

10. Kathleen Carley and Michael Palmquist, "Extracting, Representing, and Analyzing Mental Models," *Social Forces* 70 (March 1992): 601–36.

11. Roberts, "Other Than Counting Words."

12. Ibid., 69.

13. Roberto Franzosi, "From Words to Numbers: A Generalized and Linguistics-

Based Coding Procedure for Collecting Textual Data," *Sociological Methodology* (Fall 1988): 263–98.

14. Gilbert Shapiro and John Markoff, *Revolutionary Demands: A Content Analysis of the Cahiers de Doleances of 1789* (Stanford, Calif.: Stanford University Press, 1998).

15. Gerhard Deffner, "Microcomputers as Aids in Gottschalk-Gleser Ratings," *Psychiatry Research* 18 (Spring 1986): 151–59.

16. Roberts and Popping, "Computer-Supported Content Analysis," 283 (emphasis added).

17. Many computer programs for qualitative data analysis offer substantial and even ingenious support for qualitative coding tasks, but these programs offer little support for quantitative coding. Although these programs may be appropriated for some quantitative coding tasks, they are not widely applicable to the needs of content analysts.

18. Deffner, "Microcomputers as Aids in Gottschalk-Gleser Ratings."

19. Roberto Franzosi, "Strategies for the Prevention, Detection, and Correction of Measurement Error in Data Collected from Textual Sources," *Sociological Methods and Research* 18 (May 1990): 442–72.

20. William Evans, "Teaching Computers to Watch Television: Content-Based Image Retrieval for Content Analysis," *Social Science Computer Review* 18 (Fall 2000): 246–57.

21. Roberto Franzosi, "Computer-Assisted Content Analysis of Newspapers: Can We Make an Expensive Research Tool More Effective?" *Quality and Quantity* 29 (May 1995): 157–72.

22. Bernard Berelson, "Content Analysis," in *Handbook of Social Psychology,* ed. G. Lindzey (Reading, Mass.: Addison-Wesley, 1954), 488–518, quote on 518.

23. Oli R. Holsti, *Content Analysis for the Social Sciences and Humanities* (Reading, Mass.: Addison-Wesley, 1969), 194.

24. Cuilenberg et al., "Artificial Intelligence and Content Analysis."

25. Hesse-Biber et al., "HyperRESEARCH."

26. Gunter L. Huber and Carlos Marcelo Garcia, "Computer Assistance for Testing Hypotheses about Qualitative Data: The Software Package AQUAD 3.0," *Qualitative Sociology* 14 (Fall 1991): 289–306.

27. David P. Fan, *Predictions of Public Opinion from the Mass Media: Computer Content Analysis and Mathematical Modeling* (Westport, Conn.: Greenwood, 1988).

28. Unlike many other systems discussed in this chapter, Fan's system provides no online support for human coding. Rather, a human intervenes after each iteration (or "filtration") to review search results and to specify search criteria for the next iteration.

29. See Philip J. Stone, "Thematic Text Analysis: New Directions for Analyzing Text Content," in *Text Analysis for the Social Sciences: Methods for Drawing Statistical Inferences from Texts and Transcripts,* ed. C. W. Roberts (Mahwah, N.J.: Erlbaum, 1997), 35–54; Weber, *Basic Content Analysis.*

30. Evans, "Teaching Computers to Watch Television."

31. Christian Bauer and Arno Scharl, "Quantitative Evaluation of Web Site Content and Structure," *Internet Research* 10 (Spring 2000): 31–41.

32. But see William Evans, "Content Analysis in an Era of Interactive News: Assessing 21st Century Symbolic Environments," in *The Electronic Grapevine: Rumor, Reputation,*

*and Reporting in the New On-Line Environment,* ed. D. Borden and K. Harvey (Mahwah, N.J.: Erlbaum, 1988), 161–71.

33. Gilbert Shapiro, "The Future of Coders: Human Judgments in a World of Sophisticated Software," in *Text Analysis for the Social Sciences: Methods for Drawing Statistical Inferences from Texts and Transcripts,* ed. C. W. Roberts (Mahwah, N.J.: Erlbaum, 1997), 225–38.

# PART 3

# Computers, Social Science, Humanities, and the Impact of New Social Terrain

WENDY PLOTKIN

# 5 / Electronic Texts in the Historical Profession: Perspectives from Across the Scholarly Spectrum

**Historians have relied** on manuscripts and printed books, journals, newspapers, and other documents at least since the time of Gutenberg. They have used these sources to obtain and analyze information and to disseminate it. In the last forty years, the computer has increasingly integrated itself into the historian's world through scholarly communication online, access to textual, visual, and audio material in electronic form, and processing of quantitative data.[1]

Scholarly communication has moved from the spoken word and the printed page to the computers in scholars' offices and homes. The advent of e-mail through national telecommunication networks such as the Internet has speeded up and expanded communication between scholars. Much cheaper than long distance phone calls and more convenient than the postal service, e-mail has allowed scholars to exchange their thoughts in one-to-one messages, discipline-defined discussion groups, and electronic newsletters and journals. One-to-one messages are easily exchanged at the convenience of the scholar, crossing continents and time zones within minutes. This has speeded up communication between historians and increased the feasibility of frequent, shorter messages.

Online history discussion groups have evolved on topics ranging from social history to the U.S. Civil War. The first generation of discussion groups was fairly informal and marginal in terms of scholarly content.[2] In late 1992, H-Net, or Humanities on Line, was created. H-Net was established to achieve a variety of objectives, including improving the quality of online discussion groups in history. In its first seven years of existence it started up or affiliated with more than 100 edited scholarly discussion groups in history and the humanities, ranging from American studies and Australian–New Zealand history to the history of the American West and of women. In becoming one of the leading historical Internet resources in the world, it now offers online discussion among scholars, reviews of books and other media, and Web sites with syllabi, bibliographies, and links to other Web sites.[3] The editors are drawn from the international academic community and range from highly respected senior scholars to younger scholars, usually with their Ph.D.'s, eager to engage in the newer technologies in teaching and research. These editors ensure that the discussions sustain a high scholarly level. Thus they are faced with the challenge of shaping a new medium that is less structured than a classroom or conference panel but more structured than the chat lists found across the Internet. This has raised issues of the degree of control they should exercise, in situations ranging from attempts by Holocaust deniers to dominate the Holocaust forum to charges of censorship from those whose postings are rejected or returned for editing by the editors. Compromises must be made between opening up intellectual discussion to an international and interdisciplinary community and ensuring that the openness does not lead to casual chatter and loose historical claims that waste the time of busy scholars. Assisting in the effort to sustain quality and garner resources for each list are editorial boards that include leading scholars from around the world.[4]

How have these forms of electronic communication affected historians? In a 1992 article about the impacts of computerization on the historian, librarians Matthew B. Gilmore and Donald O. Case argue that history is an unusually individualized discipline that "militates against extensive use of that technology which is cooperative and generalizable." Thus, they view the expansion of electronic networking as less likely to affect historians than scholars in other disciplines.[5]

Others argue that historians will adapt to the greater accessibility offered by electronic communication by increasing their collaborative efforts.[6] H-Net's popularity, with more than 60,000 subscribers in ninety countries from around the world, suggests that many historians are now comfortable in communicating in this new medium.[7] Because of the tendency of history departments to hire historians from a variety of disciplines, it has been difficult for historians in the same field to concentrate in the same location. As location becomes less of a factor, historians may find themselves influenced at an earlier stage in their work by the work of others, possibly resulting in the convergence in subject areas.

The Internet also may enhance communication between scholars and students. The ease with which a student can engage in intellectual dialogue with a professor through e-mail allows the student to develop conceptual understanding and writing skills. It contributes to a collegiality among faculty and students that contact in the classroom alone does not allow.[8]

Historians have shown a willingness to share and discuss approaches to teaching on the Internet. H-Net includes the H-Teach, H-WorldCiv, H-Survey, H-MMedia, and H-High-S (high school teaching) networks, all for pedagogical discussion.[9] Syllabi and course materials are available in increasing abundance on the Internet. Edward Ayers's "Valley of the Shadow: Living the Civil War in Virginia and Pennsylvania" includes his narrative of Civil War life, links to primary papers, and appropriate images.[10] Architecture, history of art, and urban history courses are making available their materials on the Internet.[11]

Distance learning has arrived in the form of online universities and online courses offered by traditional universities. Hailed by administrators as the salvation of budget-strapped educational institutions, a number of virtual universities have already been created—the Michigan Virtual University, the Kentucky Commonwealth Virtual University, Western Governors University (WGU), and the California Virtual University.[12]

WGU is an example of the unusual organization of many of these institutions, free from the constraints of physical location. It is not an individual institution but a consortium of universities in eighteen Western U.S. states and the U.S. territory of Guam, established by the governors of these states in 1995. WGU and its affiliate institutions include more than two dozen undergraduate-level history courses. These courses are taught by faculty associated with campus-based institutions such as Oklahoma State University and Brigham Young University. Ranging in price from $240 to more than $10,000, the courses are markedly different from traditional university courses in a number of ways. Many of the courses are independent, done by students on their own, involving minimal to moderate interaction with the professor and other students. Furthermore, courses are open-ended: Students may start the classes at any time and have up to a year take the exams to prove a competency in the course, with a certain number of competencies leading to degree. Paid consultants grade the exams, so it appears that the primary role of the class professor is to put together the materials for the course.[13]

This model is not the only one for online education. Professor E. L. ("Skip") Knox has offered Internet history courses on the Renaissance, Western Civilization, and the Crusades since 1995. He requires intensive and structured online group discussion among the students and asks them to read the lectures that he makes publicly available on the Web. He engages in detailed discussion with the students individually and in a group, alerting students who are falling behind or performing substandard work and working out a solution. He grades all assignments and provides detailed feedback to students, thus offering as much or more attention than is provided in on-campus courses. Knox is a staunch defender of this form of online education and argues that it is superior to the traditional, campus-based courses he used to teach.[14]

Opposition to distance education has been fierce, directed at the philosophical and economic claims made on its behalf. Many argue that a liberal education calls for interpersonal interaction, and virtual universities deny this opportunity to students. On-campus instructors have a strong intellectual and personal stake in in-person teaching and are angered at directives to adopt new strategies that have been developed without their involvement. Along with those concerned with accreditation of universities, they say that a great deal of experimentation and evaluation is needed to compare the advantages and disadvantages of campus-based and online education. The harshest critics, such as historian David Noble, argue that distance education is but one more manifestation of the corporatization of higher education, a phenomenon that has prioritized economies of scale and profits over the dissemination of high-quality education to the nation's students.[15]

Teaching is not the only area in which the Internet has affected the history profession, however. Historians are also increasingly using the Internet for scholarly communication and research. Their efforts include electronic periodicals, article preprints, archival information, and primary documents. The catalyst for this online publishing is the development of the World Wide Web, a major improvement over earlier means of offering information online.[16] The Web has revolutionized the Internet by allowing the average scholar to obtain these documents with ease and view them on screens in familiar fonts that imitate the appearance of books. Its appeal is enhanced by its ability to incorporate text, images (stationery and moving), and audio material.[17]

Taking advantage of this improved technology, scholarly associations are using the Internet for their newsletters and journals. The American Historical Association (AHA), the Organization of American Historians, and many other associations have created Web sites. The AHA has put portions of its *Perspectives* newsletter online, as have the Conference on Latin American History (CLAH) and American Society for Legal History (ASLH).[18] The Chinese Urban History Association's *Wall and Market* and the *Chinese Environmental History Newsletter* are sent directly to subscribers, the former for a small charge and the latter free of charge. These newsletters include scholarly articles as well as news, in many cases approaching the standards of historical journals.[19]

The typical Web site of a scholarly organization or academic department is similar in content to a newsletter in its provision of a wide assortment of professional information. With the advent of the Web, it is easy and cheap to distribute information in smaller increments.[20]

The movement of historical journals to the Internet has been accelerating in recent years. More and more of the established U.S. and European historical journals, such as the *American Historical Review* and the *Journal of American History,* are available on the Web. This change occurred only after an initial wariness based on a variety of objections to the electronic environment: poor readability and portability, a reduction in the quality of content, the loss of archival copies, violation of copyright, and a decreasing ability to cover costs. Readability and portability have been considered to be inferior in electronic editions, perhaps because of the state of the technology and the novelty of the new medium. Quality can be lessened by the ease of distribution, which may dissolve the determination to carefully channel and screen the content on the Internet. According to Sara Bearss of the Conference of Historical Journals, "Issues of quality control remain a paramount concern. Many of the print editors are troubled by the demand for speed in electronic formats. Will editing for content, copy editing, and careful checking of citations and facts be squeezed out by the impetus for speed and immediacy?"

Some also express fear about the loss of a "canonical" copy of journals, either because of the technological obsolescence of the electronic medium on which they are stored or the ease with which electronic texts can be changed. As various versions of the journal appear online over the years, who will maintain the original version, where will it be stored, and how will its publishers authenticate it?

Finally, the ease of duplication of electronic text creates concerns about an increase in copyright violations through attempts to obtain online versions without paying the subscription fees. These fees are needed to cover the costs of publishing journals, and in the case of some newsletters they are the major source of income for the associations that publish them.[21]

Two major initiatives—Project Muse and JStor—have promoted the publication of scholarly journals online. Project Muse has been putting the Johns Hopkins University Press's prestigious journals on line since 1995, including *Reviews in American History* and *English Literary History.* Institutions subscribe, and only those who are part of the institution can access the Internet versions.[22] Whereas Project Muse distributes current issues of these journals, JStor is creating electronic editions of back issues of major historical journals. Included are the *American Historical Review, Journal of American History, Journal of Modern History,* and the *William and Mary Quarterly,* from their beginnings through 2000.[23]

A third initiative, the Making of America project at Cornell University and University of Michigan, involves disseminating nineteenth-century journals on the Web. As part of this project, the universities have placed the *Atlantic Monthly* (1857–1900), *Harper's New Monthly Magazine* (1889–96), and *North American Review* (1816–1900) on the Web, along with several dozen other U.S. periodicals of the era.[24]

On the heels of this cautious investigation of the Internet by the mainstream journals, historians and scholars in ancillary disciplines have experimented with electronic journals. The record of this new breed of journal is mixed in terms of survival and reputation.

Classical and medieval scholars have taken to the Internet with great enthusiasm, establishing the *Bryn Mawr Classical Review* in 1990 and *The Medieval Review* in 1993.[25] In 1993, the University of Tasmania launched *Electronic Antiquity: Communicating the Classics,* explaining,

> Distance, above all, is what has motivated us to undertake to produce *Electronic Antiquity: Communicating the Classics.* Australia, New Zealand, South Africa, Asia, their distance from the libraries and the universities of the northern hemisphere is, for those of us who live in this region, a major difficulty. Even within these countries size, population and geographical diversity can make simple communication difficult, at times near impossible. Electronic transmission offers us one way of realistically and speedily communicating not just with the rest of the world, but also with one another.

The journal has published semiannually since 1993.[26]

*Cromohos,* the *Cyber Review of Modern Historiography,* is an Italian online journal devoted to modern historical culture from the end of the fifteenth century to the present. The journal includes articles in Italian and English and is overseen by editors from two Italian universities and an international editorial board. Since its inception it has attempted to blend the best of the traditional and innovative in its use of the Internet. For example, it has created *ELIOHS,* an electronic library of the classics of historiography, and a guide to historical resources on the Internet.[27]

The *Electronic Journal of Australian and New Zealand History,* one of the earliest peer-reviewed electronic journals, was established by two leading professors from the region in 1995 and has published approximately thirty articles and sixty book reviews.[28]

A peer-reviewed publication, the *Journal of Southern Religion,* has been published by the University of Virginia since 1998 and includes leading scholars in U.S. history among its contributors.[29] *Essays in History,* a peer-reviewed graduate student journal of the University of Virginia department of history, has been published online since 1991, exclusively so since 1994.[30]

Not all electronic journals have endured, although the older issues remain available on the Web. *Chronicon,* edited at the University of Dublin and emphasizing Irish history, released two issues in 1997 and 1998 but has been quiescent ever since.[31]

Although these periodicals are increasingly professional in their preparation, with some incorporating peer review and respected editorial boards, most are not as prestigious as their older printed counterparts. In part this lack of prestige results from their newness and the fact that only a few have accepted the standard means of ensuring quality in their early stages. The acceptance of electronic journals will depend to a large degree on their willingness to incorporate peer review and rigorous editing in their production. At the same time, it is likely that they will experiment with a variety of innovations, including increasing interaction between authors and readers, distributing articles and reviews continuously rather than in periodic packages, and incorporating hypertext and hypermedia.[32]

The computer and the Internet offer more than communication between scholars. They also facilitate historical research. Archival materials of most institutions in the United States are now catalogued through the Online Computer Library Center (OCLC) First Search service (major institutions) and the National Union Catalog of Manuscript Collections (smaller institutions) Web page.[33] Furthermore, hundreds of archives and collection libraries have created Web pages that include lists of and finding aids for their collections. The Library of Congress is slowly converting its 1,600 registers of large manuscript collections to electronic form, and the National Archives and Records Administration already has in-depth descriptions of its records on the Internet.[34] Some of the smaller archives and special collections of libraries have fully computerized finding aids, and many more are moving toward this.[35] Bell & Howell Information and Learning (formerly University Microfilms International), a major source of microfilm editions of archival sources, has extensive information on its collections online.[36] In addition to allowing extensive investigation of research resources, these records are valuable sources of historical information. The National Archive and Records Administration (NARA) descriptions of the records of the nation's federal agencies, for example, offer excellent summaries of the statutory history of the agencies and the functions they were established to achieve.

The most exciting development in the use of the Internet and computers in history is the increasing availability of full-text primary documents, both published and unpublished. Since the late 1950s, several academic projects have taken on the task of converting entire corpora or collections into electronic form. Gateways such as "EuroDocs: Western European Primary Historical Documents" introduce one to the vast number of resources. These cover all eras in European civilization, from the Greek and Roman periods to medieval, Renaissance, and modern Europe, and include images as well as texts. Perseus offers a fascinating scholarly site on Greek and Roman life, and the Thesaurus Linguae Grecae CD-ROM, produced at the University of California of Irvine, consists of "the entire corpus of Greek classical literature from Homer to 600 A.D.," including approximately 3,500 authors and 9,500 literary works.[37]

The Labyrinth and the Internet Medieval Sourcebook are major sites that include the *Electronic Beowulf* and elegant illustrated medieval manuscripts from Oxford University and elsewhere. Renaissance Europe is represented by "Plague and Public Health in Renaissance Europe."[38] Historic maps, such as those of dozens of Dutch cities in the seventeenth century, are available. "Maps of Paris" includes a range of maps of the capital city from 1721 to 1870.[39]

One of the largest archives of materials associated with European history is the American and French Research on the Treasury of the French Language (ARTFL) at the University of Chicago. ARTFL makes available online and through CD-ROMs a corpus of almost 2,000 French literary, historic, and scientific works ranging from famous authors such as Molière and Racine to rare works. The works include a small selection of medieval, Renaissance, and seventeenth-century texts and a much larger volume of modern works from the eighteenth through the twentieth centuries.[40]

An archive of the works of Marx and Engels is available, as well as many other primary texts in European history.[41]

Interest in electronic texts in U.S. and British history is growing.[42] In 1990, the Library of Congress launched its American Memory program, serving as a testbed for digitizing and distributing primary documents to the public. The program has placed on the Internet many of the Library's collections, including the Thomas Jefferson papers, U.S. Congressional Documents and Debates from 1774 through 1873, images and text of documents of the National American Women's Suffrage Association (1860–1920), narratives of California residents (1849–1900), African-American pamphlets (1820–1920), early films of New York City by Thomas Edison, and a variety of photograph collections.[43] Eventually, American Memory flowered into the National Digital Library Program (NDLP), an ambitious program to digitize a much larger portion of the Library's collections. In 1996, the National Digital Library Federation (NDLF) was established as a collaboration of twelve research libraries, the Library of Congress, the National Archives and Records Administration, the New York Public Library, and the Commission on Preservation and Access. The federation aims to coordinate and support the efforts of all libraries to make their collections accessible electronically and to use electronic media for their preservation.[44]

The Model Editions Partnership, begun in July 1995, is creating electronic editions of major U.S. papers projects, including the documentary history of the first federal Congress, the Lincoln legal papers, the Nathanael Greene papers, the documentary history of the ratification of the Constitution, the Margaret Sanger papers, the papers of Elizabeth Cady Stanton and Susan B. Anthony, and the Henry Laurens papers. The electronic editions will incorporate essential elements of scholarly editing while augmenting these with electronic enhancements such as customized indexes, links to related annotative material, and various views of the documents (e.g., with and without standardized spelling and names).[45]

The National Archives has encouraged the creation of Web sites for each of the presidential libraries it oversees. Some, such as the Franklin Delano Roosevelt site, include the full text of substantial materials from the library, including formerly classified materials from the 1933–1945 period, files dealing with U.S.-Vatican relations during World War II, and German diplomatic files dealing with U.S.-German relations in the 1930s and 1940s.[46]

The works of many American literary figures from the nineteenth and early twentieth century are being made available, a rich source for U.S. intellectual and social historians. Examples include the Walt Whitman Hypertext Archive, which aims to put the complete works of Whitman on the Web, along with critical commentary and biographical information; many of the works of nineteenth-century U.S. novelists, poets, and essayists are already online. Other impressive social history projects include the annotated collection "Urban Planning, 1794–1918: International Anthology of Articles, Conference Papers, and Reports" from Cornell University, an electronic edition of Jacob Riis's *How the Other Half Lives,* and the "Lower East Side Project," a Web site devoted to important turn-of-the-century U.S. speeches, papers, and articles of urban reformers.[47]

Historical texts and multimedia histories are also being created on CD-ROMs, which, unlike the majority of Internet offerings, may be costly. Accessible Archives, a company in Pennsylvania, has published CD-ROM versions of the *Pennsylvania Gazette,* Benjamin Franklin's colonial newspaper, and its successors; "The Civil War: A Newspaper Perspective"; "African-American Newspapers: The 19th Century"; and *Godey's Lady's Book,* a significant nineteenth-century magazine for women.[48]

This is just a sample of the historic texts available in electronic form.[49] The establishment of national clearinghouses for electronic texts such as the

Center for History and New Media (CHNM), Center for Electronic Texts in the Humanities (CETH), and the Institute for Advanced Technology in the Humanities (IATH) is likely to increase the support and technical assistance for creating electronic texts.[50]

How they will be used is important. One of the main advantages of electronic texts is the low cost and ease of dissemination. Thus, many of the text projects described in this chapter have the goal (shared with microfilm and microfiche projects) of broadening access to valuable primary materials instead of requiring costly trips to archives.[51]

Another feature that adds value to electronic texts is hypertext, or three-dimensional text, as one scholar calls it. With hypertext, one can link different texts together merely by selecting a word or words within the original texts. Thus, one could link passages from the electronic Adams and Jefferson referring to a specific event, person, or idea to compare the authors' views on the subject. One could track changes in legislation as it is amended by linking the various versions of the amended sections to each other.

Hypermedia, requiring somewhat more sophisticated software, allows linking of nontextual media such as photographs, paintings and even moving pictures in a textual work. This is useful for many research projects when one wants to view places or objects as well as to analyze them.

Electronic texts have another unique quality: the ease with which information within them can be identified, organized, and analyzed. Using electronic texts, scholars can search in systematic or random fashion for words, phrases, and concepts. Both word-processing programs and specialized software have been designed for this task. This software allows a scholar to search a text or group of texts for a specific word, such as all uses of the word *suicide* by Durkheim. Each occurrence of the word is identified and can be displayed in context. More sophisticated software programs allow the scholar to engage in complex Boolean searches, searching texts using two or more words occurring together or separately. For example, one might search the papers of Elizabeth Cady Stanton for passages using the words *abolition* and *women* to identify sections about female antislavery advocates.[52]

This ability to search offers a number of advantages. It acts as a secondary index, supplementing the print publication's index and customizing it to the needs of the individual scholar. As important is the capacity to collect all occurrences of a subject of interest to the scholar within a single text or from a wide assortment of texts. Traditionally, the historian transcribed by hand or typewriter each such occurrence onto cards or sheets of paper or use a copy machine. With an electronic text, the scholar can scroll through the various occurrences, transfer them to electronic note cards, or print them out together without any transcription. The time saved on this single task is significant, especially as the amount of text increases. Consider being able to perform these operations on the "Minutes of the Executive Council of the American Federation of Labor, 1893–1955" or congressional material about new deal economic policies from 1933 to 1938, now available only on microfiche.

The computer is merely a tool; the task of conceptualizing or drawing conclusions is still left to the historian. In that sense, the computer is conservative, facilitating but not changing the traditional work of the historian. It is also transparent in that its use may not show up in the scholarly essay or monograph because the scholar's method of organizing and analyzing concepts is essentially unchanged.

Some historians and social scientists have chosen to move beyond traditional textual analysis. They have undertaken conceptual analysis through quantification of textual material. In this sense, they are drawing on the tradition of content analysis, an approach used by a small number of political scientists and historians in the last thirty years. Especially in the late 1960s and early 1970s, a variety of texts were rigorously analyzed in terms of their themes and language. For example, a U.S. political scientist examined colonial and British newspapers from the 1730s through the 1770s (the prerevolutionary and revolutionary periods) for their use of *American, British, colonial,* and similar words. He was interested in the relationship between a growing American nationalism (as indicated by changes in the uses of these words) and critical revolutionary events such as the Stamp Act Crisis or the Boston Tea Party. A Latin American historian systematically searched the speeches of a nineteenth-century authoritarian Ecuadorean leader to identify the sources to which the leader attributed his authority, such as the church or the constitution. These studies used the computer for statistical analysis because the technology was not yet available for easy access to electronic texts.[53]

Content analysis never achieved significant status as a method within the historical community. It may be that traditional historians believed that content analysts sacrificed too much of the complexity of a text in classifying its contents. They also may have attributed too much significance to small or skewed samples of texts. It is also likely that the effort of classifying texts and entering the data into the earliest computers was not justified by the results they found.

Although their methods may have fallen short, there is great validity in the aims of content analysts. Their work complements that of traditional historians in its attempt to confirm the hypotheses included in more traditional studies. In traditional studies, the level of discussion generally does not extend beyond vague concepts of comparison such as "greater than" or "lesser than." Although these studies are invaluable for presenting interpretations, their being put to the test of a more rigorous analysis can enhance the understanding of the text and provide new insights, even if they do not result in a new interpretation.[54]

Various approaches are being tested to improve textual analysis, including the work of the Text Encoding Initiative (TEI), an international initiative established in 1987. The TEI is one of many efforts throughout the electronic world to develop standard means of encoding texts. At its simplest level, the TEI encourages encoding of the most basic structures within a text (title page, chapters, chapter titles, paragraphs, and appendixes) to facilitate the presentation in print and online.[55] The TEI also has the more ambitious objective of allowing the computer to assist the scholar in analyzing a text. Ever since electronic texts became available, scholars have developed their schemes to mark them up, to set off important portions of the texts to be picked out by the computer for analysis. Although the initial interest in encoding was expressed by linguistic and literary scholars, historians have begun to acknowledge the value of encoding as well. Encoding dates, names, places, political offices, organizations, occupations, currencies, and other discrete historical items facilitates the analysis of these texts using the computer. More complex encoding of concepts similar to that done in creating indexes is also possible, although it is not done often today. Historical projects using the TEI include the Model Editions Partnership, the American Memory Project, "Documenting the American South; or, The Southern Experience in 19th-Century America," "African-American Women Writers of the 19th Century," and the "Dutch Golden Age."[56]

At the outer edges of computer-assisted textual analysis is the application of artificial intelligence to text interpretation. Several scholars from France and England have explored this higher-level use of computers in relation to analyzing textual descriptions of paintings included in seventeenth-century English probate papers, the belief systems of French public and private figures of the fourteenth and fifteenth centuries, and the attitudes of conqueror and conquered in post-Columbian America.[57]

The advantages of electronic texts for analysis thus range from making traditional methods easier and faster to potentially using the computer to count and conceptualize. Several questions have arisen about how these texts can be made most useful for analysis.

One of these is the level of accuracy to be obtained in transcription from other media. Keyboarding, conversion of printers' typesetting tapes, and scanning are the primary means of entering text onto electronic media. All are error-prone, as is preparing texts for printed media. Various projects differ in the importance they assign to accuracy.

Another issue is the level of encoding in electronic texts. The rawest form of electronic text is the plain ASCII version, which is the verbatim transcription of text onto electronic media. Many electronic text creators have gone beyond this ASCII version to help the researcher use and analyze the text. Often, text is combined on a single CD-ROM with a search program that allows the user to take advantage of analytical tools. This bundling of text and search program has been criticized by some scholars, who argue that it interferes with the ability to use one's preferred search programs. In addition, it prevents the combination of the text with other texts or the application of additional analytical tools by the scholar. Other electronic text publishers have encoded the ASCII text to assist in the searches, using standards such as the TEI, described earlier. No consensus exists as to which of these strategies is superior; it may be that all three are needed to satisfy a variety of users.

A third debate is the amount of annotation or critical apparatus to be applied to archival documents. Electronic texts are more malleable in terms of their editing and distribution than are printed texts. Thus, they lend themselves to the possibility of a greater variety of editions, with various levels of annotation. The value of widespread dissemination is considered to be greater than the need for editorial interpretation, although ultimately the interpretation is deemed necessary to make the documents most understandable and useful to historians and the public.[58]

A fourth debate is whether page images should be included along with searchable text. Images use much more electronic memory, so their inclusion may raise the costs of any products in which they are included and the demands on the users' computers. On the other hand, some consider transcribed text alone insufficient for the purposes of analysis; as described later in this chapter, these critics need to see the physical text itself (or its representation through digital imagery).[59] As memory and storage space become cheaper, publishers may choose to incorporate both, although the quality of images remains an issue.[60]

A fifth debate is over the most appropriate means of dissemination. CD-ROMs and the Internet are the two most common methods. CD-ROMs are favored by those who prefer a more traditional package for pricing and marketing reasons. CD-ROMs are like books or records in that they are discrete objects and are easier to price and more portable.[61] Even so, many CD-ROMs are licensed like software rather than sold outright because of the great possibility for duplication. CD-ROMs also allow the packaging of text with a search program, which many of those new to electronic texts prefer.

On the other hand, distribution via the Internet and other networks is a goal for many projects. For many, the ideal is for free distribution, in the spirit of creating a rich information and collaborative culture.[62]

Some scholars challenge the advantages of electronic texts, criticizing both the capacities and characteristics of electronic media. For example, the capacity of the computer to improve on unassisted textual analysis is still in question. Gilmore and Case note that a scholar engaged in an authorship study abandoned the computer in favor of his own intellectual efforts. Was this scholar typical in his frustration with the computer? Are there certain types of cases in which the computer is essential in an analysis? For example, authorship studies, including Mosteller's and Wallace's study of the *Federalist Papers,* have been considered good candidates for computer-aided analysis.[63] In the absence of a survey of historians who have used the computer for textual analysis, this is a difficult question to answer. Extensive experience is needed with the tools described here to be able to truly evaluate their helpfulness to historians. It is important to include in any survey of satisfaction those who use textual analysis tools to pursue traditional tasks as well as those who attempt more difficult and unusual applications.

Gilmore and Case also assert that the digitized text can never adequately replace the document itself. Some scholars have responded to this concern by developing elaborate means of describing the physical appearance of the document within the text. Others insist that images of the physical text accompany its transcription.[64]

Another concern is the durability of electronic texts and the stability of the hardware and software needed to read them. One study of the problem observed,

> The great advantages of digital information are coupled with the enormous fragility of this medium over time compared to traditional media such as paper. The experience of addressing the Year 2000 issue in existing software systems, or data losses through poor management of digital data are beginning to raise awareness of the issues. Electronic information is fragile and evanescent. It needs careful management from the moment of creation and a proactive policy and strategic approach to its creation and management to secure its preservation over the longer-term.[65]

An intensive international effort is under way to address this issue, led by two U.S. organizations: the Commission on Preservation and Access (CPA) and the Record Libraries Group (RLG). In 1996, the two agencies commissioned *Preserving Digital Information: Report on the Archiving of Digital Information,* produced by experts in archival practices and technology. The report included horror stories of the loss of significant data through obsolescence in the 1960s and 1970s. It noted that "technological obsolescence represents a far greater threat to information in digital form than the inherent physical fragility of many digital media." Rather than using this experience as a reason to recommend traditional means of storage, the study called for "building—almost from scratch—the . . . deep infrastructure . . . that will enable us to tame anxieties and move our cultural records naturally and confidently into the future." It called for the establishment of digital archives, with the primary mandate to preserve digital information, distinct from the digital libraries and other creators and disseminators of digital information.[66]

Great Britain, Australia, and other European countries are involved in similar initiatives to ensure the long-term preservation of digital information.[67]

Obviously, the function of the electronic copy is critical in determining the standards that should be applied to it. If it is an archival copy, then long-term considerations are paramount. If it is an attempt to increase the accessibility of the primary document and is one of many copies, then these standards may be less important.[68]

Ironically, despite the improved accessibility of electronic texts, accessibility itself is a concern. The number of computers owned by scholars has increased tremendously in recent years. Their use in primary and secondary education has made them more desirable as personal items for scholars with children, and prices continue to drop relative to income. Also, despite the budget limitations of many colleges and universities, personal computers and workstations probably will be among the last amenities to go.

Thus, with certain exceptions, electronic dissemination is likely to increase access to many types of documents. These exceptions are the poorer schools and families in the more developed countries and entire undeveloped nations. Much concern has been expressed about the inability of struggling nations to take advantage of the communication revolution because of the cost of computers. It will be important to ensure that hard copies of sources are available to scholars in these countries and to provide financial assistance to enable them to upgrade their computer facilities.[69]

Access in undeveloped countries is improving. In 1996, it was estimated that "about half of all internet users in the world are in the United States, 25 percent are in Europe and the rest are scattered throughout different countries."[70] A 1997 survey estimated that "among country and global top level domains above the 10,000 mark, the most rapidly growing included: Malaysia, Turkey Russia, Korea, Russian Fed., Ukraine, China, Indonesia, Argentina, Hong Kong, Thailand, and New Zealand."[71] A 1994 article in the *Chica-go Tribune* portrayed the development of new networks in Latin America, led by women's groups. The article described Isis International, "one of the primary networks for women's information and communication in the world," which "has offices in Chile and the Philippines and reaches about 150 countries via letter, telephone, fax, and e-mail."[72] The United Nations and other international agencies are including Internet access among the services they offer to developing nations.[73]

The use of electronic texts in the history profession is dependent on more than acceptance by historians. Others in the scholarly world must accept them as well. Archivists, for example, have acknowledged both the opportunities and drawbacks of electronic texts. As described earlier, the National Archives has embraced electronic dissemination. However, reservations still exist. The cost of digitization may reduce the funds available for more traditional archival purposes. Archives that derive income from famous documents are less likely to digitize these for understandable reasons. They also are concerned about the authenticity of archival documents on the Web. Is the document one sees on the screen the same as the one originally digitized at the archives, or has it been manipulated in some fashion? Encryption, the technology for ensuring the authenticity of a document, is still not up to the standards many desire. Furthermore, some archivists argue that there is a need for context in offering documents. They worry that the Internet too easily divorces the document and its context or provides an inferior attempt at context.[74]

Scholarly editors similarly express reservations, especially about the added cost and time needed to develop electronic editions. The technological learning curve and labor intensiveness are deterrents for some creators of critical editions in print form.[75]

Academic librarians are also vital to scholarly communication and have taken the lead in the electronic revolution. Led by the Library of Congress National Digital Library Project, they have even assumed the role of electronic publishers.[76] This is not inconsistent with past practice. As the repositories of many of the nation's special collections of primary published and unpublished documents, libraries have traditionally taken steps to make these collections more accessible through printing and microfilm.[77] The Library of Congress assigns as much, if not more, importance to making its collections accessible to Congress and other audiences as to adding to its collections.[78]

Several academic libraries have created specialized electronic text centers to collect and disseminate electronic texts. Such centers have proliferated, with almost twenty-five of them currently located in the United States, Canada, and Australia alone. Columbia University was among the first to establish an Electronic Text Service devoted solely to supplying and assisting humanist scholars with electronic texts on CD-ROMs. In addition, the Columbia University law library established a "virtual library" that allows electronic access to the standard law books. The universities of Virginia and Michigan also pioneered in making electronic texts available to faculty and students, especially in a networked environment. Many other libraries allow students to access electronic texts from their Web sites and maintain CD-ROM stations and a supply of textual CD-ROMs.

Digital libraries, a more ambitious attempt to make increasing amounts of text available through the Internet, are also being created at Carnegie-Mellon and Stanford Universities, the University of California at Berkeley and Santa Barbara, the University of Illinois at Champaign-Urbana, and University of Michigan.[79]

On the copyright and fair use front, librarians have taken the lead in recommending revisions of the current copyright law to take advantage of the increased accessibility in the electronic environment. Many librarians have become concerned about the copyright confusion and licensing restrictions that have emerged in the electronic environment. In cooperation with the Coalition for Networked Information and the Association of Research Libraries, they have been prominent among copyright activists. Library organizations have testified in favor of maximum application of fair use doctrine to materials on the Internet and were active opponents of certain provisions of the Digital Millennium Copyright Act and the Copyright Term Extension Act that were perceived as antagonistic to the dissemination of material on the Internet.[80]

Libraries have also worked to develop online journals independent of commercial print publishers, although primarily in the physical and biological sciences. This is largely a response to the rapid rise in the cost of commercial scientific journals in recent years; high costs have prompted librarians to cancel subscriptions to the most expensive journals and to explore electronic dissemination through the Internet. Through the Coalition for Networked Information, created by the Association of Research Libraries, CAUSE, and Educom, the librarians have drawn up a number of alternative pricing and ownership schemes to further the goal of widespread access to electronic periodicals. Whether this will affect the historical profession, in which the price of journals has stayed somewhat lower than that of scientific journals, remains to be seen.[81]

Despite librarians' enthusiasm for the potential of electronic libraries, there are many obstacles to easy library transition. Although they have long used computers in their work, librarians' efforts have been devoted primarily to acting as intermediaries with reference tools such as indexes and bibliographies. Incorporating electronic texts into libraries is a significant step, raising issues of cost competition with printed publications, technological training of staff and users, and integration into information and cataloguing systems. Libraries are increasingly short of resources, and any investment in electronic equipment or textual material may divert funds from printed publications. As telecommunications and electronic texts are introduced, library professionals and paraprofessionals will need to be trained in their use. The ability to adapt to the use of these resources will vary among librarians.[82]

The attitude of the academic computing center toward electronic texts is also important. In many schools, these centers were slow to respond to the increased use of computers in the humanities, continuing to serve the scientific and mathematical communities instead. Other centers, such as those at Princeton and Georgetown Universities, have taken a lead in providing services to the humanities community.

Scholarly publishers are also affected by the potential expansion of electronic texts. University publishers, in particular, are struggling financially as rising costs and reduced subsidies are squeezing out the economic viability of publishing the traditional monograph. They may not be able to afford the investment in training, time, and money that would be needed to turn to electronic publishing of primary papers, secondary sources, or journals.[83] Both costs and uncertainty limit experimentation in the new medium, as observed by a veteran university press editor: "The old saw that no publishing technologies but papyrus and clay tablets have ever fully died out, while true, I think begs a larger set of questions about the nature of the new medium, the implications of the new (inevitable) payment mechanisms, and the consequent challenges to publishers, authors, and librarians alike."[84] The Association of American University Presses (AAUP) maintains a Web page with a link to a Scholarly Electronic Publishing Bibliography.[85]

Despite the uncertainty, esteemed university presses are experimenting with electronic publication. A search of the current online AAUP catalog reveals more than seventy releases in which the primary publication is a CD-ROM or a print publication accompanied by a CD-ROM. New works such as the *Encyclopedia of Kentucky* are being produced, and older works such as the University of Chicago's massive *The Founder's Constitution* are being reissued on CD-ROM.[86]

The History E-Book Project of the American Council of Learned Societies is boldly confronting the issues associated with electronic publishing. Responding to the vulnerability of the scholarly monograph, the project "will collaborate with five Learned Societies and seven University Presses" to "convert to electronic format 500 backlist monographs of major importance to historical studies—books that remain vital to both scholars and advanced students, are frequently cited in the literature, and are currently not widely available." In addition, it will "publish 85 completely new electronic monographs that use new technologies to communicate the results of scholarship in new ways."[87]

The commercial publishers, with more capacity to take on the challenge of electronic publishing, have also shied away from it. When they have become involved, the effects have often been less than desirable. Voyager Company, a publisher that specializes in CD-ROMs, has produced one of the exceptions, the CD-ROM version of a well-known social history textbook published by Pantheon Press in 1992. The *Who Built America?* CD-ROM uses hypermedia to travel from many points in the text to electronic primary sources, to still and moving graphics, and audio. Unlike many other commercial historical CD-ROMs to date, *Who Built America?* was created by respected scholars and has been received positively in the scholarly community.[88]

Unfortunately, other commercial CD-ROMs generally are accorded a low rating by historians. Reviews of these CD-ROMs indicate disappointment in many of the products. Although most reviewers appreciate the multimedia aspects of the CD-ROM, they deplore the low quality of the text, often obtained from inferior, out-of-copyright sources and lacking attribution to an individual author. Thus, despite the use of hypermedia, the commercial CD-ROM market has been left to those least likely to add scholarly value to these products.[89]

The failure to engage in electronic publishing on a large scale exists despite print publishers' possession of valuable assets in the world of electronic publishing, particularly copyrights and electronic versions of these publications created as part of print publication. Offsetting these advantages are their concerns about markets, retailing outlets, and competition with their traditional profit base. Is there a market for electronic texts, and how can it be tapped? Will publishers need to provide additional support to academic customers in using these state-of-the-art products? If a market does exist, success may turn sour because sales of print publications may plummet with the rapid dissemination of electronic versions in a spurt of copyright violations.

Copyright is a crucial concern, as is evident in the contentious process to amend the Copyright Act of 1976 to reflect the changed environment created by electronic publication. The long period of time it took to amend the copyright statutes revealed the conflicts between publishers and others such as librarians who want maximum freedom of distribution of electronic materials.[90]

The concerns of print publishers about electronic publishing have had two effects on the availability and quality of electronic texts. The availability has been greatly restricted because of the difficulty of obtaining electronic rights to copyrighted print publications (including critical editions of primary sources) and the high cost of electronic data entry. One philosopher-turned-publisher has taken on the former issue by producing a highly respected critical electronic edition of philosophical works. This is intensive, specialized work, however, and may not catch on.

The quality of electronic texts also has been affected by the lack of scholarly involvement in their creation and by the choices made by some electronic publishers of older and less well-respected editions of works whose copyright restrictions have expired.[91]

All the issues concerning converting older printed texts to digital form may be moot for materials released since the mid-1960s. The conversion of most government offices and businesses to electronic communication means that much of the critical communication that will serve as the basis for future historical study is already—and, in some situations, only—available in electronic form. A congressional study estimated that 75 percent of all federal transactions would be handled electronically by the year 2000. Certainly, a large amount of the diplomatic and domestic policy making that is going on today within and between nations is done via electronic communication.[92] Even at a lower level of policy making, significant information may be found in the electronic communication between senior officials. A study of the e-mail of a U.S. Naval Laboratory in Maryland found information of interest to future historians in many of these messages.[93]

The significance of government e-mail to historians has been highlighted by federal court cases initiated in 1989, collectively known as the "PROFS" cases.[94] These involved representatives of the Reagan, Bush, and Clinton administrations, the National Security Council (NSC), NARA, the AHA, and the Organization of American Historians. Reagan administration officials were discovered to have destroyed electronic records concerning the Iran-Contra scandal and other controversial NSC activities. This set off a series of lawsuits leading to an injunction against the destruction of remaining records and a court ruling requiring NARA to develop guidelines to ensure the preservation of electronic records, including e-mail, in all federal agencies. NARA complied by amending the relevant portion of the Code of Federal Regulations in 1996. The two-year comment period on the changes revealed the continuing chasm of opinion over the significance of e-mail and the desirability of long-term preservation of sensitive electronic policy-making documents. The arrival of electronic documents as legitimate records was evidenced to a certain extent in September 1996. At this time, Congress passed the Electronic Freedom of Information Act (FOIA), which requires that federal agencies respond to requests for electronic records.[95]

Furthermore, the federal government is disseminating tremendous amounts of textual and statistical information on the Web. Since 1995, the Government Printing Office (GPO) has offered the full texts of the *Congressional Record,* the *Federal Register,* General Accounting Office (GAO) Reports, and Comptroller Decisions and links to the documents of many other agencies. These documents serve as easily accessible source material for the present generation of political scientists and evidence for later generations of historians, assuming that issues of authenticity and representativeness are resolved satisfactorily. Most state and many local governments also have Web sites that contain information on local agencies and important documents.[96]

In addition, an increasing amount of important contemporary textual material is being disseminated commercially through CD-ROMs and online services as well as the Internet. *The New York Times* and *Wall Street Journal* are among many newspapers that are available in electronic form via commercial database services.[97] The transcripts of television news are available, including those of the Cable News Network (CNN) and the "McNeil News Hour."

What will be the effect of this expansion in electronic texts on the conversion of existing manuscripts and printed publications? It is likely that the availability of this electronic material will increase the demand for computer-aided textual analysis tools. It may also result in technology that will reduce the cost of converting printed publications to electronic texts, allowing more conversions of existing documents of historic interest.[98] Obviously, much remains to be seen.

## NOTES

1. See Dennis A. Trinkle, ed., *Writing, Teaching, and Researching History in the Electronic Age: Historians and Computers* (Armonk, N.Y.: M.E. Sharpe, 1998); Dennis A. Trinkle, Dorothy Auchter, Scott A. Merriman, and Todd E. Larsen, *The History Highway: A Guide to Internet Resources* (Armonk, N.Y.: M.E. Sharpe, 1997); and Daniel Greenstein, *A Historian's Guide to Computing* (Oxford, England: Oxford University Press, 1994) for U.S. and British perspectives on history and computing. The American Historical Association has included a section on computers in its monthly newsletter, *Perspectives,* since 1989 and has produced two excellent volumes on the subject: Janice L. Reiff, *Digitizing the Past: The Use of Computers and Communication Technology in History* (Washington, D.C.:

American Historical Association, 1999); and Janice Reiff, *Structuring the Past: The Use of Computers in History* (Washington, D.C.: American Historical Association, 1991). Journals explicitly dealing with the topic include the *History Computer Review* (formerly the *History Microcomputer Review*), the *Journal of the American Association of History and Computing,* and the *Social Science Computer Review.* The *History Computer Review* may be contacted at Department of History, Pittsburg State University, Pittsburg, Kansas 66762; it is establishing a Web site at <http://www.pittstate.edu/hist>. The *Journal of the American Association of History and Computing* is an electronic journal established in 1998, available at <http://mcel.pacificu.edu/JAHC/jahcindex.htm>. The *Social Science Computer Review* is published by Sage Publications and has an informational page with tables of contents of issues since 1996 at <http://hcl.chass.ncsu.edu/sscore/sscore.htm>.

2. For early articles about the Internet and history discussion groups, see Richard W. Slatta, "Historians and Telecommunications," *History Microcomputer Review* 2:2 (Fall 1986): 25–34; David R. Campbell, "The New History Net," *History Microcomputer Review* 3:2 (Fall 1987): 25; and Norman R. Coombs, "History by Teleconference," *History Microcomputer Review* 4:1 (Spring 1988): 37–40.

3. The H-Net Web site is at <http://www.h-net.msu.edu>. Also see Melanie S. Weiss and Mark L. Kornbluh, "H-Net: Humanities and Social Sciences OnLine," *History Teacher* 31:4 (1998): 533; "H-Net Teaching Resources Archive," *Perspectives* 34:1 (January 1996): 20; and Steven A. Leibo, "Noteworthy: "H-Net and the Internationalization of Scholarship," *Perspectives* 33:5 (May 1995): 23. An interesting discussion of the H-Net Book Review project and its impact on traditional book review publishing is available in David Burrell, "Negotiating Book Reviews: A Study of Technology, H-Net, and the Emergent Status of a Contemporary Print Form," at <http://dave.burrell.net/book.html>.

4. The author is one of the founders of H-Net and its first list, H-Urban. This paragraph is based on her experiences as an editor since H-Urban's inception in February 1993.

5. Matthew B. Gilmore and Donald O. Case, "Historians, Books, Computers, and the Library," *Library Trends,* Spring 1992, 667–87.

6. See Mark Olsen, review of *History and Computing I,* ed. Peter Denley and Deian Hopkin (Manchester, England: Manchester University Press, 1987), and *History and Computing II,* ed. Peter Denley, Stefan Fogelvik, and Charles Harvey (Manchester, England: Manchester University Press, 1989) in *Computers and the Humanities* 24 (1990): 499.

7. "What Is H-Net" at <http://www2.h-net.msu.edu/about/>.

8. See the excellent essay by John Semonche, "Time Traveling: Historians and Computers," *History Microcomputer Review* 11:2 (Fall 1995): 10, on this and other aspects of online communication. See also Karen L. Murphy and Mauri P. Collins, "Communication Conventions in Instructional Electronic Chats," *First Monday* 2:11 (November 3, 1997), at <http://www.firstmonday.dk/issues/issue2 11/murphy/index.html>.

9. H-Net Teaching List information is available at <http://h-net.msu.edu/~teach/teach.html>.

10. See Jeffrey R. Young, "A Historian Presents the Civil War, Online and Unfiltered by Historians," *New York Times,* June 29, 2000, D8. The article notes that approximately 3,000,000 people had accessed the Web site since 1995 and that a CD-ROM would be issued in August 2000. The "Valley of the Shadow" Web site can be accessed at <http://jefferson.village.virginia. edu/vshadow2/>.

11. The architecture and art history courses are at <http://www.uic.edu/classes/arch>. See also "Reading a Community: Doing Urban History at the Local Level," available at <http://www.uoguelph.ca/history/urban/sitemap.html>. This includes lectures, links to related resources, and an international bibliography on urban history.

12. "Virtual Universities Look for Ways to Build School Spirit," *Chronicle of Higher Education,* February 4, 2000, A47.

13. Western Governors University (Education without Boundaries) home page at <http://www.wgu.edu/wgu/index.html>. From that page, see also "About WGU" and links, "Academics," "Associate of Arts," and "Catalog" to search for the history courses being taught. Only a few of the classes explicitly indicate any degree of interaction with the professor or among students, so it is not clear from the Web catalog how much interaction actually occurs. In most cases, the course description is silent on this, and in some cases, mostly at Brigham Young University, it is stated that the work is "independent."

A disturbing aspect of the degree of independence allowed in these courses is evident in Jeffery R. Young, "A Virtual Student Teaches Himself," *Chronicle of Education,* May 7, 1999, A31–A32. A computer consultant who is working toward a degree at Western Governors University observes that to prepare to take a competency exam in Western civilization, "He might ask a friend who's taken a course on the subject what textbook he used, and read that. Or he might just read a faded two-volume set on his bookshelf: *Civilizations Past and Present,* published in 1944 by what was then the U.S. War Department."

14. Scott Jascik, "Historians Differ on Impact of Distance Education in Their Discipline," *Chronicle of Higher Education,* January 21, 2000, A43; E. L. Skip Knox, "The Rewards of Teaching On-Line," paper presented at the 2000 meeting of the American Historical Association, at <http://www.h-net.msu.edu/aha/papers/Knox.html>; "Western Civilization: A Course in European History," at <http://history.boisestate.edu/westciv>; "Asynchronicity," handouts distributed at Educom '96, at <http://history.boisestate.edu/westciv/admin/papers/asynchronicity.htm>; "Real Problems in the Virtual World," paper presented at Educom '96, at <http://history.boisestate.edu/westciv/admin/papers/realproblems.htm>; "The Pedagogy of Web Site Design," *ALN Magazine* 1:2 (August 1997), at <http://www.aln.org/alnweb/magazine/issue2/knox.htm>; and "Real Problems in the Virtual World (Updated)" at <http://history.boisestate.edu/westciv/admin/papers/psa.htm>. For an earlier description, see Ellis L. "Skip" Knox, "The Electric Renaissance: A Course in the Ether," *Perspectives* 31:2 (February 1993): 5–8, 10. See also Stephen E. DeLong, "The Shroud of Lecturing," *First Monday* 2:5 (May 5, 1997), at <http://www. firstmonday.dk/issues/issue2 5/delong/index.html>.

A somewhat negative experience with Internet teaching is described in a paper by Janet Smarr of the University of Illinois at Urbana-Champaign: "CIC Women Writers of the Renaissance Project," presented October 26, 1996, at the "Networking the Humanities" Conference of the Consortium of Humanities Centers and Institutes. On other Internet-taught courses, see postings to H-MMedia@h-net.msu.edu from John Saillant of Brown University on April 13, 1996 (African-American religion), and the H-Canada cross-posting on March 14, 1996 (these are available from the Discussion Logs of these lists at <http://www.h-net.msu.edu>).

15. See Florence Olsen, "Authors Argue That 'Distance Education' Is an Oxymoron," *Chronicle of Higher Education,* June 23, 2000, A49; and John Seely Brown and Paul Dug-

uid, *The Social Life of Information* (Cambridge, Mass.: Harvard Business School Press, 2000), the subject of Olsen's article. A large number of articles on distance education have been published in *The Chronicle of Higher Education* in recent years, including Lawrence Biemiller, "U. of Utah President Issues a Pointed Warning about Virtual Universities" (October 9, 1998), A32; "Role of Accreditors in Distance Education Is Debated at Conference" (February 12, 1999), A21; Dan Carnevale, "Assessing the Quality of Online Courses Remains a Challenge, Educators Agree" (February 18, 2000), A59; Florence Olsen, "'Virtual' Institutions Challenge Accreditors to Devise New Ways of Measuring Quality" (August 6, 1999), A29; Jeffrey R. Young, "A Virtual Student Teaches Himself" (May 7, 1999), A31–A32; Jeffery R. Young, "Rising Demand for Distance Learning Will Challenge Providers, Experts Say" (October 11, 1999), available at <http://chronicle.com/free/99/10/99101103t.htm>; Dan Carnevale, "Professor Says Distance Learning Can Increase Colleges' Income" (October 14, 1999), available at http://chronicle.com/free/99/10/99101403t.htm>; "Student's F's Highlight Problems in Electronic Course at U. of Iowa" (November 26, 1999), A67; Beth McMurtrie and Katherine S. Mangan, "Education Dept. and Career Schools Clash Over Accrediting of Distance Learning" (December 17, 1999), A36; Jeffrey Young, "Faculty Report at U. of Illinois Casts Skeptical Eye on Distance Education" (January 14, 2000), A48; Dan Carnevale, "New Master Plan in Washington State Calls for More On-Line Education" (February 4, 2000), A50; Sarah Carr, "A Distance Education Advocate Calls for Better Financing for Such Programs" (February 4, 2000), A50; and Sarah Carr, "Chapman U. Administrator Studies Distance Learning's Effect on Faculty Pay" (March 3, 2000), A46.

On the views of David Noble, see his extensive essay "Digital Diploma Mills: The Automation of Higher Education" in *First Monday,* which is an online peer-reviewed journal dealing with the effects of the Internet on international society, at <http://www.firstmonday. dk/issues/issue3 1/noble/>. Books by Noble include *America by Design: Science, Technology, and the Rise of Corporate Capitalism* (Oxford, England: Oxford University Press, 1979), *Forces of Production: A Social History of Industrial Automation* (Oxford, England: Oxford University Press, 1986), and *The Religion of Technology: The Divinity of Man and the Spirit of Invention* (New York: Penguin, 1999).

16. The Web still uses some of the earlier technologies for transferring information (e.g., FTP and Gopher) but in a manner that hides them from the user.

17. See Andrew McMichael, Michael O'Malley, and Roy Rosenzweig, "Historians and the Web: A Beginner's Guide," *Perspectives* 34:1 (January 1986): 11, also available at <http://chnm.gmu.edu/chnm/beginner.html>. The Web version of "Historians and the Web" includes links to many historical sites on the Internet.

18. *Perspectives Online* is available at <http://www.theaha.org/perspectives/index.cfm>. All post-1993 issues of the CLAH newsletter except the current issue are available to the public at <http://h-net.msu.edu/~clah> (the current issue is restricted to CLAH subscribers). The ASLH newsletter is at <http://h-net.msu.edu/~law/aslh news>. A gateway to electronic newsletters and journals on the World Wide Web is <http://ejournals.cic.net/toc.Topic.html> (organized by discipline). See also the *ARL Directory of Electronic Journals and Newsletters* at <http://arl.cni.org/scomm/edir>.

19. Kristin Stapleton [kestap01@ukcc.uky.edu], "Chinese Urban History News," on H-Urban [H-Urban@uicvm.uic.edu], May 19, 1995; Helen Dunstan [HIDUNSTA@ruby.

indstate.edu], private e-mail messages to Wendy Plotkin [U20566@uicvm.uic.edu], July 5 1995, and June 19, 1996. According to Dunstan, the online version of the *Chinese Environmental History Newsletter* is much more popular than the print version, which she attributes to the ease of subscription (via an e-mail request) as much as to the lack of a charge. For a list of electronic discussion groups on the Web, see the *Directory of Scholarly and Professional E-Conferences* at <http://www.n2h2.com/KOVACS/>.

20. A list of many of the historical societies with Web sites is available at <http://www.lib.uwaterloo.ca/society/history soc.html>. The Center for History and New Media provides a link to "History Departments around the World" at <http://chnm.gmu.edu/chnm/departments.taf>.

21. See Michael Grossberg, "History Journals in the 21st Century" (1997) at <http://www.theaha.org/perspectives/issues/1997/9705/9705NOT.CFM>; "History Journals and the Electronic Future: The Final Report of a Conference Held at Indiana University, Bloomington, August 3–8, 1997, at <http://www.indiana.edu/~ahr/report.htm>; David Ransel, "The Present and Future of Historical Journals," *Perspectives* 33:5 (October 1995), at <http://www.theaha.org/perspectives/issues/1995/9510/9510ARC.CFM>; and Sara B. Bearss, "Book Reviewing and Journal Publication in the Electronic Age: Report of a Joint Meeting at the OAH," *Editing History* 12:1 (Spring 1996): 9. Bearss's article is one of several reporting on a March 29, 1996 meeting between representatives of the Conference of Historical Journals and of H-Net's Book Review Project. See also Michael McGiffert, "Editors and Electronics: A Survey of the Uses of Computers by Journals of History," Occasional Paper of the Conference of Historical Journals, Report No. 1, Winter 1989; and Michael Moore, "President's Column," *Editing History* 8:2 (Fall 1992): 2–3.

22. Project Muse is at <http://muse.jhu.edu/journal>.

23. Information on JStor is available at <http://www.jstor.org>; for the list of journals published, see <http://www.jstor.org/about/content.html>.

24. The "Making of America" project is lodged at two libraries: Cornell University (at <http://library5.library.cornell.edu/moa/>) and the University of Michigan (at <http://www.umdl.umich.edu/moa>).

25. The *Bryn Mawr Classical Review* is available at <http://ccat.sas.upenn.edu/bmcr/>. *The Medieval Review* is available at <http://www.hti.umich.edu/t/tmr.html>.

26. "Editorial," *Electronic Antiquity: Communicating the Classics* 1:1 (June 1993). *Electronic Antiquity* is available at <http://scholar.lib.vt.edu/ejournals/ElAnt/>.

27. *Cromohos* is available at <http://www.unifi.it/riviste/cromohs/>.

28. The *Electronic Journal of Australian and New Zealand History* is at <http://www.jcu.edu.au/aff/history/>.

29. The *Journal of Southern Religion* is available at <http://jsr.lib.virginia.edu/index. html>.

30. *Essays in History* is at <http://etext.lib.virginia.edu/journals/EH/>. Before becoming an exclusively online journal, it was published in print for four decades, and it was available in both print and electronic form from 1991 to 1994.

31. *Chronicon* is at <http://www.ucc.ie/chronicon/>. An earlier online electronic journal in European modern history, the *On-Line Modern History Review,* lasted for only a few issues.

32. See note 18 for information on indexes to electronic journals. Many of the jour-

nals included in these indexes are only partially online: They publish Tables of Contents, article abstracts, selected articles and books reviews, and subscription information on the Internet.

33. The OCLC is at <www.oclc.org>; most university libraries subscribe to its First Search catalog, so access to this catalog is available to those affiliated with the universities. The National Union Catalog of Manuscript Collections is at <http://lcweb.loc.gov/coll/nucmc/>.

34. The Library of Congress Manuscript Finding Aids, which currently cover about 200 collections, are available at <http://lcweb.loc.gov/rr/mss/f-aids/mssfa.html>; see <http://lcweb.loc.gov/rr/ead/eadhome.html> for a more general discussion of finding aids available electronically from the Library of Congress.

The National Archive and Records Administration (NARA) finding aids are available at <http://www.nara.gov/guide/>.

35. See Tulane University's "Ready, 'Net, Go!: Archival Internet Resources" at <http://www.tulane.edu/~lmiller/ArchivesResources.html>.

36. UMI's Research Collections is at <http://www.umi.com/hp/Support/Research/>.

37. Beverly T. Watkins, "A Data Base of Ancient Greek Literature Revolutionizes Research in the Classics," *Chronicle of Higher Education,* September 18, 1991, A24–A27. See also Michael Neuman, "The Very Pulse of the Machine: Three Trends toward Improvement in Electronic Versions of Humanities Texts," *Computers and the Humanities* 25 (1991): 365. The Perseus Project, a collection of Greek and Roman texts and images, is at <http://www.perseus.tufts.edu/>. The Dante Database (*La Commedia* and commentaries) is at <http://www.nyu.edu/library/bobst/research/etc/dante.htm>.

38. "Labyrinth" is available at <http://www.georgetown.edu/labyrinth/index.html>. The "Plague" project is at the Institute for Advanced Technology (IATH) at the University of Virginia, an innovator in applying technology to research and teaching. Information on the project is available at <http://jefferson.village.virginia.edu/osheim>.

39. General Dutch maps are at <http://grid.let.rug.nl/~welling/maps/maps.html>; the city maps are at <http://grid.let.rug.nl/~welling/maps/blaeu.html>. "Maps of Paris" are at <http://www.columbia.edu/cu/arthistory/courses/parismaps/>.

40. The ARTFL project is on the World Wide Web at <http://humanities.uchicago.edu/ARTFL/ARTFL.html>. See also John Price-Wilkin, "Text Files in Libraries: Present Foundations and Future Directions," *Library Hi Tech* 9:3 (1991): 11–12; Neuman, "Very Pulse of the Machine," 366; "ARTFL Preparing CD-ROM of Database" and "MOPS: ARTFL by E-Mail," *The ARTFL Project Newsletter* 7:1 (Winter 1991–92): 1.

41. The Marx/Engels Web site is at <http://www.eserver.org/marx/>.

42. For a comprehensive collection, see Rutgers University's "American and British History Resources on the Internet," <http://www.libraries.rutgers.edu/rul/rr gateway/research guides/history/history.shtml>.

43. The American Memory Web site is at <http://memory.loc.gov/ammem/amhome. html>. The American Memory project serves as a source of information for other digital projects and has made available a series of technical papers at various stages and on various aspects of the project at <http://memory.loc.gov/ammem/ftpfiles.html>. For early impressions of the American Memory project, see Beverly T. Watkins, "'American Memory,' Coming Soon to America's Campuses," and "Scholars, Librarians, and

Technologists Urged to Join in Using Electronic Information," both in *Chronicle of Higher Education*, November 27, 1991, A18–A20, A21.

44. See the "National Digital Library Program" at <http://memory.loc.gov/ammem/dli2/html/lcndlp.html>; "A Periodic Report from the National Digital Library Program, November/December 1995 (No. 4)," at <http://lcweb.loc.gov/ndl/nov-dec.html#pilot> and "National Digital Library Federation Constituted as a Charter Organization (Adopts Three-Point Agenda)," press release, August 16, 1996 (available at <http://lcweb.loc.gov/loc/ndlf/news8-96.html>); "Mission and Goals: National Digital Library Federation" (available at <http://lcweb.loc.gov/loc/ndlf/agree.html>); "NDLF Planning Task Force Final Report, June 1995" (available at <http://lcweb.loc.gov/loc/ndlf/plntfrep.html>).

45. The Model Editions Partnership Web site is at <http://mep.cla.sc.edu>. The partnership's director, David Chesnutt, is a former president of the Association for Documentary Editing (ADE), the editor of the Henry Laurens Papers, and a leading advocate of electronic texts and their encoding. For his views on the value of historical editions in print and electronic form, see "Quid Pro Quo: Today's Challenges in the Editorial Community," *Documentary Editing*, March 1993, 1–3, and "The Papers of Henry Laurens: Editing in the Digital Age," paper delivered at the American Historical Association meeting in Washington, D.C., in 1993.

46. The NARA Presidential Libraries Web site is at <http://www.nara.gov/nara/president/address.html>. The Franklin Delano Roosevelt library is at <http://www.fdrlibrary.marist.edu/>.

47. The Walt Whitman Hypertext Archive is available at <http://jefferson.village.Virginia.Edu/whitman>. "Urban Planning: 1794–1918" is at <http://www.library.cornell.edu/Reps/homepage.htm>. *How the Other Half Lives* is available at <http://tenant.net/Community/Riis/contents.html>; the Lower East Side project at <http://tenant.net/Community/LES/contents.html>.

48. The Accessible Archives is at <http://www.accessible.com/>. The *Pennsylvania Gazette* CD-ROMs cover the periods 1728–50, 1751–65, 1766–83, and 1784–1800. For the author's review of the first disk, see "Research and Reference Tools: Reviews," *Journal of American History* 80:4 (March 1994): 1572–73. For a general discussion of historical CD-ROMs, see Roy Rosenzweig's review essay "'So What's Next for Clio?': CD-ROM and Historians," *Journal of American History* 81:4 (March 1995): 1621–40. This review is available at the Center for History and New Media Web site established by Rosenzweig at <http://chnm.gmu.edu/chnm/clio.html>. The site also includes a list of more than 200 historical CD-ROMs. The *History Computer Review* and its predecessor, the *History Microcomputer Review*, have been among the best sources of CD-ROM and Web site reviews since 1985.

49. The most comprehensive introduction to historical electronic texts, including links to many of them, is Andrew McMichael, Michael O'Malley, and Roy Rosenzweig, "Historians and the Web: A Beginner's Guide," at <http://www.gmu.edu/chnm/beginner.html>. See also Beth Juhl, "Red, White and Boolean," *Choice* 35:8 (April 1998), at <http://www.ala.org/acrl/choice/apress.html>, offering a comprehensive review of all electronic historical materials, including full texts. Also valuable are Avra Michelson and Jeff Rothenberg, "Scholarly Communication and Information Technology: Exploring the Impact of Changes in the Research Process on Archives," *American Archivist*, May 1, 1992; John

Daly, ed., *Workshop on Electronic Texts: Proceedings,* June 9–10, 1992, Library of Congress, at <http://lcweb2.loc.gov/ammem/etext.html>; Neuman, "Very Pulse of the Machine"; and Price-Wilkin, "Text Files in Libraries."

50. The CHNM Web page is at <http://chnm.gmu.edu/>. It is one of the best sites from which to start a search for historical resources on the Internet, including far more than are described here. The CETH Web page is at <http://www.ceth.rutgers.edu> and the IATH Web page is at <http://jefferson.village.virginia.edu>.

51. For the importance of access, see Beth Luey, "Wedding the Past to the Future: Planning a National Database for Our Documentary Heritage," *Documentary Editing* 17:4 (December 1995): 101–4; Martha L. Benner, "'The Abraham Lincoln Legal Papers': The Development of the Complete Facsimile Edition on CD-ROM," *Documentary Editing* 16:4 (December 1994): 100–107; David Chesnutt, "Presidential Editions: The Promise and Problems of Technology," *Documentary Editing* 16:3 (September 1994): 70–77, and "Historical Editions in the States," *Computers and the Humanities* 25:6 (December 1991): 377.

52. Reiff, *Structuring the Past,* 19–23, 62–66, and Richard Jensen, "Text Management," *Journal of Interdisciplinary History* 22:4 (Spring 1992): 711–22, are especially useful in providing an overview of textual analysis tools.

53. Richard L. Merritt, *Symbols of American Community, 1735–1775* (New Haven, Conn.: Yale University Press, 1966); Peter H. Smith, "Political Legitimacy in Latin America," in *New Approaches in Latin American History,* ed. Richard Graham and Peter H. Smith (Austin: University of Texas Press, 1974), 225–55.

54. Charles M. Dollar and Richard J. Jensen, *Historian's Guide to Statistics: Quantitative Analysis and Historical Research* (New York: Holt, Rinehart & Winston, 1971), 205–14, 267–68; Reiff, *Structuring the Past,* 31; Daniel Scott Smith, "Notes on the Measurement of Values," *Journal of Economic History* 45:2 (June 1985): 213–18; Price-Wilkin, "Text Files in Libraries," 8. See Greenstein, *A Historian's Guide to Computing,* 183–87, for an excellent discussion of the strengths and limitations of computer-assisted textual analysis.

55. In this use, the TEI is similar to HTML, the markup language of the World Wide Web, both of which use the Standardized General Markup Language (SGML) as the metalanguage, or base. Marking up structures allows those who are "printing" these documents (online or print) to designate special fonts for titles and other headings.

56. The TEI has created a consortium to govern its affairs, with a Web site at <http://www. tei-c.org>. Other online descriptions include John Price-Wilkin, "Using the World-Wide Web to Deliver Complex Electronic Documents: Implications for Libraries," *Public Access Computer Systems Review* 5:3 (1994): 5–21, available at <http://info.lib.uh.edu/pr/v5/n3/pricewil.5n3>. Scholarly literature on the TEI includes three special issues of *Computers and Humanities* (29:1–3 [1995]), edited by Nancy Ide and Jean Veronis, on "The Text Encoding Initiative: Background and Contexts"; in particular, see Lou Burnard and Daniel Greenstein, "Speaking with One Voice: Encoding Standards and the Prospects for an Integrated Approach to Computing in History," *Computers and the Humanities* 29:2 (1995): 137–48. Other discussion of the use of the TEI in encoding historical texts is in Chesnutt, "Presidential Editions"; Model Editions Partnership *Prospectus* ("2.5 Conforming to Relevant Standards" and "4 Why Mark-Up Is Important"); and Daniel I. Greenstein, ed., *Modelling Historical Data: Towards a Standard for Encoding and Exchanging Machine-Readable Texts* (Göttingen: Max-Planck-Institut für Geschichte, 1991). *Model-*

*ling Historical Data* is also useful in explicating the European approach to text analysis that has been developed in the last twenty years, an alternative approach to that offered by the TEI that is associated with many of the historians affiliated with the Association for History and Computing (ACH).

For a critique of text encoding based on issues of time and expense, see Ann Gordon, "I Already Have a Job: An Editor/Historian Contemplates Electronic Editions," in *Conference Abstracts: Posters and Demonstrations,* ACH/Association for Literary and Linguistic Computing (ALLC) joint international conference, University of California at Santa Barbara, July 11–15, 1995. Technical critiques of the TEI are available in abstracts of Claus Huitfeldt, "Why SGML Is Prescriptive and Interpretive," and Mark Olsen, "Text Theory and Coding Practice: Assessing the TEI," papers presented at the panel "Encoding, Interpretation, and Theory" at the 1996 meeting of the ACH/ALLC, available at <http://gonzo.hd.uib.no/allc-ach96/Panels/Giordano/molsen.html>. The Model Editions Partnership is at <http://mep.cla.sc.edu/>, the American Memory project at <http://memory.loc.gov>, "Documenting the American South" at <http://metalab.unc.edu/docsouth/aboutdas.html>, the African-American Women Writers' Project of the 19th Century at <http://digital.nypl.org/schomburg/writers aa19/>, and the Dutch Golden Age at <http://www.etcl.nl/goldenage/>.

57. Michelson and Rothenberg, "Scholarly Communication and Information Technology," 40–43.

58. Chesnutt, "Presidential Editions," 76.

59. See B. Burningham, "Attitudes of the Canadian Research Community toward Creating and Accessing Digitized Facsimile Collections of Historical Collections," *Computers and the Humanities* 33:4 (1999): 409–19. This article describes a study undertaken by the Canadian Institute for Historical Microreproductions (CIHM) to determine whether historians would prefer images or searchable text if only one format was possible. The overwhelming demand was for the images, even at the loss of searchability, if an index searchable by subject, author, and title accompanied the images.

60. Manfred Thaller, Abstract of "Text as a Data Type," paper presented at "Digital Manuscripts: Editions v. Archives" panel at ACH/ALLC 1996 meeting, available at <http://gonzo.hd.uib.no/allc-ach96/Panels/Thaller/thaller2.html>. The Walt Whitman Hypertext Archive offers a good example of a project that incorporates both images and electronic searchable text. See, for example, "I celebrate myself" at <http://jefferson.village. virginia.edu/whitman/works/leaves/1867/text/frameset.html>.

61. See Juhl, "Red, White and Boolean": "The ability to deliver Web-based products outside the libraries and campuses must also be measured against the comparative speed and dependability of a stand-alone CD-ROM."

62. See Chesnutt, "Presidential Editions," 76. Chesnutt also comments on the problem of speed on the Internet, although over time it is likely to be faster to download a text than it is today. In addition, the Internet is beginning to acquire many of the attributes of CD-ROMs that may make it a more promising climate for pricing and charging. For example, it is possible to limit access to a World Wide Web site to those who have paid a fee; the technology of Java and newer Internet programs also allows programs to be packaged with texts. Thus, Project Muse can make valuable assets available online by charging fees and restricting access to those who pay. Many of these issues are discussed in the

proceedings of the three conferences held to date by the Association of Research Libraries and the Association of American University Presses (AAUP) on electronic texts. The proceedings have been published in the following volumes: *Scholarly Publishing on the Electronic Networks: Proceedings of the Second Symposium, December 5–8, 1992* (Washington, D.C.: Association of Research Libraries, 1993), available at <http://arl.cni.org/scomm/symp2/1992.toc.html>; *Gateways, Gatekeepers, and Roles in the Information Converse: Proceedings of the Third Symposium, November 13–15, 1993* (Washington, D.C.: Association of Research Libraries, 1994), available at <http://arl.cni.org/symp3/1993.toc.html>; and *Filling the Pipeline and Paying the Piper: Proceedings of the Fourth Symposium* (Washington, D.C.: Association of Research Libraries, 1995).

63. Gilmore and Case, "Historians, Books, Computers, and the Library," 681; Susan Hockey, *A Guide to Computer Applications in the Humanities* (Baltimore: Johns Hopkins University Press, 1980), 134–35.

64. Gilmore and Case, "Historians, Books, Computers, and the Library," 683. See also Burningham, "Attitudes of the Canadian Research Community." The History of Science CD-ROM conference held in Rome in December 1991 strongly affirmed the need for a physical image to be included with the textual transcription of the document. Robert H. Kargo to Wendy Plotkin, May 11, 1992.

65. Neil Beagrie and Daniel Greenstein, "A Strategic Policy Framework for Creating and Preserving Digital Collections," Arts and Humanities Data Service, Version 4.0, July 14, 1998, available at <http://ahds.ac.uk/manage/framework.htm>.

66. John Garrett and Donald Waters, eds., "Preserving Digital Information: Report of the Task Force on Archiving Digital Information," commissioned by the Commission on Preservation and Access and the Record Libraries Group, Inc., May 6, 1996 at <http://www.rlg.org/ArchTF/index.html>. See also Jeff Rothenberg, "Avoiding Technological Quicksand: Finding a Viable Technical Foundation for Digital Preservation" (Washington, D.C.: Council on Library and Information Resources, 1998), at <http://www.clir.org/pubs/reports/rothenberg/contents.html>.

The National Historic Publications and Records Commission (NHPRC), one of the major funders of documentary editing projects in U.S. history, has had an ambivalent attitude toward digitization. In 1992, it published a study that called for the continued use of microfilm as the primary medium for disseminating primary documents, with almost no mention of electronic dissemination. This recommendation probably was based in part on the traumatic experience of archivists with microfilm. In its early days, microfilm was very unstable, and a number of preservation disasters occurred. Since then, microfilm has undergone great improvement and is governed by the recommendations of the American National Standards Institute. Archivists are thus wary of experimenting with new media, aware of the loss of a portion of the Vietnam archives caused by the extinction of all machines that could read their obsolete magnetic tape. See Ann D. Gordon, *Using the Nation's Documentary Heritage: The Report of the Historical Documents Study* (Washington, D.C.: National Historical Publication and Records Commission, 1992); Ann D. Gordon, "A Future for Documentary Editions: The Historical Documents Study," *Documentary Editing* 14:1 (March 1992): 6–10 (in which the author describes the need to "balance the medium's obvious appeal against its uncertain future" and recommends further research into the topic); conversation with Ann Gordon, September 10, 1992.

Despite the initial caution indicated in this study, the NHPRC has supported electronic editions on an experimental basis. It has financially supported the Model Editions Partnership, a major demonstration of the use of electronic media in critical editions, and the CD-ROM edition of the Abraham Lincoln Legal Papers, a project that carefully considered the relative merits of microfilm and CD-ROM dissemination and chose the newer medium. Martha L. Benner, one of the editors, describes in some detail the debate within the archival community over the desirability of microfilm and electronic distribution and the Lincoln Papers' reasons for deciding on a CD-ROM for dissemination in Benner, "'The Abraham Lincoln Legal Papers,'" 100–101, 104. Benner notes, "It would take around 20 discs to store 250,000 images and the database [describing the documents] as compared to slightly more than 200 reels of microfilm for the same number of images alone" (100–101).

In 1996, the NHPRC formally adopted a policy encouraging the development of electronic editions in new projects and the approximately forty print projects it was already funding. see "NHPRC Revises Plan and Approves Grants for State Records Boards, Documentary Publishing, and Electronic Records Research and Redevelopment (November, 1996)" at <http://www.nara.gov/nhprc/comnov96.html>. However, it retracted this policy in 1999, issuing a new statement: "The National Historical Publications and Records Commission generally regards projects to preserve endangered records, to provide basic access to significant historical materials (e.g., to arrange and describe the materials), and to compile documentary editions as a higher priority than projects to convert materials and existing finding aids to electronic form or projects whose main purpose is to make digitized materials available via the Internet. At this time, therefore, the Commission prefers not to spend its limited funds on projects that primarily involve digitization activities." See "NHPRC: November, 1999 Commission Meeting" at <http://www.nara.gov/nhprc/comnov99.html>.

67. Beagrie and Greenstein, "A Strategic Policy Framework"; National Archives of Australia, "Managing Electronic Records, 1997 Edition" at <http://www.naa.gov.au/recordkeeping/er/manage%5Fer/intro.html>; Hartmut Weber and Marianne Dorr, "Digitisation as a Method of Preservation? Final Report of a Work Group of the Deutsche Forschungsgemeinschaft (German Research Association)," at <http://www.knaw.nl/ecpa/ecpatex/reports.htm#weber>.

68. See Anne Kenney, "Digital Image Quality: From Conversion to Presentation and Beyond," presentation at the Scholarly Communication and Technology Conference (organized by Andrew W. Mellon Foundation), April 24–25, 1997, at <http://www.arl.org/scomm/scat/kenney.html>. This highly technical paper discusses the tradeoffs involved in selecting the quality of the digital image. See also Peter B. Hirtle, "The National Archives and Electronic Access," *The Record* (NARA's newsletter), May 1995, at <http://webgopher.nara.gov/0/about/what/record/vol1no5/vol1no5.txt>; Foe Bauman, "National Archive Brings Past to Life by Putting Photos, Documents on the Web," *The Record*, January 1998; and other columns in "NARA Online" at <http://www.nara.gov/publications/record/>.

69. See "U.N. Fears Divisive Impact of the Internet," *New York Times*, June 29, 2000; Katie Hafner, "Common Ground Elusive as Technology Have-Nots Meet Haves," *New York Times*, July 8, 1999; and Barbara Crossick, "A New Measure of Disparities: Poor Sanita-

tion in Internet Era," *New York Times,* May 12, 1998. For earlier expressions of concern, see Daniel Eisenberg, "The Electronic Journal," *Scholarly Publishing* 20:1 (October 1988): 55; Kenneth S. Warren, "Information Deluge and Information Drought," *Scholarly Publishing* 23:4 (July 1992): 223–30; Ian Montagnes, "Sustainable Development in Book Publishing," *Scholarly Publishing* 23:4 (July 1992): 231–41 (deals primarily with print publication in developing countries); Beth Luey, "The Concerned University Press: An Academic Experiment," *Scholarly Publishing* 23:4 (July 1992): 263 (deals primarily with marketing print publications to developing countries); Anne B. Piternick, "Electronic Serials: Realistic or Unrealistic Solution to the Journal 'Crisis?,'" in *A Changing World: Proceedings of the North American Serials Interest Group, Inc.,* ed. Susanne McMahon, Miriam Palm, and Pam Dunn (New York: Haworth, 1991), 25 (discusses access of southern European nations).

70. Erez Navaro, Adel Gureli, Ozlem Gursel, and Kathryn Starnella, "Internet Access in the World," written as part of a group project for the class "Communication Technology, Community and Identity" at Northwestern University during the fall of 1996, at <http://pubweb.acns.nwu.edu/ena346/group paper.html>. The source of this estimate is Phil Noble, "International Cyberspacing: Use of the Internet Worldwide" *Campaigns and Elections* 17:7 (July 1996): 29.

71. "Internet Survey Reaches 19.5 Million," *CSS Internet News,* August 26, 1997, included in e-mail posting on Sustainable Development Networking Programme Coordinators List, August 29, 1997, at <http://www3.undp.org/lstarch/mgrs/msg00983.html>.

72. "Latinas Lead the World in Networking," *Chicago Tribune,* July 10, 1994, sec. 6, 1 and 11.

73. Erez Navaro, Adel Gureli, Ozlem Gursel, and Kathryn Starnella, "Internet Access in the World," at <http://pubweb.acns.nwu.edu/ena346/group paper.html>. There is an extensive amount of information on the World Wide Web about Internet access in undeveloped countries, much tied to the issue of economic and human resource development. See Murali Shanmugavelan, "Information Technology in (IT) in Developing Nations," available at <http://www.fao.org/waicent/faoinfo/sustdev/CDdirect/CDre0050.htm>; Sustainable Development Department, Food and Agriculture Organization of the United Nations, "The Internet and Rural Development: Recommendations for Strategy and Activity," at <http://www.fao.org/sd/cddirect/CDDO/chapter2.htm>.

74. See Stefan Aumann, Abstract of "Digital Archives," paper presented at panel "Digital Manuscripts: Editions v. Archives" at 1996 ACH/ALLC meeting, available at <http://gonzo.hd.uib.no/allc-ach96/Panels/Thaller/aumann.html>. Copyright concerns also constrain archival electronic dissemination. Private collections—that is, unpublished papers donated by private individuals and organizations—carry the most stringent copyright protection of all documents because they are not subject to the fair use provisions of the Copyright Act of 1976. Thus, they are least available to the researcher. This protectiveness has persisted into the electronic age. See Helen Humeston, "Archives, Optical Discs, and the Copyright Act of 1976," *Archival Issues* 18:1 (1993): 15–30.

75. See Luey, "Wedding the Past to the Future," 104; Gordon, "I Already Have a Job."

76. See Perry Willett, "The Victorian Women Writers Project: The Library as a Creator and Publisher of Electronic Texts," *Public-Access Computer Systems Review* 7:6 (1996): 5–16, at <http://info.lib.uh.edu/pr/v7/n6/will7n6.html>.

77. The Library of Congress first began to publish print editions of its collections in 1904. In 1938, financially assisted by the Rockefeller Foundation, the Library established "a Photoduplication Service for the purpose of 'competently supplying distant investigators with microfilm and other photoduplicates of materials otherwise not available for use outside Washington.'" In 1943, it began microfilming the papers of Thomas Jefferson. See "Jefferson's Legacy: A Brief History of the Library of Congress: The Collections," available from the Library of Congress Web site at <http://lcweb.loc.gov/loc/legacy/colls.html>.

78. "The Mission and Strategic Priorities of the Library of Congress, FY 1997–2004," available at <http://lcweb.loc.gov/ndl/mission.html>. This includes the statement, "The Congress has now recognized that, in an age in which information is increasingly communicated and stored in electronic form, the Library should provide remote access electronically to key materials. For the general public, the Congress has endorsed the creation of a National Digital Library Program through a private-public partnership that will create high-quality content in electronic form and thereby provide remote access to the most interesting and educationally valuable core of the Library's Americana collections. Schools, libraries, businesses, and homes will have access to important historical material in their own localities together with the same freedom readers have always had within public reading rooms to interpret, rearrange, and use the material for their own individual needs."

79. For electronic text centers and digital libraries, see the CETH Directory of Electronic Text Centers, at <http://harvest.rutgers.edu/ceth/etext directory/>. For older literature on the beginnings of electronic text centers, see Anita Lowry, "Machine-Readable Texts in the Academic Library: The Electronic Text Service at Columbia University" in *Computer Files and the Research Library,* ed. Constance C. Gould (Mountain View, Calif.: Research Libraries Group, 1990), 16–23; and Price-Wilkin, "Text Files in Libraries," 15–43. The volume *Gateways, Gatekeepers, and Roles in the Information Omniverse: Proceedings from the Third Symposium, November 13–15, 1993,* includes descriptions of the University of Virginia Electronic Text Library and Project Janus at Columbia Law School (a "virtual" law library) as well as other initiatives discussed in this chapter, such as Project Muse. It is available at <http://arl.cni.org/symp3/1993.frontmatter.html>. On digital libraries, see the Digital Libraries Initiative at <http://dli.grainger.uiuc.edu/>.

80. The Association for Research Libraries has a special Web page devoted to copies of its newsletter articles that deal with copyright, at <http://arl.cni.org/newsltr/copy.html>. These articles document the positions of the library community on copyright since 1996. For example, see Arnold P. Lutzker, "In the Curl of the Wave: What the Digital Millennium Copyright Act and Term Extension Act Mean for the Library and Education Community," April 1999, at <http://arl.cni.org/newsltr/203/curl.html>. That article begins with the statement, "In the coming 18 months, the library and education community faces a series of fast-paced public policy forums where significant copyright and other intellectual property issues will be addressed." Among the provisions on which the library community obtained some exemptions was the ability to use material in the twenty-year period of copyright protection added through the act. According to Lutzker, "It was posited that the overwhelming majority of works are neither commercially exploited nor readily accessible in the marketplace after several decades, much less seventy-five years (or seventy years after an author's death). Yet, for researchers and scholars, access to such

works from the library's collection are important and no limitation should be made on such noncommercial uses." The June 1997 issue of the Association of Research Libraries newsletter is devoted to the topic of copyright in the digitized environment and the efforts of the National Humanities Alliance. It is available at <http://arl.cni.org/newsltr/192/192toc.html>. See also "Educational Community Articulates Principles for Managing Intellectual Property in the Digital Environment" (June 1997) at <http://arl.cni.org/newsltr/192/nha.html>.

81. See "Create Change: A Resource for Faculty and Librarian Action to Reclaim Scholarly Communication" at <http://www.arl.org/create/home.html> for current essays and views on the relationship between journal prices, electronic journals, and the ability of libraries to afford other forms of traditional material. For earlier literature on the topic, see Eldred Smith, "A Partnership for the Future," *Scholarly Publishing* 22:2 (January 1991): 83–92; Ann Okerson, "With Feathers: Effects of Copyright and Ownership on Scholarly Publishing," *College and Research Libraries* 52:5 (September 1991): 425–38; "OSAP Develops Electronic Publishing Workshop," *ARL* 160 (January 2 1992): 12.

82. Many of these issues are addressed in the three volumes of the proceedings of the joint Association of Research Libraries/AAUP symposia on electronic publishing described in note 62. See the special issue on "Keeping the Pace: How Librarians Retool for Changing Times" in the Association for Research Libraries electronic journal *Leading Ideas: Issues and Trends in Diversity, Leadership, and Career Development* 14 (May 2000), at <http://www.arl.org/diversity/leading/indexalt.html> for a comprehensive look at the effect of technological change on librarians. See also Brett Sutton, ed., *Literary Texts in an Electronic Age: Scholarly Implications and Library Services* (Urbana: University of Illinois at Urbana-Champaign, Graduate School of Library and Information Science, 1994).

The *Public-Access Computer Systems Review* is one of the best online sources for discussion of the impact of electronic media on librarians and library services. It is available at <http://info.lib.uh.edu/pacsrev.html>. See especially Charles W. Bailey Jr. and Dana Rooks, eds., "Symposium on the Role of Network-Based Electronic Resources in Scholarly Communication and Research," a special issue of *Public-Access Computer Systems Review* 2:2 (1991): 4–60, at <http://info.lib.uh.edu/pr/v2/n2/bailey1.2n2>. Older literature on the topic includes Stephen E. Wiberly Jr., "Habits of Humanists: Scholarly Behavior and New Information Technologies," *Library Hi-Tech* 33:9–1 (1991): 17–21; Robert D. Stueart, "Libraries: A New Role?" in *Books, Libraries, and Electronics: Essays on the Future of Written Communication,* ed. Efrem Sigal et al. (White Plains, N.Y.: Knowledge Industry Publications, 1982), 93–116; John Gurnsey, *The Information Professions in the Electronic Age* (London: Clive Bingley, 1985), 155–92.

83. Kenneth Arnold, "The Body in the Virtual Library: Rethinking Scholarly Communication," *Journal of Electronic Publishing* (January 1995), <http://www.press.umich.edu/jep/works/arnold.body.html>. The University of Michigan Press's online *Journal of Electronic Publishing,* established in 1995, is a good source for information and elaboration of the issues associated with electronic publishing, although those who contribute are more likely to be those already comfortable with the electronic medium. See also J. E. Gregory Rawlins, "The New Publishing: Technology's Impact on the Publishing Industry over the Next Decade," *The Public-Access Computer Systems Review* 3:8 (1992): 5–63, available at <http://info.lib.uh.edu/pr/v3/n8/rawlins1.3n8>.

84. Michael Jensen, "Cost Recovery and Destiny: Developing the Appropriateness Matrix," *Journal of Electronic Publishing* 4:1 (September 1998), at <http://www.press. umich.edu/jep/04-01/jensen.html>.

85. The AAUP Web page is at <http://aaupnet.org/>; the link to Charles W. Bailey Jr., "Scholarly Electronic Publishing Bibliography (June 16, 2000)" is under "Resources" at <http://aaupnet.org/resources.html>; the bibliography is at <http://info.lib.uh.edu/sepb/ sepb.html>. The AAUP established a computer committee and electronic discussion group in the early 1990s to help the presses assess the opportunities and the pitfalls of electronic publishing. A list of the current AAUP Electronic Committee members is at <http://aaupnet.org/committees.html>. An article about the organization and its use of the Internet to increase access to its catalogs is included in *Gateways, Gatekeepers, and Roles in the Information Converse: Proceedings of the Third Symposium, November 13–15, 1993* at <http://arl.cni.org/symp3/creesy.html>.

86. A review of the *Encyclopedia of Kentucky* CD-ROM is in "Research and Reference Tools: Reviews," *Journal of American History* 80:4 (March 1994): 1573–74.

87. "The History E-Book Project: Introduction," at <http://www.historyebook.org/ 2intro.html>. One of the most interesting features of the project is the planned use of the electronic medium to publish the primary materials associated with the monograph, moving beyond their mere citation in a footnote. One of the challenges is to learn how much of this material to include, in terms of cost and capacity of the medium. See "Why the Electronic History Monograph?" at <http://www.historyebook.org/4electronic%20monograph.html>.

88. An H-Net review of the CD-ROM *Who Built America?* can be found at <http:// www. unimelb.edu.au/infoserv/urban/hma/hurban/1994q2/0436.html>.

89. This generalization is based on a perusal of reviews of multimedia on the H-Net Review Web site and in the *History Computer Review.* One typical review suggests that "as long as historical CD-ROMs are written by publishers for popular audiences, not historians for scholarly audiences, the problems inherent in this CD will likely be repeated" (David Rexelman, review of "The War in Vietnam," *H-War* (February 1997) at <http:// www2.h-net.msu. edu/mmreviews/showrev.cgi?path=24>).

In his 1995 *Journal of American History* article "'So What's Next for Clio?'" historian Roy Rosenzweig reveals a similar dissatisfaction with historical CD-ROMs. Commenting on the presentation of an abundance of primary documents without commentary, he writes, "Multimedia and hypertext can offer multiple perspectives and to allow readers to draw their own conclusions, but that potential is best realized where, as in good books, readers can encounter real authors with deeply held convictions—even if the reader ultimately rejects those perspectives" (1628–1629). Thus, he calls for an informed interpretative voice in these CD-ROMs. Other commentary on CD-ROMs is available in the discussion "CD/ROMs in Higher Education" on H-MMedia in April 1996, available from <http://h-net2.msu.edu/mmedia/archives/logs/apr96>.

90. See "Who Owns What? Intellectual Property, Copyright, and the Next Millennium," *Journal of Electronic Publishing* 4:3 (March 1999), available at <http://www.press. umich.edu/jep/04–03/index.html>, for a good overview of publishers' views on copyright in the digital environment. Charles W. Bailey Jr.'s "Scholarly Electronic Publishing Bibliography" includes a section on "Electronic Commerce/Copyright Systems," at <http:// info.lib.uh.edu/sepb/pcomm.htm>, with links to many articles on the topic. See Pedro

Isais, "Electronic Copyright Management Systems: Aspects to Consider," *Ariadne* 20 (1999), at <http://www.ariadne.ac.uk/issue20/ecms/>. The *Journal of Electronic Publishing* also includes excellent articles on the topic, including Bill Rosenblatt, "Solving the Problem of Copyright Protection Online," at <http://www.press.umich.edu/jep/03-02/doi.html>. A good source on the present state of the copyright law is "The Copyright Page," at <http://www.benedict.com/>.

For information on the National Information Infrastructure Copyright Protection Act, see *NCC Washington Update* 2:29 (September 12, 1996), "Update on Copyright Legislation" and "Copyright Conference on Fair Use," available at the H-Net Web site at <http://h-net.msu.edu/ncc>. The critics' perspective is available in Page Putnam Miller, "Copyright and 'Fair Use' in the Electronic Environment," *Perspectives* 33:2 (February 1995): 5–6. The history of copyright in the United States, including the recommendations of the National Commission on New Technological Uses of Copyrighted Works (CONTU), are covered in Humeston, "Archives, Optical Disks, and the Copyright Act of 1976."

91. See Rosenzweig, "'So What's Next for Clio?"

92. Ronald W. Zweig, "Electronically Generated Records and Twentieth-Century History," *Computers and the Humanities* 27:2 (1993): 73–83. On the general impact of electronic communication on the historical profession, see Edward Higgs, ed., *Historians and Electronic Artefacts* (Oxford, England: Oxford University Press, 1998). This recent work includes essays by R. J. Morris, "Electronic Documents and the History of the Late 20th Century Black Holes or Warehouses: What Do Historians Really Want?," and Seamus Ross, "The Expanding World of Electronic Information and the Past's Future." See also the papers presented at the University of Pittsburgh's Center for Electronic Recordkeeping and Archival Research's "Working Meeting on Electronic Records," May 1997, at <http://www.sis.pitt.edu/cerar/er-mtg97.html>.

93. Carol Elizabeth Nowicke, "Managing Tomorrow's Records Today: An Experiment in Archival Preservation of Electronic Mail," *Midwestern Archivist* 18:2 (1988): 67–75.

94. PROFS was the e-mail system used by the federal government at this time.

95. An excellent overview of the litigation and the issues raised is David A. Wallace, "Preserving the U.S. Government's White House Electronic Mail: Archival Challenges and Policy Implications," presented at the Sixth DELOS Workshop: Preserving Digital Information (Lisbon, Portugal), June 19, 1998, at <http://www.ercim.org/publication/ws-proceedings/DELOS6/wallace.rtf>. See also the "Public Citizen" summary of the cases at <http://www.citizen.org/litigation/foic/foia highlight.html> and the following issues of *NCC Washington Update:* 1:8 (February 16, 1995); 1:11 (March 3, 1995); 1:22 (May 3, 1995); 1:46 (September 6, 1995); 1:62 (December 21, 1995); 2:17 (May 29, 1996); 2:18 (June 4, 1996); 2:25 (July 25, 1996); 2:30 (September 18, 1996); 2:43 (December 27, 1996); 3:4 (February 5, 1997); 3:16 (April 25, 1997); 3:20 (May 20, 1997); 3:21 (May 29, 1997); 3:26 (June 30, 1997); 3:41 (September 30, 1997); 3:44 (November 6, 1997); 3:47 (December 2, 1997); 4:7 (March 7, 1998); 4:9 (March 17, 1998); 4:10 (March 25, 1998); 4:19 (May 20, 1998); 4:28 (July 21, 1998); 4:32 (August 19, 1998); 4:33 (September 1, 1998); 4:38 (September 30, 1998); 4:42 (October 26, 1998); 5:27 (August 9, 1999); 5:39 (November 10, 1999); 6:1 (January 4, 2000); 6:6 (February 24, 2000); 6:7 (March 6, 2000), all available at <http://h-net.msu.edu/ncc>.

96. The GPO Web site is <http://www.gpo.gov>. A general gateway to federal, state,

and local Web sites is at <http://usgovinfo.about.com/newsissues/usgovinfo/blindex. htm>.

97. The availability of the *New York Times* electronic archives, as well as the abundance of online papers and reports on scholarly publishing, librarianship, and the electronic revolution, have served as a first-hand demonstration to the author of the benefits to the researcher of online material.

98. This trend is already apparent: The accuracy of scanners is increasing at the same rate that their costs are dropping.

# 6 / Social Activism through Computer Networks

**As new communication technologies** have taken hold and spread throughout societies, there has been constant debate about the positive and negative effects of these technologies on our social and political systems. A multitude of relationships between the dissemination of computer technology and various social variables have been proposed and examined. Educational systems and opportunities, work activities, and privacy rights are only a few societal characteristics that have been touched by computer technology.

Of particular interest to many social scientists is how new technologies affect inequality in society. In general, these scholars observe superior access to new technologies by those in higher socioeconomic positions. Inequality of access to technology, in turn leads to more social privilege, thus widening the socioeconomic gap between the information rich and the information poor.[1] The modern effects of computer access on inequality reflect the concerns of earlier elite theorists who felt that professionalism and privileged access to information were key elements in increasing concentration of power in the hands of a few powerful elites.

In contrast to the elite theorists, pluralists argued that power was becoming less centralized. Pluralists saw advances in technology as providing the potential for greater democratization and increased participation in political processes.[2] Some scholars have begun to observe growing attempts to use new communication technology, especially computer technology, in the interests of the less affluent.[3] In particular, as social movement activists have become more sophisticated computer users, some of the resources once monopolized by the "establishment" are being used to improve communication between activists.[4] Activists throughout the world now use their access to established networks, via the Internet and Usenet, as well as specialized networks such as Peacenet and Econet, to communicate about social movement activities and to form collective action agendas.

The range of activity in these networks is well suited to examining a number of practical and theoretical questions about social movements and the contributions of communication technology to social change. How do activists use computer-assisted communication? Does new communication technology change the way social movements are born, rise, and fall? How are dissemination patterns for both information and collective action changed by changing technology? Can computerized communication arenas provide access to information about the social movement process that has been inaccessible until now? Most importantly, can the information recorded in these forums facilitate competitive tests among contending theories of social movements and collective action?

Consider the two dominant theoretical perspectives regarding social movements and collective behavior: Resource mobilization, the dominant paradigm guiding social movement research throughout the 1970s and into the 1980s, and the more recently developed new social movement theory. Resource mobilization abandoned earlier psychological approaches to collective action and introduced resources, organizing, and rationality as the key variables explaining the emergence of social movements and collective action.[5] Despite the attractiveness of resource mobilization and its proven utility to social movement scholars, important aspects of social movements remain unexplained by resource mobilization theory. The result has been the rise of new social movement theory, which emphasizes social psychological processes, collective identity, and continuity as complements to the manipulation of resources described in resource mobilization theory.[6]

Recent debates in the field stem from the intersection of these two perspectives; therefore, the issues related to computer-assisted communication outlined in this chapter are drawn directly from both resource mobilization and new social movement theory. Not only can the researcher use data from activist computer use to examine resource mobilization processes, such as attempts to gather and allocate collective resources, plan strategies, and perpetuate the movement, but she or he can also observe processes related to the formation of collective identities and solidarity.

Despite its potential, computer-assisted communication has not been investigated systematically as a contributor to social movements and collective behavior. Nevertheless, there appears to be a burgeoning interest in the role of computer networks in activism;[7] therefore, the purpose of this chapter is to outline key issues in need of investigation that could shed light on the role of technology and communication in social movements and inform theoretical debates in the field of social movement scholarship.

## COMPUTER STRUCTURES FOR ACTIVISM

Social movement activists use computers to communicate with other activists in several complementary ways. These methods range from the unorganized and individualistic use of electronic mail to systems professionally organized specifically to nurture activism. The most informal method involves the personal use of electronic mail. Activists send items of interest to friends, colleagues, and fellow activists, who may be spurred by the message to act. In addition to acting themselves, people who receive the message can to forward it to acquaintances. The result is an effective information network defined by personal ties and powered by electronic mail forwarding. Using this method, activists can relay messages to thousands of like-minded computer users in a very short time.

A related method also takes advantage of electronic mail technology. In this case an organization or individual sets up a clearinghouse for information related to a particular movement. People then send information relevant to their movement to the clearinghouse address. Interested people subscribe to the clearinghouse service, which upon receipt of a contribution automatically sends an electronic mail message to all its subscribers containing the text of the contribution. These listservs are a very efficient way for activists to send information to hundreds or even thousands of activists whom they have never met. After the message is sent through the clearinghouse service, the personal message forwarding process takes over as activists forward to their acquaintances all or part of the information they have received. The clearinghouse method takes more organization and sustained commitment because activists must take responsibility for starting the clearinghouse, maintaining subscription lists, monitoring the content of contributions, and ensuring the proper functioning of the service.

With the advent and popularization of the World Wide Web, activists and activist organizations have created thousands of home pages that provide information on activist concerns and activities. Web pages are superior to previous modes of electronic communication because they allow people to distribute formatted text and graphics easily. Furthermore, the ease of navigating the Web via point-and-click hypertext links encourages use by activists who are less technically knowledgeable. The Web is more limited, however, with regard to interactivity. Activist Web pages usually consist of static documents that can be updated only by the author, and the technical knowledge necessary to maintain even a low degree of interactivity is beyond most activist users.

The final method is the most formal of the four and involves computer networks dedicated to activism. The networks may be as small as local bulletin board systems or as large as the international Institute for Global Communications (IGC), which houses thousands of computer "conferences," bulletin boards, and Web pages related to activists' concerns.[8] Beyond what is necessary for maintaining a clearinghouse service or individual Web pages, these networks must also purchase and maintain hardware and provide facilities to house the system. Larger systems employ paid staff to maintain equipment and software, solicit users, and perform fiscal accounting functions. Through electronic mail, Web pages, chat functions, and conferences dedicated to specific movement interests, these networks provide to activists— who normally would never meet or communicate with each other—an inexpensive forum for discussing issues, advertising activities, and providing information about the development of social movement organizations. Other computer services (e.g., Microsoft Network (MSN), America Online) also provide conferencing, chat, Web, and electronic mail functions that are used by activists; however, organizations such as IGC are dedicated to activism.

## SPECIAL CHARACTERISTICS OF COMPUTER-ASSISTED COMMUNICATION

### Speed and Cost

Computer networking technology changes and enhances the character of social movements in a number of ways. Because it is the collective nature of social movements that separates them from other types of human activity, any technology that changes the collective character of a movement has important ramifications for its processes and effects. Computerized networks alter the nature of social movements mainly through the speed and ease of information transfer. Information can be transmitted to thousands of nodes all over the globe, almost effortlessly and very inexpensively, in minutes or even seconds.

The speed-to-cost ratio involved in disseminating information is truly an advance over previous systems of communication. After startup investments, information can be sent to thousands of other activists for only a few cents or sometimes even for nothing. Access to computer networking facilities of friends, employers, and universities sometimes makes startup costs negligible as well. College students, for example, routinely co-opt the computing resources of their universities to coordinate protest against the university itself. The time and resources involved in sending a message to thousands of people through the network amount to only a small fraction of what it would take to achieve the same result through the telephone. Similarly, the time and money involved in distributing the same information through the mail—even within one country—would be prohibitive.

An example of this process occurred in late 1992 when Mattel released a new Barbie doll called "Teen Talk Barbie." These dolls were programmed to say different things that were supposed to be related to being a teenage girl. One sentence the teen Barbie spouted was "Math class is tough." Recognizing that this message reinforced the prevailing socialization of young women to fear math and to feel unable to perform mathematical tasks, an association of scholars mounted a campaign to get Barbie to stop saying "Math class is tough." Part of this attempt was an electronic mail message sent to academics explaining the situation, urging action, and providing names and addresses at the Mattel headquarters. By the time this message reached me, it had been forwarded three times and I was a member of a list of ninety people who received the message. If the message had reached me through a similar pattern of forwarding, it could have reached a maximum of more than 65 million computer sites from just three forwards! Although it is unlikely that each person who received the message forwarded it to ninety people, the point is still clear: The ease of forwarding messages and sending the same message to multiple sites can result in a tremendous dissemination of information in a very short period of time. When traversing international boundaries, the transmission of information via the Internet has even greater cost-related advantages. Recent international coordination of protest against the World Trade Organization is but one striking example.

The advantages of speed and ease are inextricably connected with the disadvantages of information overload, however. Although information reaches thousands of nodes, the question remains whether the information is digested by the audience or passed over like so much junk mail.

## Accuracy

One important asset the computer network has is the accurate replication of information to the thousands of nodes it touches. Because of forwarding capabilities, original messages can travel through many network nodes without the slightest distortion. The result is widespread dissemination without the misinformation that typically results from pass-along methods of infor-

mation distribution. Given social movements' tendencies to rely on informal networks to distribute information about the grievances and activities
of the movement, the computer network is a substantial advance in communication procedures. Social movement campaigns that rely heavily on details
such as accurate addresses or phone numbers can expect these details to be
distributed more accurately and easily by electronic means than by word of
mouth. In the Barbie incident, accurate information about the exact nature
of the problem, how to respond, and where to direct responses reached every person who received the message. The result of the Barbie campaign was
a promise by Mattel to replace dolls that made the math statement and to
volunteer Barbie for promath advertising.

## Interactivity

The ability of computers to expand levels of interactivity is one of the key
characteristics that change the way social movements use communication
technology. Using computers, activists have access to time-shifted interaction, simultaneous interaction, and easy connections to other ideologically
aligned people whom they may not know personally. All these interactive
characteristics can facilitate the operation of social movements and combine
to provide advances on earlier communication methods used by activists.

**THE MICROSOCIAL ROLES OF COMPUTER CONFERENCING**   One important
function of computer conferences such as those that exist on IGC's Peacenet
and Econet relates to the microsocial processes that sustain social movements.
As many scholars have observed, movements must exploit communication
resources to achieve their goals. Communication must be able to "generate
sympathy among bystanders" and maintain "legitimacy and efficacy" among
movement participants.[9] Each of these functions can be observed directly in
activist conferences. In fact, these two functions often are the main activity
in movement-related computer-assisted dialogue. One conference on IGC's
Peacenet dedicated to the pursuit of gay and lesbian rights contains many
articles reporting developments throughout the world that extend greater
rights to the gay and lesbian population. Furthermore, efforts are made to
enhance activist efficacy by attributing these changes directly to the action
of people within the movement. Amnesty International is one of the most
active organizations in attempting to maintain efficacy among its activists
as it tracks and reports its group's letter-writing efforts. Highlighting these
successes helps to encourage future activism and strengthens support for the
organizing body.

Given the broad range of issues subsumed under the IGC networks, activists also have an opportunity to send their message to "third-party audiences," people not directly involved in their own organization. Gaining at least silent support for a movement's goals and actions is essential for movement success. Without gaining tacit support, movements are likely to encounter insurmountable resistance and cannot move forward on their agendas. Again, this function is evident in activist networks in which urgent issues regarding specific movements are advertised in general interest conferences and activists are encouraged to read material outside their specific area of involvement. Although Amnesty International's overt attempt seems to be to find letter writers, the latent effect of their solicitations is to spread information about the appalling conditions, torture, and human rights violations endured by political prisoners throughout the world. The result is strong pro–Amnesty International feelings that lend strength to the Amnesty International agenda.

Although social psychological grievances have never seemed to be strong predictors of the emergence of social movements, McAdam, McCarthy, and Zald point out the important role these grievances play in producing the pool of potential activists: "The more integrated the person is into the aggrieved community, the more readily he or she can be mobilized for participation."[10] Although having a sympathetic attitude toward a movement does not necessarily compel one to become an activist, such an attitude is an important underlying prerequisite. The announcements, conversations, and reactions in computer conferences certainly facilitate awareness of movement issues and often are designed to elicit appropriately sympathetic attitudes, thereby moving the reader into the pool of potential activists.

Another function of computer networking apparent in the text of activist conferences is direct recruiting through calls to action and solicitation of funds. Given what we know about activists becoming involved in new movements partially as a result of their involvement in other movements and organizations, we might view a computerized forum such as Peacenet as a virtual breeding ground for movement activists. Both direct involvement in conversations with other activists and simply reading announcements and information about protest activity can convince activists to take on new causes, develop new identities, and be socialized into new roles. This type of computer networking allows a person to access information about new issues and movements while investing only small amounts of time and energy.

**MASS MEDIA VERSUS COMPUTER NETWORKS**    Social movement activists have long depended on the successful use of the mass media to achieve their goals and get their message to potential movement participants. Although this method of disseminating information about grievances is inexpensive and reaches a very broad audience, activists often have trouble getting media attention and often have to resort to radical behavior to do so. Furthermore, generally they must turn control of the movement's message over to reporters and editors who may be unsympathetic or may distort the movement's message.[11]

In addition to this loss of control over the message of the movement, mass media function differently from computer networks with regard to the process of coordinating action. The mass media essentially involve one-way communication and do not necessarily attempt to coordinate action. The computer network has the ability to reach people who are separated by great geographic distances (just as the media do), but it also allows them to return communication. The result is that along with purposeful coordination of action, there are opportunities to clarify and solicit agreement on plans of action. However, the computer network also loses some of the effect of mass media because of the limited and selective audience it serves. Thus, although some coordinating gains are made by computer networks, it is unlikely that computer technology will be able to reach even a small percentage of those whom traditional mass media can.

**DENSITY OF AGGRIEVED POPULATIONS**    Many social change theorists and social movement scholars posit that density of a particular population facilitates the growth of collective behavior. One classic example is the movement of blacks from southern rural areas to urban environments as a precipitating condition for the civil rights movement.[12] Computer networks that allow two-way communication can facilitate an artificial density of an aggrieved population.[13] When people discover others who share like concerns and problems, the solidarity and community that typically arise from dense populations are the result. This dynamic is demonstrated clearly in the men's movement conference on Peacenet, where men who want to discuss issues relevant to progressive men's identities are able to find others like themselves. Through networking with others who share similar concerns, these participants develop a collective identity and are encouraged to become active in the movement. Although it is debatable how much computers precipitate mass action by creating artificial density, indicators of this dynamic do exist. Rather than precipitating the kind of uncoordinated mass action that occurred in many local sites after the Rodney King verdict (propelled by mass media accounts), computers are facile at cheaply coordinating actions such as Amnesty International's letter-writing campaigns, for which both a sense of outrage and detailed information are needed to carry out effective action. Private communication networks, such as America Online and MSN, are evidence that this type of aggregation and identity development can be facilitated as technology becomes available to wider audiences.

**COALITIONS AND COORDINATION**    Another area of social movement scholarship that activist computer networks are ideally configured to study is the connection between different social movement organizations (SMOs) within a broader movement. McAdam, McCarthy, and Zald call these broad groupings of SMOs pursuing similar goals social movement industries (SMIs).[14] Furthermore, given the broad membership of large communication networks such as IGC, it is possible to examine the connections not only between SMOs within an SMI but also across different SMIs. It is clear that the groups focusing on gay and lesbian rights are not in the same SMI as groups promoting bans on nuclear power. But it is equally clear that some activists are involved in both efforts and that there is ideological overlap between such activists' agendas. A large, diverse umbrella organization such as IGC provides a unique opportunity to study this overlap both in membership and in ideology. In most conference-related networks, participants subscribe to certain conferences in which they intend to participate regularly. Examining overlapping subscriptions to different groups' conferences within an SMI and across SMIs would provide an excellent representation of activist connections and the overall network. Furthermore, combining this type of network analysis with qualitative analyses of the content of both narrowly focused conferences and more generalist ones can provide information about the ideological sympathies of participants in the movements.

Beyond simply mapping out the network, there has been a call for research to assess "under precisely what conditions we can expect competing SMOs to cooperate".[15] The computer network is an ideal research site to begin addressing this question. Because only a small portion of movement activity takes place in this setting, the researcher working with activist networks is unlikely to answer the question completely. However, she or he will find a record of information that is difficult to find elsewhere: recorded interactions between members of different SMOs and SMIs under conditions of both collaboration and competition.

IGC itself is somewhat of an advance on the previous status of organizing in the social movement arena. It is doubtful that an umbrella organization with such a large and diverse membership has ever existed, much less endured or enjoyed the growth that IGC has. Whereas previous coalition organizations have been created for a singular purpose or under a single ideological identity, IGC—although it certainly has an ideology—is held together mainly through what can be considered a tactic or a resource: communication. Co-alitions that have organized around a single goal often cannot maintain their own existence after the goal has been removed, either through success (e.g., the antipornography organizations analyzed by Curtis and Zurcher)[16] or through a structural change that makes immediate pursuit of the goal no longer reasonable (e.g., the defeat of the equal rights amendment).[17] With no immediate direction left for the group, the attempt to refocus often ends in divisive reactions, particularly because groups united for one purpose some-times are made up of smaller groups that have little else in common ideo-logically. However, if ideology is not the force that brought an organization or individual into another organization, ideological changes (either inside the group or in the political climate) are much less likely to determine future participation. Thus in IGC or Peacenet, the umbrella remains stable because of what it provides to its participants: communication. Unless an easier or more efficient means of communication evolves to compete with these or-ganizations, it is unlikely that the umbrella will fold.

## CHARACTERISTICS OF COMPUTER-USING ACTIVISTS

Despite the amazingly long reach of computer networks, implications for mobilization to action are limited because the population of computer us-ers, although growing, is still sparse and specialized in its orientation. One reason for sparse membership in activist networks is that startup costs are prohibitive for many activists and potential activists, limiting mass access to the networks. This problem is especially acute in less developed areas, where computers are especially difficult to access. Although the prices of comput-ers and modems continue to fall, and many people can avoid these costs by accessing networks through educational or work facilities, many others sim-ply cannot participate because of their economic situations.

An even more significant obstacle is the time and effort needed to master the technical details of participating on the network. Certainly, the Web significantly reduced the learning curve for end users of the Internet. On the other hand, as the Web technology continues to advance, the complexity of maintaining an effective Web presence more and more requires trained com-puter experts, something many activist organization cannot afford. And even with the interface simplifications brought by the Web, computers can scare off potential users, thus limiting the reach of the network. These limits of-ten are also greatest in populations who might have the greatest need for the political clout offered by protest. The U.S. Department of Commerce reported in 1998 that less that 10 percent of households with incomes under $25,000 used the Internet, whereas around 60 percent of those with incomes over $75,000 were online. The same study found a growing digital divide between the races, with blacks and Hispanics lagging significantly behind whites and Asians in computer ownership.[18]

Beyond just learning how to use computers and access networks, users must also become aware of the activist potential of the computer and locate these social movement forums within the computing world. Owning a computer and knowing how to operate its communication apparatus does not guarantee that activists will discover or become involved in organizations such as IGC.

One process that can help overcome the elite user problem depends on the connection of computer-using actors to activists in noncomputer movement environments. If activists who participate on the network act as nodes, linking nonusers to the computer format and eventually to other nonusers who are connected to other nodes, the network disseminates information throughout the movement. This model is used by the AFL-CIO's LaborNet to connect union leaders throughout the United States, thereby indirectly linking the larger constituency.[19] Those who participate on the network can gather information from the network and transfer it to other activists through more traditional means. Likewise, these network nodes can gather information from traditional means and local activists and then post it on the network.

Analyzing conference records allows easy observation of activists posting information about movements operating in their own local areas. The complementary end of the process is much less certain. Computer records do not tell how well activists collect information from the network and then use the information to further traditional means of collective behavior. If the people who participate on the Net are not involved in organizations other than computer conferences, the implications of the network for mass action are diminished.

## CONCLUSION

The ultimate effects of improved communication through computerization on inequality and access to political power are difficult to predict. Nevertheless, it is clear that this technology is changing some of the contexts and processes of social movements. These changes both propose challenges and provide opportunities for understanding social movements and other types of collective behavior. Access to computer-mediated communication has become an important resource for activists and will continue to grow as a tool for activism. Understanding attempts to distribute access to this social movement resource and attempts to curtail mobilization by preventing or limiting access are important concerns with which resource mobilization scholars must grapple. Resource mobilization scholars must also examine the process of coordination that is unique to computerized communication. New social movement scholars likewise will find fertile data from computer sources with regard to identity-building processes and attempts to develop solidarity.

Possibilities for examining intersections of resource mobilization and new social movement theories also exist within the computer domain. Analyzing the activity of computer-using activists as they attempt to establish a connection between the network and nonusers provides an important interface between these two theoretical approaches. The node activist's sense of responsibility in carrying out this essential resource mobilization function probably is rooted in the strength of his or her identity and ideological commitment to the social movement.

This essay touches only a few issues related to social movements that can be investigated through computer networks. Among important issues neglected herein is the notion of abeyance structures,[20] which sustain movements in times when mass support is not evident. Computer networks are full of movements that appear to be in abeyance yet can be sustained through a small number of activists on the network even if the activists are widely scattered geographically and have no opportunity for face-to-face communication.

Another important issue not addressed here involves the position of a particular identity group within a given movement and the attempts of this group to influence the larger movement. Historical examples include Morris and McAdam's discussions of the role of women in the civil rights movement and Ryan's discussion of minority women in the contemporary women's movement.[21] Particularly salient recently have been data on the place of African Americans, Latinos, and bisexuals within the gay and lesbian movement as well as the position of gay and lesbian activists within other movements such as the Irish National Liberation Movement and the Irish Republican Army and within the African National Congress in South Africa. All these issues are discussed extensively and passionately in activist computer conferences. Finally, a last issue that might be investigated using data from computer networks is the rise of a new movement through the development of grievances within a "parent" movement.[22] For example, the information discussed in the various gay and lesbian conferences, and particularly in those dedicated to bisexual issues, allows us to observe the development of the bisexual movement within, and as a reaction to, the gay and lesbian movement.

The computer activist network is a largely untapped resource for data about social movements that can provide a great deal of information about the processes of social movements. Perhaps the most attractive feature of these computer networks is the accurate and easily traceable path left by activists. Although collective behavior and social movement attitudes often develop in observable settings, records of such events sometimes are difficult to obtain and often rely on participants' memories. Actions and attitudes that develop on computer networks allow systematic data collection that often is not available in other social movement forums. However, it should be recognized that the records on communication networks often are incomplete. Participants communicate with others outside the computer network and spend time thinking about and working on movement activity completely independent of the computer. Nevertheless, records of communication that occurs on the network can be much more complete than records of analogous written communication in earlier movements, and these data provide an essential supplement to more traditional types of data about collective behavior and social movements.

## NOTES

1. Everett M. Rogers, *The New Media in Society* (New York: Free Press, 1978); Angela G. King, "Closing the Digital Divide," *U.S. News and World Report* 128:21 (May 29, 2000): 23–36.

2. Peter Bachrach, *The Theory of Democratic Elitism: A Critique* (Boston: Little, Brown, 1967); Kenneth Laudon, *Communication Technology and Democratic Participation* (New York: Praeger, 1977).

3. Michael F. McCullough, "Democratic Questions for the Computer Age," *Computers in Human Services* 8 (1991): 9–18; Howard Rheingold, *The Virtual Community* (New York: Harper, 1993).

4. Manuel Castells, *The Information Age*, vol. 2: *The Power of Identity* (Oxford, England: Blackwell, 1997); Kevin A. Hill and John E. Hughes, *Cyberpolitics: Citizen Activism in the Age of the Internet* (Lanham, Md.: Rowman & Littlefield, 1998).

5. John D. McCarthy and Mayer Zald, *The Trend of Social Movements in America: Professionalization and Resource Mobilization* (Morristown, N.J.: General Learning Press, 1973); J. Craig Jenkins, "Resource Mobilization Theory and the Study of Social Movements," *Annual Review of Sociology* 9 (1983): 527–53.

6. Alberto Melucci, *Nomads of the Present: Social Movements and Individual Needs in Contemporary Society* (Philadelphia: Temple University Press, 1989); Alberto Melucci, *Challenging Codes* (Cambridge, England: Cambridge University Press, 1996).

7. Hill and Hughes, *Cyberpolitics;* Craig Calhoun, "Community without Propinquity Revisited: Communication Technology and the Transformation of the Urban Public Sphere," *Sociological Inquiry* 68 (1998): 373–97; Mario Diani, "Social Movement Net-

works, Virtual and Real," paper presented at the conference "A New Politics," Centre for Cultural Studies and Sociology, University of Birmingham, 1999; Daniel J. Myers, "Media, Communication Technology, and Protest Waves," paper presented at the conference "Social Movement Analysis: The Network Perspective," Ross Priory, Scotland, 2000.

8. Institute for Global Communications, *IGC User's Manual* (San Francisco: IGC/Tides Foundation, 1991); Institute for Global Communications, *IGC Internet's Progressive Gateway*, <http://www.igc.org>, accessed May 24, 2000.

9. Doug McAdam, John McCarthy, and Mayer Zald, "Social Movements," in *Handbook of Sociology*, ed. Neil Smelser (Newbury Park, Calif.: Sage, 1988), 695–737.

10. Ibid.

11. Pamela E. Oliver, "Bringing the Crowd Back In: The Nonorganizational Elements of Social Movements," *Research in Social Movements, Conflict, and Change* 11 (1989): 1–30.

12. Aldon Morris, *The Origins of the Civil Rights Movement: Black Communities Organizing for Change* (New York: Free Press, 1984).

13. Howard Rheingold, *The Virtual Community* (New York: Harper, 1993).

14. McAdam, McCarthy, and Zald, "Social Movements."

15. Ibid.

16. Russell Curtis and Louis Zurcher, "Stable Resources of Protest Movements: The Multi-Organizational Field," *Social Forces* 52 (1973): 53–61.

17. Barbara Ryan, *Feminism and the Women's Movement* (New York: Routledge, 1992).

18. King, "Closing the Digital Divide."

19. Montieth Illingworth, "Workers on the Net, Unite!: Labor Goes Online to Organize, Communicate, and Strike," *InformationWeek*, August 22, 1994, 17–23.

20. Verta Taylor, "Social Movement Continuity: The Women's Movement in Abeyance," *American Sociological Review* 54 (1989): 761–75.

21. Morris, *Origins of the Civil Rights Movement;* Doug McAdam, *Freedom Summer* (New York: Oxford University Press, 1986); Ryan, *Feminism and the Women's Movement.*

22. Steven M. Buechler, "Beyond Resource Mobilization?: Emerging Trends in Social Movement Theory," *Sociological Quarterly* 34 (1993): 217–35.

# PART 4

# Philosophical and Ethical Concerns of the Culture of Computing

H. JEANIE TAYLOR
AND CHERIS KRAMARAE

# 7 / Creating Cybertrust: Illustrations and Guidelines

**Just as many historians** now recognize that there was no Renaissance for European women in the fifteenth century,[1] many of us are realizing that without attention to the concerns and activities of women in the current communication renaissance we will have only partial, distorted, and thus seriously flawed intellectual and academic achievements.

We are more than interested in the grand computing challenges for social science. We have listened with a great deal of attention as users and promoters talk about the personal and academic freedoms possible with the new communication programs and the opportunities for new kinds of research and teaching offered by the new computer technologies. We have participated in university committees designed to enhance the amount of collaborative computer work we can do. We have provided workshops to critique old computer programs and prepare new ones. We continue to be hopeful about the ways computers can be used in our university research and teaching. However, much of what we see happening in computer use seems a replication if not an intensification of the problems many women and people of color experience in face-to-face communication and in social science work. Without more attention to these problems, the new academic work is likely to be critically flawed.

We write as feminists who try to collaborate with others to transform communication in ways that will overturn the disempowering structure of patriarchy and will imagine and enact new structures. It is not enough, we think, to identify problems and then work merely for a small voice for women and people of color (getting a word in edgewise, adding some Web sites on the Internet). We believe that we need also to articulate new visions to advance the possibility of a more sane and just world.[2] We work for an intellectual and academic renaissance for both women and men.

Here, after reviewing some of the history of gender and Internet research, online problems, and some of the proposed solutions, we offer guidelines to assist us all in making what happens on our campuses and on the Internet truly innovative and useful and not, in too many ways, the same old stuff.

We realize that what is included when people talk about computers and the Internet is huge and that not all we write will be directly applicable to all the projects and programs discussed in this volume and elsewhere. We also realize that some of the issues we discuss have legal implications, of particular interest to women, that cannot be dealt with adequately here.[3] We do not profess to know all the relevant global concerns (although, working with many others, we are making a start on them). What we do offer is material we believe important to anyone interested in assessment of technological developments.

Our experience is that many information technology projects that are assumed to be gender neutral actually have very different impact on women and men. Especially in times of rapid technological changes, gender divisions and hierarchies are accented in ways not necessarily intended by the people supporting, controlling, or evaluating the changes. Many issues demand our attention as we use and try to interpret the new cyberworld.[4] Here we explore some of the problems women have experienced in computer-mediated communication (CMC) as an example of the ways in which gender hierarchies are being perpetuated in new technologies. We then offer some recommendations for change and some tools for individual researchers and institutions to use in designing and evaluating academic projects that involve the new technologies. In a review of many of the specific problems women are having online, we have pointed out that universities and other institutions have taught sex discrimination, if not explicitly and deliberately, at least very well.[5] We are now suggesting that the so-called Information Revolution is a time and a global project that *could* be recognized by administrators, students, and teachers as a major opportunity to change, in a fundamental way, what is being taught.

## EARLY ONLINE CONVERSATIONS

Because some commentators on social relationships on the Internet have argued that CMC breaks down traditional gender assumptions—suggesting that once women are present in nearly equal numbers to men any earlier discriminatory practices will end—we think it important to trace some of the history of online gender interaction research and commentary, a history that indicates that the problems are not temporary and trivial but persistent and important.[6] Susan C. Herring, a linguist who has studied online conversations, concludes that "numerical parity is important, but it does not in and of itself create social parity, which can only exist in an environment of tolerance and respect for diversity among users."[7]

Writing in 1991, Angela Gunn argued that women were the Other on most of the computer network systems in the world rather than integral decision makers and participants.[8] She and other critics writing about the interaction on the rapidly expanding number of bulletin boards were aware that in most online messages and conversations, although indicators of race, age, physical disabilities, and appearance may disappear, the sex of the writer is still apparent in the signatures on most networks and that the modes of interaction were predominantly male and hierarchical. In the early 1990s women were the decided minority online.

Some of these women talked and wrote about their online experience. They reported that men monopolized the talk and set the agenda for the kinds of interaction that would take place, just as they customarily did in face-to-face interaction. The supposed egalitarianism of electronic communication was not experienced as the reality of women in many discussions. In their empirical studies, researchers found that in CMC interaction the men were more likely than women to participate a lot, to introduce more successful topics, and to receive more responses.[9]

Women discovered that gaining the floor in an electronic discussion could be as problematic as gaining the floor in an academic meeting. In writing about interaction and gender in general, Susan Gal argues, "Even among status equals and in mixed-sex groups, the interactional constraints of institutional events such as meetings are not gender neutral but weighted in favor of male interactional strategies. Although organization of the meetings *masks* the fact that speakers are excluded on the basis of gender, it simultaneously *accomplishes* that very exclusion."[10] In an essay specifically about interaction at computer conferences, Marilyn Cooper and Cynthia L. Selfe came to a similar conclusion.[11]

## HOSTILE ENVIRONMENTS

The climate of the early public online discussion groups was such that many women felt excluded and silenced. Yet there was little serious recognition or discussion of this as a basic problem for the developing Internet. When explicit sexual harassment occurred or exclusionary language or conversational practices were used, the complaints women made often were dismissed or received in a hostile manner. It was difficult for women individually to have an impact on general online behavior, of course.

A discussion in the *Computer Underground Digest,* an electronic journal, provides an example of how the early discussion lists were unwelcoming to women.[12] In response to an article by Mike Holderness in the *London Times Educational Supplement* that explored issues of gender bias and sexual harassment in the context of evaluating the online discussion lists as an "invisible college," one network participant (Larry Landwehr) advised women, "If you can't stand the heat, ladies, then get out of the kitchen."[13]

Even in the early days of the expansion of FREENET, the community-based system devoted to transcending "racial, sexual, and economic barriers" to electronic communication, there were clear examples of the acceptability of such exclusionary attitudes. In response to a question about a blatantly sexist remark in a discussion of FREENET, Tom Grudner, a key organizer of the organization, said, "This medium holds out perhaps the greatest hope we will see in our lifetime for communication which transcends racial, sexual, and economic barriers—IF WE ALLOW IT. But the key is: *if we allow it.* What we can't allow to happen is for professional victim-mongers to screw it up—people who have built enormous power- and financial-bases off of convincing people they are 'victims' through 'no fault of their own' and the ONLY way out is through them and their (inevitable expensive) programs."[14]

When women at the University of Illinois at Urbana-Champaign who were doing investigations of online interactions read Grudner's statement (which suggested that women writing about their perception of sexism online were "professional victim-mongers"), they were dismayed by the lack of support from a person who professed to be interested in creating "free" and welcoming electronic spaces for everyone.

One factor in the structure of the electronic networks that seemed to contribute to the climate being unwelcoming to women and people of color was the "distance" between participants.[15] In March 1993, the participants of the ARACHNET list carried on an extended conversation about the geography of the Internet that explored issues of distance and proximity in virtual spaces. Greg Madden, of the University of North Carolina at Chapel Hill, said, "In particular, some of the most cherished fundamental tenets of Geography are obsolete in a virtual world. For instance, the concepts of distance and proximity must be expanded if they are to apply in a virtual world. Probably most important, the 'neighborhood property,' which essentially states that things which are closer to each other are more likely to be similar than things which are farther apart, may not apply at all in a virtual world."[16]

## CREATING COMMUNITIES

Early in the 1990s, Michael Zackheim wrote, "It strikes me as phenomenal that the world-wide communications network that we so mightily employ erases many of the mysteries of the unknown—yet nurtures such a profound sense of loneliness."[17] Discussions about the geography of the Internet were accompanied by discussions about the concept of online communities. In the early 1990s, many of us argued that creating hospitable communication networks or communities, both virtual and real, was important if women were to establish mature discourse online. This seemed to mean that at least for some time there would be a need for segregated forums on the Internet (such as Systers, the list for women in computer science). The research of the past two decades had made clear that men were more likely to be interested in having mixed sex conversations than women were. Women in mixed-sex groups were more likely to give men plenty of space and time considerations. Although separatism was not necessarily what women wanted for all online discussions, until gender equity becomes a reality in a wide variety of settings, some women suggested that they needed access to some women-only safe forums for conversations if they were to create electronic communities.

Judy Smith and Ellen Balka envisioned a feminist computer network that would connect them in just this way:

> For those of us who are part of social change movements, who often don't feel a part of much of the culture around us, we need to know there are lots more of us out here. I can live most anywhere, places where feminists are few and far between, and still be part of a feminist reality. Then I don't have to depend on the commercial media which I already know denies me information about feminist projects. Literacy is an empowerment tool for the disenfranchised; that's why so many Third World liberation groups have literacy campaigns. Computer literacy can be the same type of liberating force for women in a technological society.[18]

Of course, in the time since Smith and Balka wrote this, women in many places in the world—those who have Internet access at work or who can afford the computer equipment and the fees of access providers—have created many discussion groups and have established many electronic mail links. In the early 1990s Judith Hudson and Kathleen Turek published "Electronic Access to Research on Women: A Short Guide."[19] Additional information on discussion groups and newsgroups is available in publications such as the *Utne Reader.*[20]

These communities women created were not all women-only forums. Many individuals and groups tried to foster an environment that was welcoming, in which the ethics of electronic communication and standards for inclusion are openly and thoughtfully discussed. For example, on April 1992, organizers at Lewis and Clark College, Oregon created an Electronic Gender Salon where papers on gender and electronic communication were circulated and discussed by a group of subscribers during a two-week period. Attention was paid to participation by gender, and issues of equity were raised continually. However, even within this carefully crafted environment, the prevailing climate of online discussion was evident, with men dominating the conversation more and more as the conference continued.

The *Utne Reader* launched a global network of Email Salons patterned after their face-to-face Neighborhood Salons, which were designed to foster "small group dialogue." The electronic promotional announcement (April 1993) for the Email Salons lists the following advantages, included here because the list contains guidelines that may still be appropriate, especially perhaps for online courses.

1. Participation is purposely kept small (25 people), which encourages all members to get to know one another. This in turn helps minimize the lurking, the flaming, and the posturing that can often plague other forms of online group communication;

2. Email Salon discussion topics change from time to time, at the discretion of the participants. This creates a more relaxed atmosphere of learning through real dialogue. Virtually all other forms of online group communication are top-based which inevitably leads to discussions in which most "participants" are silent while a few dominate.

3. We actively seek international participation for the Email Salons. Having one or more members from other cultures in your Email Salon can offer a diversity of perspectives that few face-face salons can match.

In addition to encouraging cultural diversity, the Utne Salons tried for gender balance in the makeup of each group, a policy that created a great deal of heated discussion as some interested men realized that they had to wait for more women to join before other men would be admitted.

There were numerous examples of electronic communication being used to facilitate social activism and connection in the late 1980s and early 1990s. In Montana, Judy Smith at WORD, Inc. was in daily contact with the women her agency serves and with other activist organizations using the Big Sky Net and Handsnet.[21] SeniorNet was providing round-the-clock connections for older adults across the country.[22] The Indigenous People's Computer

Network was established to provide news and information of interest to Native Americans. By envisioning and articulating alternative potential uses of electronic communication, women and minority men were trying to make a difference in the way information technologies were used and developed. For example, Leslie Weisman, author of *Discrimination by Design* (1992), called upon women to consider how the new information technologies could make the world a safer place for women, a question not addressed in many of the CMC forums at the time (or now).[23]

Many of us were trying to determine how to help ensure access for most people, not just an elite. We imagined computer terminals connected to community systems in laundromats, homeless shelters, daycare centers, and so on, with sufficient support so that most people in the United States would have access to the Internet; at the same time we realize that access to machinery does not automatically mean access to computer interaction.[24]

As in other conversations, some women have learned to be assertive and to ignore or overcome harassment, but many others have found that mixed-sex conversations online can quite suddenly turn frustrating and personally demeaning.

Wondering whether the methods of harassment in synchronous (real-time) chat discussions might differ significantly from those of asynchronous (e.g., e-mail-based) communication, Susan C. Herring (1999) studied two extended interactions, one on an asynchronous discussion list and the other on an Internet relay chat (IRC) channel. Her analysis discovered similar patterns over time: initial situation, initiation of harassment by men, resistance by women to the harassment, and escalation of harassment by the men, eventually concluding in an accommodation by targeted participants to the dominant group norms or silence from the targeted women. Herring notes that although the episodes she studied might be considered extreme cases of sexual harassment, equally or more extreme cases are being reported in other recent CMC research.[25] Noting that men often dominate face-to-face interactions also, Kimberly Dawn Blum points out that in online environments, male domination can last for days. This problem has particular implications for online learning environments, she suggests.[26] Women who want to be respected as scholars (which means avoiding being known as a troublemaker or as someone who questions the actions of respected men in the field) may be very hesitant about publicly pointing to online sexist behavior. There are still no generally accepted grievance procedures for sexual harassment on the Internet.[27] Of course, we are aware of the discussions about how virtual environments such as IRC can allow all of us to deconstruct and reconstruct gender and break out of the binary gender categories. The lack of physical presence online and the possibility of creating one's body through writing text has received a lot of attention in the popular media.[28] In the past, at least, most of the players in these real-time discussions have been young, heterosexual males, some of whom say they gender-switch to see whether they can get away with their descriptions of female self or who say that they play female to have intimate discussions with women. Although some people find that gender switching gives them a sense of freedom and power and a way of breaking gender molds, others worry about the deception possible in these virtual spaces.[29]

We continue to find evidence that the kinds and extent of problems experienced by many women online vary, depending on how public the forum and how cohesive the community of users, with greater "distance" between participants leading to greater disrespect for the humanness of other participants. This "distance" also makes it more difficult to do anything about these problems because there is no recognizable community that can be approached to invoke community standards.[30] It therefore becomes even more important to instantiate such standards at the points where institutions such as universities interface with the Internet.

We have mentioned some of the problems. What can we do to make a difference in the way women experience electronic communication in the future?

We can work to create real communities that focus on the electronic world. Although it has become difficult to know where the center is, those of us who feel marginalized in the university community or who find ourselves both insiders and outsiders in the academic world not only need to create spaces that promote our own competence in these areas but must also use our vision from that intermediate space to affect the way systems are created to include other marginalized people. Recognizing the importance of addressing the issues raised by the new information technologies as they are affecting universities, we (with Dale Spender) founded a working group of women on the campus of the University of Illinois at Urbana-Champaign, which we believe can serve as an example of the type of organizing and planning that can benefit women on other campuses. After four years of monthly face-to-face meetings, Women, Information Technology, and Scholarship (WITS) has become primarily an online support and information-sharing link for women. Through the years our experiences in working together have changed many of our lives in beneficial ways and have affected some campus policies.

## WITS: WOMEN, INFORMATION TECHNOLOGY, AND SCHOLARSHIP

The WITS group began meeting in September 1991. From its beginning WITS was an interdisciplinary venture.[31] The experience of women and other minorities with electronic communication is not the same everywhere on campus, of course. The distribution of hardware, know-how, and technical support is uneven, with some women in the sciences living centrally in a culture of computing and others in some areas of the humanities with comparatively little equipment and support. The WITS group was composed of about forty women faculty, academic staff, and graduate students from a wide range of disciplines, and in the course of its first years it provided stimulation, practical knowledge, and a sense of involvement in creating the electronic world for its members. Its members also felt a deep connection with one another and a sense of support from the group.[32]

Some of our overarching interests included information policies and systems for future generations of university students and faculty; freedom of information for all citizens of all nations; easing rather than exacerbating the difficulties all women and people of color face on campuses; availability of resources especially designed to benefit those who have found universities a hostile environment; and respect for diversity in policymaking that involves information technologies. We explored technical issues, devoting time to workshops and other skill-building activities. In addition to the regular colloquium sessions, subgroups of women met in focused reading groups on a variety of topics including virtual reality, women and space (both virtual and real), and feminist speculative fiction. The group saw itself building upon its strength and sense of solidarity to become an activist organization, increasing involvement of the group in issues at the campus, local, state, national, and global levels.[33]

Some of our work dealt with the limitations of online exchanges and the resulting problems. Because tone of voice, facial expressions, body posture, pauses, and so on are missing on the online discussions, use of contextualization cues such as emotive symbols may temper some of the extremes of verbal emotion that end up being vented on the discussions and may give readers some way to frame what they read in the absence of the paralinguistic cues that normally inform understanding of interpersonal interactions. But emoticons are very limited and static. The small computer video cameras now available are producing rather limited and static visual cues.

In addition to gathering examples of the problems with online hostile situations, we also wrote recommendations for dealing with serious violations of collaborative communication norms. We suggested that sometimes just calling attention to the problem is enough. For example, when complaints about sexist or racist comments are made to listserv moderators, they can return the comment in quotes followed by something like the following message: "Someone using your logon has posted remarks found offensive to others. We ask your cooperation in solving this problem. Thank you."

## INSTITUTIONAL PARTICIPATION IN THE DEVELOPMENT OF THE INTERNET

It is important that universities and other institutions that interface with the Internet take seriously their role in this development of the Internet. Because electronic communication networks are so large and decentralized and seemingly lawless and because increasingly they are dominated by businesses, it is easy to understand why universities and other institutions may not have recognized the role they can play at their institutional interface. Universities have the opportunity to change the structure of interaction on campuses and to influence the way networks will develop at the national and international level.[34]

Universities need to facilitate discussions about electronic networks both as they are being used today and as they will be used in the future, and they need to recognize the responsibility they have for influencing this development. In addition, they must help develop campus policy to address the problems we have outlined here.[35] As a start, we suggest the following:

Development and protection of women-only online forums

Training for moderators about issues of equity and access and about ways of dealing with people who express disrespect for others online

A grievance procedure (which allows class action) for complaints of sexual harassment online and open meetings of standing committees on ethics and operations

Periodic reports, to a central body, on number and types of complaints and action taken

Clarification of what will be considered offensive messages and discussion of etiquette for online communication

We are not suggesting here some tight control, some infringement of the rights of Internet users (quite the opposite, in fact, we are advocating the rights of a substantial portion of *potential* Internet users).[36] We are arguing that the electronic discussion groups have become an important arena for developing and distributing knowledge and that as such they are an extension of the physical university. Universities cannot afford to ignore what is going on in these virtual spaces; the same standards of nondiscrimination, equal treatment, and elimination of sexual harassment must be applied in these arenas.

In the early 1990s many people writing about the Internet used the North American frontier as an analogy to evoke the excitement and lawlessness of cyberspace and the potential for taking and conquering new lands. Given the vast damages, to Native Americans and the rest of the land, caused by the policies of the "frontier movement," we found the analogy very troubling. We noted the often controlling language so many people use in discussing the adventures in subduing and conquering land and other space. Many ecological issues are left unexplored. For starters, the hundreds of millions of computers worldwide use great amounts of electricity (with accompanying dangerous emissions), and the number of sheets of paper used (many of them bleached white in a process that creates dioxin, a highly toxic chemical) increases daily.[37] Computer manufacturing creates dangerous pollutants, especially for the women assembling the chips. Computers often are thrown into junk piles before they wear out, as manufacturers sell faster and smaller computers with more promised devices and functions.

Meetings in cyberspace can save some transportation costs,[38] but many other ecology issues are left by the wayside. Those of us who have computers can turn them off when they are not in use, and when buying new equipment we can choose energy-efficient hardware. But as we organize these amazing electronic networks, we need also to consider how they alter our relationship with the rest of the earth. When we talk about what we want our world to be, we need to consider what our world is.

In this chapter we offer guideline questions that may help all of us consider some of the hidden implications of our new programs and involve women and their interests in all phases of our projects. We have worked on a modification of a list of questions Maureen Ebben developed for discussion at a WITS meeting. We do not suggest that each of these questions will be equally relevant to all research projects. We also realize, in ways that research programs seldom take into account, that women's lives and concerns are not a unified mass. We need to consider class, race, age, and occupational differences, for example. We would ask whether a project seemingly equally desirable for women and men students might bring new administrative problems to high school or university secretaries or whether the question format used in an interactive CD-ROM skills test adequately represents the conversation conventions of the Latina and African-American communities.[39]

We suggest that if every academic project were to include a WITS-type component based on consideration of these and related questions and resolutions, we could much more readily talk about new, more beneficial social contact and education. The WITS group has developed a statement that expresses concern with the development of the new technologies as they affect girls and women around the word and makes policy recommendations.

A Global Alert from WITS to Potential Strategic Partners
Gender Equity in Global Communication Networks

*Introduction*

Information technology is transforming societies. Increasingly, access to information and vehicles for utilizing that information—the bases for generating wealth and power in the next decades—will accrue to those who can best utilize the global communication network. Thus, it is essential that all people have equitable and affordable access to this electronic network.

*Who We Are*

Women, Information Technology, and Scholarship (WITS) is an interdisciplinary group of women scholars and academic professionals at the University of Illinois at Urbana-Champaign that was formed specifically to explore and address gender equity issues in information technology. The women of WITS believe that women and girls—half the world's population—should have integral roles in the conception, design, content, use, implementation, economics, and legal policies of electronic communication networks on a local, national and international level. However, the current user mix, along with a social environment which discourages female usage of electronic networks, continues to exacerbate the gender gap and has put females at a stunning disadvantage globally. Women are vastly underrepresented as designers, users, and contributors on the electronic networks. Our goal is an hospitable communication environment for ALL users.

*Recommendations*

WITS has developed several policy recommendations to share with individuals and other groups helping to shape the emerging global network. We recommend:

1. That publicly funded and supported information infrastructure projects . . .
   a. be subject to systematic mandated assessment of the degree to which gender equity is reached.
   b. be conducted by gender-balanced committees of people involved in research, education, and library communities; consumer and public interest groups; and technology and information industries.
2. That new standards based in equity be developed and applied to ensure the

creation, access to, and preservation of networked digital resources for, about, and by women.

3. That network environments be accessible and hospitable to women and girls regardless of race, ethnic background, religion, cultural background, economic status, and sexual orientation.

4. That affirmative action principles be incorporated and upheld by . . .
   a. designing training and support programs for women and girls.
   b. applying and (where necessary, reformulating) current laws to guarantee women's rights in the networked environment.
   c. fostering civic networks that offer affordable and equitable access.
   d. encouraging continued research on the gendered use of electronic networks.

In the U.S. these recommendations can be considered supported by "The National Information Infrastructure: Agenda for Action" (September 15, 1993), which states that "the NII can transform the lives of the American people—ameliorating the constraints of geography, disability, and economic status—giving all Americans a fair opportunity to go as far as their talents and ambitions will take them." The Agenda principles include the following: "Extend 'universal service' concept to ensure that information resources are available to all at affordable prices. Because information means empowerment, the government has a duty to ensure that all Americans have access to the resources of the Information Age."

We urge that organizations (i.e., strategic partners or individuals at grassroot levels who are like-minded) take every opportunity to convey these recommendations to those who are involved in making network design decisions and user policies.

In view of these concerns and our recommendations, we suggest the following guideline questions as a lens that scholars in the humanities and social sciences might use for looking at their own projects as they develop, whether they are focused on research or teaching.[40] Scholars are encouraged to get input at the planning stages from women and from men of color on their own campuses and within their disciplines as they proceed with their work.

Guidelines for Development and Use of
Computer and Internet Projects

*Development*
—To what extent are women included in all stages of project planning? Does the process allow the articulation of women's need for programs that will enhance the quality of their lives?
—Who is interested in promoting this technology or program? Whose economic interests are at stake? With what impact on women's economic interests?

—To what extent is the information technology developed in the interests of women?

—To what extent is the project based on sane operating principles: in politics, an aim for justice; in nature, an aim for harmony; in education, an aim for discovery; in use, an aim for openness; in human relations, an aim for equality?

—To what extent will the project contribute to nonoppressive development?

*Accessibility*

—To what extent will the project be inexpensive and equally available to women and men students of all ages?

—To what extent will the program be readily accessible to unemployed women, disabled women, older women, and women from all racial and ethnic groups?

—To what extent will the project foster participation to the satisfaction of all users?

—To what extent will the project include a safe atmosphere for women to work?

*Empowerment*

—To what extent does the project foster the self-reliance and independence of the women users (e.g., information easily accessed without need of an intermediary, who may be unavailable, expensive, or oppressive)?

—To what extent does the project enhance women's status (e.g., social, economic, health)?

—To what extent does the project solve or create problems for women (e.g., does it increase women's mobility, does it decrease the possibilities for online harassment)?

—To what extent does the project foster a new vocabulary that releases the discourse of expertise from the hands of the professions into the vernacular?

—To what extent does the project provide service to the individual woman versus service to the status quo system?

—To what extent does the project limit women's options as much as it opens options?

—To what extent does the project include a continuing built-in process for women's shaping the program after it has been put into use?

*Societal Relations*

—To what extent does the project broaden women's traditional options?

—To what extent does the project foster fair distribution of information resources?

—To what extent does the project distribute and decentralize communication?

—To what extent does the project encourage symmetrical gender relations, participatory politics, and democratic culture?

## CONCLUSION

In this chapter we highlight a few of the issues of Internet sexism: the replication of conversational inequities, the Internet as a site of sexual harassment and displays of power, and the ways in which distance can alienate women and strip communities of intimacy and accountability. We also suggest some practices that could lessen these problems. And finally, we offer a set of guideline questions that can be used to think about the implications of all new programs and to make clearer the place of women in the process of developing policies and practices. We suggest that everyone using state or federal funds for computer work, everyone setting business policies that affect Internet users nationally and internationally, and all who are interested in creating a more just society use these or other guidelines to keep in view concerns that are too often invisible to planners and promoters.

Re-envisioning cyberspace and making room for all will not be a simple matter. It will require the minds and voices of a wide range of people, speaking from the margins, the center, and intermediate positions. In general we ask for an examination and rejection of all the forms of domination that are being created in what is called, euphemistically, an Internet and a World Wide Web. Women must work together with men who have related concerns to form a critical mass of people who are committed to raising these issues and supporting each other in critiquing the present and planning a more equitable future rather than a technical enhancement of the past.

## NOTES

1. Joan Wallace Scott writes that "an impressive mass of evidence has been compiled to show that the Renaissance was not a renaissance for women, that technology did not lead to women's liberation either in the workplace or at home" (*Gender and the Politics of History* [New York: Columbia University Press, 1988], 19). Joan Kelly's research points out that women as a group were adversely affected by the developments of the Renaissance (*Women, History, and Theory: The Essays of Joan Kelly* [Chicago: University of Chicago Press, 1984]).

2. Feminism is a particularly useful approach to understanding technology because, as Susan Leigh Star writes, "It's not so much that women have been left out, but that we are both in and out at the same time" ("Power, Technologies and Phenomenology of Standards: On Being Allergic to Onions," in *A Sociology of Monsters?: Power, Technology, and the Modern World,* ed. John Law [Oxford, England: Basil Blackwell, 1991], 50).

3. Some of these issues are discussed in Cheris Kramarae and Jana Kramer, "Net Gains, Net Losses," *Women's Review of Books* 12:5 (February 1995): 31–33.

4. See Wendy Harcourt, ed., *Women @ Internet: Creating New Cultures in Cyberspace* (New York: St. Martin's Press, 1999), and Susan Hawthorne and Renate Klein, *CyberFeminism: Connectivity, Critique, and Creativity* (North Melbourne: Spinifex, 1999).

5. Cheris Kramarae and H. Jeanie Taylor, "Women and Men on Electronic Networks: A Conversation or a Monologue?" in *Women, Information Technology, and Scholarship,* ed. H. Jeanie Taylor, Cheris Kramarae, and Maureen Ebben (Urbana, Ill.: Center for Advanced Study, 1993), 59.

6. For example, John Perry Barlow, "A Declaration of the Independence of Cyberspace," <http://www/eff/org/pub/Censorship/Internet censorship bills/barlow 0296.declaration>.

7. Susan Herring, "The Rhetorical Dynamics of Gender Harassment On-line," *Information Society* 15 (1999): 167. (This was a special issue on the rhetorics of gender in computer-mediated communication, edited by Laura J. Gurak.)

8. Angela Gunn, "Computer Bulletin Boards Not Just Boy Toy," *New Directions for Women* 7 (November/December 1991).

9. Maureen Ebben, "Women on the Net: An Exploratory Study of Gender Dynamics on the Soc.women Computer Network" (Ph.D. diss., Department of Speech Communication, University of Illinois, 1994); Susan Herring, "Gender and Participation in Computer-Mediated Linguistic Discourse," doc. ED345552 (Washington, D.C.: ERIC Clearinghouse on Languages and Linguistics, 1992); Cynthia L. Selfe and Paul R. Meyer, "Testing Claims for On-line Conferences," *Written Communication* 8:2 (1991): 163–92; and Laurel Sutton, "Using Usenet: Gender, Power, and Silence in Electronic Discourse," in *Proceedings of the 20th Annual Meeting of the Berkeley Linguistics Society* (Berkeley: Berkeley Linguistics Society, 1994), 506–20.

10. Susan Gal, "Between Speech and Silence: Problematics of Research on Language and Gender," in *Gender at the Crossroads of Knowledge: Feminist Anthropology in the Postmodern Era,* ed. Micaela di Leonardo (Berkeley: University of California Press, 1992), 186.

11. Marilyn M. Cooper and Cynthia L. Selfe, "Computer Conferences and Learning: Authority, Resistance, and Internally Persuasive Discourse," *College English* 52:8 (December 1990): 847–69.

12. *Computer Underground Digest* 5:29 (April 21, 1993).

13. Describing the Internet as "a beautiful anarchy, just about the only one left on the face of the earth" and insisting that there was no verifiable evidence that women were excluded from the conversations there or harassed in the course of them, this participant blamed women for their critiques of the interaction on the Internet.

14. March 29, 1993, Communet: Community and Civic Network Discussion List, COMMUNET@UVMVM.bitnet.

15. Michael Heim wrote, "A loss of innocence therefore accompanies an expanding network. As on-line culture grows geographically, the sense of community diminishes" ("The Erotic Ontology of Cyberspace," in *Cyberspace: First Steps,* ed. Michael Benedikt [Cambridge, Mass.: MIT Press, 1991], 77).

16. Tuesday, March 9, 1993. *greg-madden@unc.edu,* posted to ARACHNET, ARACHNET@uottawa.bitnet.

17. Michelle Zackheim, "The Café Series," *Frontiers: A Journal of Women's Studies* 8:1 (1992): editorial page.

18. Judy Smith and Ellen Balka, "Chatting on a Feminist Computer Network," in *Tech-*

*nology and Women's Voices,* ed. Cheris Kramarae (New York: Routledge & Kegan Paul/ Methuen, 1988), 88.

19. Judith Hudson and Kathleen Turek, "Electronic Access to Research on Women: A Short Guide" (Albany, N.Y.: Institute for Research on Women, 1992, 1995).

20. *Utne Reader Internet Email Salons,* utnereader@mr.net.

21. Evan Brown, "On Line in the Big Sky," *Missoula Independent,* November 14, 1991, 10.

22. Richard Adler, *Seniornet: Toward a National Community of Computer-Using Seniors,* Forum Report #5, Aspen Institute Project on Enhancing the Social Benefits of New Electronic Technologies (New York: Aspen Institute, 1988).

23. Leslie Kanes Weisman, *Discrimination by Design: A Feminist Critique of the Man-made Environment* (Urbana: University of Illinois Press, 1992).

24. See Ronnie Rosenberg's critique of many computer literacy education programs and suggestions for improvement, "Debunking Computer Literacy," *Technology Review* 94:1 (1991): 58–65.

25. Herring, "Rhetorical Dynamics," 156.

26. Kimberly Dawn Blum, "Gender Differences in CMC-Based Distance Education," <http://www.feminista.com/v2n5/blum2.html>.

27. We are encouraged by the universities, individual newsgroups, and other institutional interfaces that are finally including discussion of online sexual harassment in their institutional sexual harassment policies or codes. However, we are saddened by the often horrific experiences of many women experiencing harassment who have been unsuccessful in convincing list owners and institutional authorities that there are real problems of import to the entire electronic community.

28. See Parks and Roberts's study, which indicates that although many people have taken advantage of the Internet online communities such as multiuser object-oriented systems (MOOS) to try some gender switching, most people participating in the MOOS hadn't tried it and those who had didn't do it for long. Lynne D. Roberts and Malcolm R. Parks, "The Social Geography of Gender-Switching in Virtual Environments on the Internet," *Information, Communication, and Society* 2:4 (Winter 1999): 521–40.

29. Shannon McRae, "Coming Apart at the Seams: Sex, Text, and the Virtual Body," in *Wired Women: Gender and New Realities in Cyberspace,* ed. Lynne Cherry and Elizabeth Reba Weise (Seattle: Seal Press, 1996), 242–63.

30. We can learn a lot about these problems by considering the responses when electronic sexual harassment and rape are reported to electronic communities. For one early account that did receive attention in print media as well as electronic media, see Julian Dibbel, "A Rape in Cyberspace; or, How an Evil Clown, a Haitian Trickster Spirit, Two Wizards, and a Cast of Dozens Turned a Database into a Society," *Village Voice* 38:51 (December 21, 1993): 36–42.

31. Putting together this group, particularly finding women in the sciences and engineering who were interested in and able to participate, was a challenge. In the course of our search for members we discovered barriers to communication as we discussed the problems and their significance for women from different disciplines. We appreciate the efforts of neuropsychologist Marie Banich, who served as a bridge for us, pointing out to all "sides" the misunderstandings that were occurring in our first conversations.

32. In an electronic discussion about the WITS group, one WITS member said, "Something I love about WITS . . . is the sense of acceptance and safety in the group, at the same time we're intellectually challenging and informing each other. In other words—the feminists/womanist qualities of the group!"

33. See Taylor et al., *Women, Information Technology, and Scholarship*.

34. The various ethics committees that have formed to deal with some of the problems of interaction on the Internet need to rethink the basic divisions used in discussing "ethics," which, in the past, has meant primarily considering the good and evil categories of patriarchy. See definitions in Cheris Kramarae and Paula A. Treichler, with Ann Russo, *Amazons, Bluestockings, and Crones: A Feminist Dictionary* (San Francisco: Harper San Francisco, 1992).

35. At the University of Illinois at Urbana-Champaign, the College of Engineering adopted the following sexual harassment statement for posting in its public computer laboratories: "Sexual harassment is any statement that a reasonable person would find offensive, humiliating, or an interference with his or her required tasks or career opportunities at the University. When sexual harassment is found to have occurred, the University will vigorously pursue disciplinary action." Users of these terminals should be aware of the public nature of shared facilities and take care not to display images or play sounds that could create an atmosphere of harassment for others. Similar considerations apply to electronic mail exchanges. "Anyone who finds a particular sexually-oriented image or sound to be interfering with his or her required tasks can notify the site operator (who will remind the person displaying the material of the sexual harassment policy). If the person persists, contact the Assistant Dean for Sexual Harassment."

36. Here we use mainstream terminology. Actually, the language of individual "control" and "rights" should alert us to the problems we will have in conceptualizing and using communal networks. For discussion of the limitations of control, see Irene Diamond, *Fertile Ground: Women, the Earth, and the Limits of Control* (Boston: Beacon Press, 1994).

37. Globally, the number of Internet users is projected to reach 502 million by 2003. See "Internet Users Now Exceed 100 Million," report of article in the *New York Times,* November 12, 1999, in *Edupage,* November 12, 1999, at EDUCAUSE@EDUCAUSE.EDU.

38. Earthtrust, an organization concerned with international wildlife protection and environmental problems, has made extensive use of electronic mail to connect volunteers and organization offices.

39. For information on what is increasingly called the digital divide, see the bibliographies and reports in "Current Native American Technology and Telecommunications Projects" (1994 to present), <http://www.benton.org/Library/Native>, and National Telecommunications and Information Association (1999), "Americans in the Information Age Falling through the Net," <http://www.ntia.doc.gov/ntiahome/digitaldivide/index.html>. Gender issues are seldom included in these reports and surveys, so we focus on them here.

40. These guidelines are an expansion of those developed by Maureen Ebben for a WITS colloquium session.

# 8 / Electronic Networks for International Research Collaboration: Implications for Intellectual Property Protection in the Early Twenty-First Century

And that kind of exclusive ownership cuts directly against the grain of the technology in question. From the start, computers were seen as tools of collaboration, designed to facilitate brainstorming and data sharing

—Henry Jenkins, Technology Review (March/April 2000)

## INTRODUCTION

In the early twenty-first century, the convergence of digital computing and telecommunications is opening unprecedented opportunities for international research and education collaboration, sharing of data and information worldwide, and accelerated scientific and technological progress. Yet some scholars argue that overly expansive intellectual property rights that deny future creators and potential collaborators the raw material they need could limit the ability of the scientific, technical, and educational communities to capitalize on such opportunities.

Some were prescient about shared knowledge in the network environment becoming embroiled in issues of intellectual property protection at the beginning of the 1990s. New electronic network technology already had potential to transform international research collaboration, and a legal regime was evolving for extension of intellectual property protection to the activities of network users. Furthermore, internationalization of research had spurred interest in intellectual property as a set of ground rules for distribution of rights in international research transactions. Digitization of information and growth of research networking had accelerated this trend and raised additional issues for science and technology communities in intellectual property protection. The question was raised, "How should the intellectual products of international research collaborations in the network environment be protected in the interests of scientific and technological progress?"

Electronic networks already meant more than remote online access to large databases on mainframe computers. Distributed networks had already begun to lead to electronic equivalents for scientific publishing and to faster, less formal means of communicating intellectual advances. The result was an increasingly broad spectrum of scientific communication, ranging from informal electronic messaging to complex software environments for visualization technology in large-scale simulations. At the same time, the greatly expanded scope and connectivity of networks began to erode the barriers of time and distance for research collaboration on a global scale. James J. Duderstadt, president of the University of Michigan, envisioned "research collaboratories" as advanced, distributed research environments that would use multimedia information technology to relax the constraints of distance, time, and even reality on research collaboration.[1]

However, there were growing tensions between collaborative practices electronic networks facilitated and traditional notions of individual property rights in intellectual production: In the informal and often unpredictable intellectual collaborations of networks, authorship often was unrecorded—not to say uncompensated. Electronic technology was playing a crucial role in promoting practices in which individual contributions to dynamic intellectual products were deemphasized and effectively merged. The potential of these networks emphasized iterative intellectual practices in which more than one person contributed cumulatively over time, collaboration between two or more people across nations, and sharing of collections of information and data on a global scale.

The battle shaping up over the future of electronic networks was, on one side, between those who saw its potential for new creativity and productivity in international collaborative endeavors as a threat to individual proprietorship in information and who saw vigorous application and extension of traditional intellectual property protection to the network environment as the solution. On the other side were those who argued that the network environment might become a new intellectual commons that excessive legal control could stifle. What appeared to be needed were rules to protect intellectual products that featured collaboration and, in general, were more closely aligned with the characteristics of contemporary intellectual production in the network environment.

Today, the still primitive applications of the early 1990s—the communication networks and information services such as Internet, Bitnet, and Com-

puServe, the more sophisticated hypertext applications that were just beginning to be developed—are widely available globally.

Internet technologies are having a dramatic impact on research activities,
including the creation of entirely new forms of research. The development
of networking tools and Web servers stimulated the field of bioinformatics—
the use of computers to analyze genes and proteins—to take off and become
a key element of basic scientific research and new drug development.

Science journals have gone online, and hyperlinks replace old-fashioned
footnotes.[2] Global digital libraries enable researchers anywhere in the world
with a computer and a modem to tap into the entire database of the Library
of Congress, the Bibliothèque de France, or the British Library.

Today, there is a move toward collaboratively constructing knowledge using distributed workgroups supported by an electronic communication infrastructure. The exponential growth of knowledge has made it almost impossible for any organization to exist in isolation. Powerful computers and networks
deliver educational services to anyone at any place and any time, no longer
confining education to the campus or the academic schedule. Recently, almost
thirty countries agreed to create a distributed global biodiversity information
facility to link local digital databases that embrace the full range of biodiversity information including geographic, ecological, genetic, and molecular data.[3]

Today, the early 1990s battle over legal control of intellectual products in
the network environment rages as full-fledged warfare. Few other issues before the 106th Congress generated so much lobbying as the question of whether digital databases—collections of facts such as telephone directories, weather
reports, stock tables, and real estate listings—could be copied, repackaged, and
distributed by anyone with an Internet connection.[4]

The House Judiciary Committee had approved a bill that would establish
criminal penalties for the unauthorized use of material in databases. Opponents said the bill would allow companies with databases to control access
to public domain facts. The question of database piracy is one instance in
which Internet technology has outstripped traditional intellectual property
laws, proponents said. Before there was an Internet, the issue was pretty well
settled by copyright law. In March 1991, the US Supreme Court ruled in *Feist
Publications, Inc. v. Rural Telephone Service* that the telephone white pages
could not be copyrighted because the compilation did not involve selection
and coordination; one could use the list without permission.[5]

Today, the ease with which information on the Internet can be retrieved
and the size of the investments and potential profits blur the line between
what is protected and what is not. Companies and interest groups have cho-

sen sides on whether to adjust the level of protection upward depending on whether they primarily collect data that is put on the Internet (the stock exchanges, real estate brokers, Lexis-Nexis, eBay, American Medical Association) or use the data compiled by someone else (the Chamber of Commerce, Consumers Union, Yahoo, Schwab, research librarians).

Undoubtedly, legal scholars say, publishers will see suboptimal profits from the production of databases if Congress fails to protect them against certain forms of piracy. However, if Congress combats this risk of market failure by enforcing strong monopolies in collections of data, such an approach may end up "balkanizing the information economy by recreating the medieval economic quandary in which products could not flow across countries or continents because too many feudal monopolists demanded payments every few miles down the road."[6]

This chapter considers the implications of broad and strong traditional intellectual property protection and raises broad protection issues that emphasize alternatives to vigorous extension of traditional principles in the network environment.

The basic argument is that if taking full advantage of the potential of the network environment for collaborative research, cumulative innovation, and scientific and technological progress is the objective, intellectual property protection laws and the courts ought to be careful not to grant protection that is too broad in scope. The actual or potential harmful effects of protection can be mitigated if the law pays close attention to the extent of the author's or inventor's efforts and what they actually achieved, and to the broad nature of what was already known and in the public domain, and restricts scope accordingly. Intellectual property systems should promote liberal licensing to allow multiple players to follow initial inventors and authors and promote transformative or fair use defenses to give value-adding advances a chance over plaintiffs' intellectual products in infringement litigation.

The framework for this chapter is based on the astute analysis of theory and historical development of intellectual property rights by legal scholar Peter Jaszi in his insightful articles on authorship or romantic creativity.[7] As he and others point out, this vision of romantic creativity expands our common-sense traditional intellectual property law and doctrines in the direction of greater protection.[8] The chapter also draws on evidence that in many cases, granting broad-scope protection stifles cumulative improvements in technology and that where advance has been rapid there always has been rivalry.

## RATIONALE OF TRADITIONAL INTELLECTUAL PROPERTY PROTECTION

What do we know about current intellectual property systems that might help modernize these principles to conform to contemporary intellectual production in the network environment? Traditional theory of intellectual property protection is informed by a commonly perceived, seemingly basic contradiction of purpose that protection aims to promote access to works of authorship but confers on authors power to restrict or deny access to their works.

The rationale, stated simply, is that without protection, the social benefits of research advance often exceed the private rewards; the intellectual property system is designed to narrow the difference through monopoly grants to authors and inventors. Although new inventions contribute enormously to social welfare, the creators and developers may not gain enough to cover their costs and compensate their risk if rival firms, that have not borne the costs of development, can rapidly copy the technology. In this event, fewer inventions might occur in competitive markets. Thus, monopoly pricing of new inventions for a limited term preserves incentives for firms to supply a continuing stream of new inventions on the market.

Traditional analysis of intellectual property helps us to pigeonhole many of the overt controversies in intellectual property traceable to the basic tension between public benefits and private reward to authors and inventors to achieve those benefits. However, it does not go far enough to explain many of the conceptual challenges faced by traditional intellectual property law in a time of rapid change in modes of intellectual production.

## MYTHOLOGY OF TRADITIONAL PROTECTION

### The Early 1990s

By the early 1990s, much more reflective analysis of traditional intellectual property concepts began to argue that only demythologizing traditional doctrine would make room for protection of contemporary intellectual practices. These critiques of intellectual property doctrine emphasized that traditional concepts had historical basis in individual authorship as a privileged category of intellectual activity that generated intellectual products of special social value and entitled practitioners (authors or inventors) to unique rewards and privileges.

For specially privileged and gifted authors, all benefits from intellectual advances—some of which might have become available to competitors in the marketplace—were included in private rewards in the prices authors charged buyers for intellectual products. However, the reward system based on the author as an individual solely responsible for original work tends to mislead when applied to iterative, collaborative, and other kinds of multiauthor intellectual practices. Prices for their intellectual properties charged by authors may be too high because individual orchestration may not be the best production process for those intellectual products.

## Expansion of Traditional Intellectual Property during the 1990s

Despite these admonitions, the strengthening and broadening of traditional intellectual property rights during the 1990s was remarkable. When Stanley Cohen and Herbert Boyer invented the gene-splicing technique in 1973, they resisted the suggestion of the Stanford University patent officer to patent. "My initial reaction . . . was to question whether basic research of this type could or should be patented and to point out that our work had been dependent on a number of earlier discoveries by others," Cohen explained.[9] The cumulative nature of scientific knowledge meant that even the most outstanding discovery was heavily dependent on the work of many others, and to patent a discovery would be to lay claim to the freely given intellectual property of others.

In 1980, however, patents became a primary legal instrument for research discoveries financed by the public sector and performed by U.S. universities. By 1997, the number of university patents issued had already doubled the early 1990s number, reaching more than 2,400 patents.[10] The increase far exceeded the rate of growth of total U.S. patenting.

The Cohen-Boyer patent is nonexclusively licensed to all takers at a low fee. But exclusive licenses on universities' broad basic patents may deter and complicate follow-on research. Research tools such as the Harvard mouse may lead to blockages on downstream research and commercial product development as upstream owners set up tollbooths that increase costs and inefficiencies for follow-on innovators.[11]

Authorship was involved in rationalizing the extension of copyright protection to computer software in 1980.[12] Copyright in a work protects only expression, leaving the idea free for reuse; the problem is that the distinction between idea and expression proves difficult to articulate in practice. The question of where and how to draw the line was at the center of debate over the proper scope of copyright protection for computer software, much of it revolving around the 1986 decision in *Whelan Associates. v. Jaslow Dental Laboratory.*[13] The *Whelan* court relied on decisions finding the infringement of one audiovisual work by another, where the two displayed the same total look and feel.

The court assumed that intellectual production of software was similar enough to audiovisual works that software authors should have the same control over subsequent adoptions as audiovisual authors. However, software seems more an intellectual product that results from successive elaborations of an idea over time and less a discrete intellectual product in which a broad scope of protection is not a serious hindrance to elaborations by future authors. Advancing software technology often entailed the ability to use a number of already developed components and hence either the ability to negotiate a license or an environment where litigation was not a serious threat.

A decade ago, the field of software functioned without patents. Early on, the courts, as in a 1972 Supreme Court ruling, compared software's logical steps to "mental processes" that not only could not be patented but had to be preserved in the public domain as the "basic tools of scientific and technological work." Over time, though, this position eroded. By the end of 2000, the Patent Office had granted almost 100,000 software patents.[14] The 1998 Federal Circuit ruling in *State Street Bank & Trust Co. v. Signature Financial Group Inc.* endorsed software patentability without qualification.[15]

This strengthening of intellectual property rights was especially prominent in the United States. But through 1994 negotiations regarding GATT, the Agreement on Trade-Related Aspects of Intellectual Property Rights (TRIPS Agreement), the United States was pushing on other countries its beliefs about strong, broad intellectual property protection.[16] Other countries were going along, not always simply as a reaction to the pressure but also because of an honest belief on the part of many parties that in the long run strong intellectual property protection would promote scientific and technological progress.

In reaction to *Feist*, the U.S. Supreme Court ruling that copyright protection did not extend to databases that did not involve some "creative" selection and organization of data, the European Union in March 1996 enacted a database directive that granted special rights to the owner of a database, even if the database did not meet the standards of copyright protection under the directive.[17]

Europe and the United States sponsored initiatives in the international forums of the World Intellectual Property Organization (WIPO) also calling for creation of a new form of legal protection for the contents of data-bases aimed to protect database owners against unauthorized extractions, uses, and reuses of the whole or substantial parts of its contents.[18] The draft law never reached the conference's floor; it was deferred by the hostility of other national delegations and the vocal opposition of U.S. scientific orga-nizations.

Whether the U.S. Congress should give databases greater legal protection became a controversial issue.

## The Late Twentieth Century

The potentially enormous negative impacts of traditional intellectual prop-erty law and, in particular, the image of the romantic author on property rights in research collaborations and cumulative improvements on original works did not go unnoticed as the decade unfolded. *Shamans, Software, and Spleens: Law and the Construction of the Information Society,* the widely re-garded 1996 work by James Boyle, said that "we are driven to confer proper-ty rights in information on those who come closest to the image of the ro-mantic author, those whose contributions to information production are most easily seen as original and transformative."[19] He argued that this had negative consequences; it led to having too many intellectual property rights, conferring them on the wrong people, and undervaluing the interests of both the sources of and the audiences for the information commodified.

In an analysis parallel to authorship inquiries, Roberto Mazzoleni and Richard R. Nelson thoughtfully reviewed alternative theories about the func-tions of patents and their underlying assumptions.[20] Traditional patent the-ory fits a discrete model of technical advance. The basic invention may be amenable to tailoring for different uses or customers; however, the invention does not point the way to wide-ranging subsequent technical advances.

However, this characterization is inappropriate when technical advances are cumulative in that today's advance lays the basis for tomorrow's. In such chains of invention, the ability to operate the most advanced version is based on the ability to do things that were the subject of earlier inventions.

Unless licensed easily and widely, such patents tend to limit the range of potential users who have access to all components of the technology. Also, there is no reason to assume that when blockages arise industries will always turn to the deadlock-breaking solutions, patent pooling, and cross-licensing.

What follows briefly surveys cumulative intellectual products, multiauthor collaborations, and digital collections of information and data in networks for the effects of across-the-board strengthening of intellectual property rights and provides suggestions for intellectual property rules alternative to those of traditional, authorial protection.

## PROTECTION FOR CUMULATIVE INTELLECTUAL PRODUCTS

### Protection for Internet-Based Bioinformatic Research Tools

Intellectual production that is the basis for traditional copyright protection focused on incentives for creating discrete intellectual products; it neglected to consider whether different incentives might be needed to advance intellectual production of the more cumulative kind that has come to typify intellectual software production.

Today, bioinformaticians churn out software tools to find genes and other significant features in DNA sequences and to compare DNA, RNA, and protein sequences.[21] The explosion has been triggered not only by the supply of data spewing from the genome projects but also by demand from biologists with Internet access. More than 500 different bioinformatics tools are available over the Internet, and their number is growing constantly as software developers working in the life sciences update and produce useful new applications.[22]

Many of the new data-mining research tools are cumulative improvements over techniques in machine learning and artificial intelligence. The hottest research tool, known as hidden Markov models, springs directly from statistics and linguistics. But granting broad protection to statistical software programs may preclude development of future data-mining algorithms without engaging in infringement or making sometimes complex licensing arrangements with owners.[23]

The issues of patent protection of computer algorithms useful in bioinformatics applications are fast developing alongside copyright issues. Although most of the attention regarding the 1998 *State Street* decision (in which Federal Circuit once again confirmed the qualification of such computer programs as patentable subject matter) has revolved around e-commerce business methods, implications for bioinformatics are equally striking. Several categories of bioinformatics-related software applications came to the center stage as subject matter for which patent protection appeared feasible: the database architecture for genetic information; algorithms specially designed to search, manipulate, and manage data meaningfully; and user-friendly interfaces to facilitate information requests and provide readily understandable results.

Such patent positions cause concern because bioinformatics-related soft-

ware applications may be viewed as upstream research tools on which owners may stack tollbooths on the road to subsequent downstream research and
commercial product development. The problem is likely to become increasingly serious in computer software, legal scholars say, where the practical limit
on claim breadth seems to be only the imagination of the claim drafter.[24] An
example is a recent patent claiming the use of computer-implemented artificial neural networks for identifying binding motifs of polypeptides; the patent
is based on one example of the technique.[25] When the U.S. Supreme Court
last explored this issue in 1966 in *Brenner v. Manson,* it rejected a broad claim.
Such a patent, the Court said, may confer power to block off whole areas of
scientific development without compensating the public.

In dealing with this issue, legal scholars say, it is crucial to balance incentives
to initial innovators against incentives to follow-on innovators. Experience
suggests that this balance is weighted too much in favor of the initial innovator, and the utility doctrine, for example, which was at issue in *Brenner v. Manson,* should be used to restrict the patenting of very fundamental concepts.[26]

Fortunately, the general trend appears to be toward liberal licensing of
these research tools. For example, eBioinformatics, Inc. enables researchers
worldwide to take advantage of bioinformatics software applications over the
Internet, using a pay-as-you-go access model. Also, the evolution of patent
protection may reflect that related to other database browsers: The dynamics between Netscape and Microsoft, involving methods of viewing Internet
materials, or between Lexis-Nexis and the West Group involving ways of
accessing legal databases, may provide useful paradigms for development in
the bioinformatics arena.

## Transformative or Fair Use Defenses in the Network Environment

Fair use analysis also mitigates the problem in cumulative improvements
caused by broad protection. The doctrine was created in the 1840s in *Folsom
v. March.*[27] Transformation of the taken material was necessary to make it fair
use, the Court found, and this is the basis for the rule that a fair use must be
a transformative use. Copyright would protect the first author against thieves
but not against those whose investment of their borrowings from the initial
source produced a higher net yield.

The unanimous 1994 Supreme Court decision in *Campbell v. Acuff-Rose
Music Inc.* held that a derivative work's purpose and character should be judged
primarily by whether and to what extent it is transformative, that is, the extent to which the derivative work adds something new, with a further purpose
or different character, that alters the preexisting work with new expression,

meaning, or message.[28] Viewed in this light, a defendant's use of the intellectual product will constitute infringement or free riding on plaintiff's efforts only when the defendant's use of the information is not transformative.[29]

Although fair use analysis applies specifically to copyright protection, patent law limits infringement through a parallel inquiry: The Supreme Court long ago ruled that if a defendant so transformed a device that the claims of the patent, literally construed, ceased to represent her invention, she is not an infringer on "reverse equivalents" grounds.[30] Once a court completes assessment of the protected product, it would consider the advance in the accused product. Analysis along these lines might have reduced the blocking effect of patents in certain fields.

However, legal scholars say that fair or transformative use provisions can be undermined in the network environment if applications such as digital libraries—which promote sharing information—require users to authenticate themselves and then track and regulate what the users do with the information.[31] Fair use defenses have been deliberately constructed as gray areas of the law so that the legality of an act may depend on multiple factors that judges will weigh together if litigation occurs. The public interest in copyright law does not go away just because the work is in digital form.

But when the rock band Metallica filed suit against Napster Inc., whose popular MP3-sharing software lets users exchange music files over the Internet, Napster sought refuge from charges of copyright violations under the Digital Millennium Copyright Act (DMCA).[32] The DMCA says Internet service providers (ISPs) are not liable for piracy committed by users on their services.[33] Some called for an amendment to the act that would crack down on emerging Internet technologies such as Napster.[34] They held that services such as Napster should be forced to gather identifiable user data such as addresses and should be required to block users who violate the law.

Others were convinced that Napster is lawful to begin with and, more importantly, that any efforts to shut it down would prove futile. Napster will be replaced by a host of decentralized Internet-mounted software technologies or networks. These perform Napster-like functions without needing a Web-based hub site. They offer no easy target for a suit because there is no Web site to shut down.

But what about the larger question? Companies already offer digital technologies that can supply "wraps," in which copyrighted music or movie or video files can be sealed at the behest of their copyright holders. Because they can continue to wrap the copyrighted files even after payment has been made, they can limit the number of times the consumer can open the file, they can dictate the brands or genres of machine or computer that will be permitted to play the work, and they can limit or bar the consumer from copying the work, either in whole or in part.[35]

Armed with this sort of unprecedented technological control over their works, authors and publishers will no longer need to permit consumers to use their works in ways that, until now, consumers have taken for granted and copyright law has declined to protect, deeming them legitimate, noninfringing fair uses of copyrighted material.

The DVD case pitted the movie industry against Internet journalist Eric Corley, who posted a descrambling code, called DeCSS (descramble content scrambling system) on his Web site, 2600.com, the self-proclaimed "hacker journal." DeCSS descrambles the encryption system used by the film industry to keep people from making copies of DVD movies.[36] The prosecution argued that DeCSS violates the DMCA, which prohibits the circumvention of technologies used to protect copyrighted materials. The defense insisted that DeCSS, which was written as part of an open-source project to allow the Linux operating system to play DVDs, merely provides consumers with the rights to fair use (such as taping a CD so that you can play it in your car) they have traditionally enjoyed.

The movie industry won; the U.S. District Court ordered a permanent injunction against the hacker Web site.[37] The Court's comments made a thoughtful contribution to the debate over these issues. However, that debate may no longer be about the role of government after the digital revolution has rendered intellectual property rights unenforceable. Rather, it may be about the role of government now that the digital revolution threatens to render intellectual property rights absolute.

Digital library builders clearly will need to keep track of emerging legal issues likely to affect their libraries of digital works and take some responsibility for how these issues are resolved. But laws vary from country to country; "international copyright," in the sense of a uniform law binding all nation states, does not exist. Rather, at present we have a system of interlocking national copyrights, woven together by the principle of national treatment.[38] Some legal scholars ask whether this would require reengineering of certain parts of the information infrastructure to zone cyberspace to conform to national boundaries so that national policies can be preserved in cyberspace.

Also involving claims of fair use, raising questions of originality and of whether pointing to another's work can be a work in itself, hyperlinking and related suits involving "unauthorized" use of Web sites have proven legally complex.[39] Legal problems are sure to arise for scholars as scientific authors increasingly cite references by hyperlinking "without permission" to other Web sites.[40]

Online auction company eBay worried that another company would take its listing for, say, a set of Wedgwood china and the listings on all the other auction sites for a set of the same china and provide a new list for comparative shoppers. eBay said that the prices and availability of its items change minute by minute. The competing Web site could have misinformation. For these reasons, eBay sued a company called Bidder's Edge, and a U.S. District Court issued a preliminary injunction preventing Bidder's Edge from using eBay's data.[41]

Some legal scholars were concerned that the ruling could affect hyperlinking and more generally the free flow of information over the Internet.[42] It might mean that everybody has a right to pick and choose who comes to their Web site and for what purposes. More troubling, the decision may make the whole concept of search engines tenuous. Under one interpretation of the Court's ruling, anyone who is not authorized to come to a site could be deemed a trespasser after the fact. Thus, anyone who wants to block access to a search engine can do so or can give preferential treatment to a search engine.

### Licensing Digital Works

A fair use defense did not work in the seminal ruling in which a New York district court ruled against MP3.com's personalized service in response to a recording industry copyright violation suit.[43] "The complex marvels of cyberspatial communication may create difficult legal issues," the judge said, "but not in this case."[44] My.MP3.com subscribers can pop a physical CD into their disc drives and have digital copies instantly appear in their music collections. MP3.com gets the digital copy from its database of 80,000 predigitized CDs, many of which belong to the major music labels. The record companies alleged that copying and distributing their CDs was unlawful.

The Court disagreed with MP3.com's contention that copying the CDs from its database is permissible under the fair use doctrine. The Court also dismissed MP3.com's claim that giving the consumer a digital version of a CD was simply a "functional equivalent" of storing user CDs for members.

Soon afterward, Warner Music Group and BMG, two Big Five labels, settled their copyright infringement claims against MP3.com.[45] They issued the music download site a license to use their copyrights for its My.MP3.com service, which requires MP3.com to pay the labels each time a copyrighted song is uploaded to the system and each time a song is streamed. The deal sets a dramatic precedent for the future of music and other digital works. MP3.com said license fees would be recouped through advertising and additional CD sales rather than through a subscription fee to users.

Although some prominent music acts such as Metallica and Dr. Dre sided with the labels against the free download site, rock star and actress Courtney Love said, "Stealing an artist's music without paying for it is absolute piracy. And I'm talking about major-label recording contracts, not Napster." Love is among the musicians raising the revolutionary notion that the Internet may offer them a better shake than the labels, which they accuse of imposing burdensome contracts.[46]

Scientists are also proposing that current practices by publishers holding copyright and in some cases limiting other distribution of journal articles be reexamined. They believe that scientific authors—especially of works based on government-supported research—should give prospective publishers a nonexclusive license to use their work in a value-added publication in traditional or electronic form. But the author should retain the right to distribute informally, such as through a Web server for direct interaction with peers. In many instances, they say, publishers enforce tighter controls over Internet copyright, dissemination, and pricing than exist in the traditional print world, and this conflicts with the new environment for communicating about science.[47]

## COLLABORATIVE WORKERS

### Intellectual Workers

THE IDEOLOGY OF AUTHORSHIP    Early eighteenth-century British laws that first identified authors as bearers of portable legal rights in intellectual productions were never intended to benefit working authors. Authorship was used as a maneuver to justify alienating the rights of intellectual workers to their productions and entitling publishers to benefit from commercial exploitation of these products.

Before 1710, authors typically sold their manuscripts for lump sum payments; afterwards authors parted with rights in their works on the same basis or (with increasing frequency) exchanged those rights for a promise of royalties at contractually fixed rates. Authorship continues to be deployed to support a regime that disassociates intellectual workers from a legal interest in their productions: the work-for-hire doctrine. This rule awards ownership of works produced within the scope of employment to the employer.[48]

The Supreme Court's 1989 pronouncement on the subject, *Community for Creative NonViolence v. Reid* makes the point that in work-for-hire cases, the crucial inquiry is into the hiring party's "control over the manner and means" by which the intellectual product is accomplished.[49] In this decision,

the Court identified circumstances supporting the conclusion that the commissioned artist was the author of his own sculpture. However, the outcome
should only emphasize that the convention is one that often deprives intellectual workers of authorship.

Courts also continue to marginalize works executed by mere "hired arti-
sans," thus undercutting the claims of these intellectual products to legitimacy as independent products of authorship. The "true" artist is one who
had escaped "division of labor" and united reason and imagination in a har-
monious alliance that represents the whole person. An example of this tendency is provided by the 1992 court decision in *Rogers v. Koons.*[50]

Before comparing the substantial similarity of the two works in question
to determine infringement, the Court compared the differences in working
methods of the two artists: Rogers was a complete artist who has a studio
where he makes his living in creating, publishing, and otherwise making use
of his rights in his photographic work. Koons's production of intellectual
works was characterized by extreme division of labor: Certain European studios execute his porcelain works, other studios make his mirror pieces, and
a small studio in Italy carves the wood sculptures. In effect, the case for infringement was strengthened by an emphasis on the difference in working
methods of the people who created the intellectual products.

## FACULTY INTELLECTUAL PROPERTY RIGHTS TO ONLINE COURSES

Traditionally, there was no discussion between faculty and universities of intellectual property protection of teaching because teaching traditionally was
nonreplicable: It could not extend itself outside what might be called the single performance.

Today, because of the rapid growth of Web-based distance education programs, these rights are becoming a hot issue, and institutions have been working to spell out who owns and controls the materials that appear online.[51]
Some universities are sharing the spoils of ownership with faculty members—
as an incentive for them to create online courses—and others are not.

If software is viewed as traditional scholarly publishing, then professors
own the work.[52] However, the university has ownership claims if the program
is seen as an invention, or a work for hire. Copyright laws hold that an employer owns a creative work that falls within the bounds of the worker's
employment, such as a program that helps a professor grade papers, legal
experts say. In addition, universities could claim ownership if a professor
creates the software as an assigned project or uses university resources, including grants awarded by the school.

No clear blueprint has yet emerged. Some faculty unions are beginning to look to other fields, such as the movie and recording industry, for ideas. The unions in the entertainment industry have been fighting for the rights to be paid for repeated performances for years, and they are trying to learn how they can work with that. In such an approach, a faculty member would own the rights to online instructional materials and could sell access to various online colleges. In fact, the day when professors make deals as rock stars and athletes do may not be far off.

But many professors are not comfortable with a world of free-agent academics. One of the dangers they see in modeling contracts and agreements off other industries is the insensitivity to the kind of language used in higher education. The word *employee* is not a popular term for a university professor. "I would really like to think that I'm a scholar or an educator," some faculty say. Institutions that are keeping their hands on potential royalties acknowledge that the ownership guidelines may have deterred some potential online instructors and that unions probably will raise the issue at future contract talks. It will become more contentious as time passes, many conclude.

## Multiauthor Collaboration

DISAGGREGATING MULTIAUTHOR COLLABORATION    Traditional protection fails with the most obvious form of multiauthor creativity: intellectual collaborations. Although copyright law has a category for works created by several authors working together on a preconcerted basis, the consequences that flow from the categorization as a work as one of joint authorship reflect the individualistic bias of traditional protection. In effect, a joint work has several individual authors. Each joint author must possess and should retain the legal prerogatives associated with individual authorship. Far from acknowledging the extent to which participation in a collaboration entails surrender of individual prerogative, law assumes the continued dominance of individual authorship.

Also, in many instances law refuses to acknowledge existence of joint authorship. The 1976 Copyright Act substantially narrowed the range of circumstances in which what might be called a collaboration in the lay sense is recognized as a joint work in the legal sense. Before 1976, courts held that joint authorship need not be the result of face-to-face collaboration, as when lyrics are added to an existing tune. By contrast, the 1976 Copyright Act defines joint authorship so as to require the intention at the time of the writing is done that the parts be combined into an integrated whole.

Temporality aside, the requirement for joint works that the contributions be intended to be merged into inseparable or interdependent parts of the whole is restrictive, although it is not new. The insistence of the law on disaggregating collaborations rather than protecting them as joint works is apparent in recent decisions concerning whether the contribution of each joint author must be protectable, copyrightable work.

Most courts have answered in the affirmative, as revealed in the 1990 decision *Childress v. Taylor*.[53] Childress, a stage performer, conceived of the idea of a play based on the life of Moms Mabley, a legendary black entertainer. After assembling extensive documentation on Mabley's life, she persuaded Taylor to prepare a script incorporating her ideas and research.

Childress allegedly misappropriated the contents of the script for her own play, and Taylor brought suit. The Court ruled for Taylor as "sole author" of the contested work on grounds that Childress's ideas and research did not represent a copyrightable contribution to the disputed work. In 1991, the Court of Appeals revisited *Childress v. Taylor* and conceded that copyright policy does not dictate a clear answer to whether each contribution to a joint work must be copyrightable. It is difficult to see why the contributions of all joint authors need be copyrightable. An individual creates a copyrightable form of expression; the resulting work is no less a valuable result of the creative process simply because the idea and the expression came from two different people.

The Court of Appeals came as close as anything in law to acknowledging the complexities of collaboration and the reimagination of collaboration by individualistic assumptions of authorship. However, rather than confronting the reality of prevailing practice and revising protection to take account of collaborative production, the Court retrenched into insisting on copyrightable contributions for all "joint" authors.

In the wake of the 1997 *Thomson v. Larson* decision and the Second Circuit Court of Appeals' affirmation of that decision, which denied dramaturg Lynn Thomson's claim to joint authorship status with playwright Jonathan Larson and her request for an interest in the royalties, questions about the *Childress* test for joint authorship were being raised.[54] One conclusion was that the provisions of the Copyright Act concerning joint authorship should be read broadly enough to support and promote collaboration between artists. To deny an artist protection under the act by not examining a collaboration from all angles, including how the collaborators work together, is to risk denying an artist an economic incentive to continue to collaborate.[55]

COAUTHORSHIP IN BIOLOGY    Today, joint authorship tensions arising between researchers who devote themselves to sequencing genomes and those who interpret their results are creating a demand for new approaches to collaboration and coauthorship in biology.[56] It has become a well-established tradition among the publicly funded genome-sequencing community to place sequence data on public and freely accessible databases as the sequences are generated. There is nothing to stop others from using those data to do good science.

Do people putting data and analysis freely on the Web prejudice their chances of publication? The journal *Nature* believes that genomics databases, like preprint servers and conferences, represent a form of intracommunity networking from which all researchers benefit. *Nature* does not count them as prior publications. If an exciting result is picked up from such a source by the media, that does not necessarily disqualify a paper from consideration as long as researchers have not preempted peer review or publication by encouraging prior publicity.

However, the problem, from the point of view of those doing the sequencing, occurs when they are continuing their sequencing while others, perhaps better placed to annotate the sequence, are free to use it to publish biologically useful information. What rights of first publication do the sequencers then have? As the discoverers of the sequence, they surely deserve some credit in the subsequent elucidation of function, credit that should extend beyond a simple reference to the database Web site. Yet once someone else has annotated their sequence data, the sequencers' own ambitions in that direction have effectively been preempted. One could argue that those involved in sequencing cannot have both prompt openness and self-protection and that, once the data are publicly available, it is open season.

Others might propose the opposite extreme: that the sequencers have the right to coauthorship on papers that spring directly from their efforts. That seems to amount to an extension of publishing practice in biology to recognize the fact that distinct but interdependent roles—in effect, collaboration—are played by those who produce basic information and those who accomplish interpretation.

Such relationships are already common in the physical sciences; for example, in astronomy the developer of a new detector is sometimes, by agreement, included on initial papers that emerge from the application of that device. In high-energy physics, huge collaborations are necessary, and everyone gets due credit by a listing of the hundreds involved. Although these particular examples may not translate directly to biology, they suggest a way forward.

## DATABASE PROTECTION

### Copyright Protection of Databases

The Supreme Court held by a unanimous vote in *Feist* that to pass the constitutional threshold, copyrightable works must possess "some minimal degree of creativity." (See also "Introduction" and "Expansion of Traditional Intellectual Property during the 1990s" earlier in this chapter.) Feist, a firm that specialized in publishing regional telephone directories, was refused a license to use Rural's directory, which covered a small part of the larger geographic area to be encompassed in Feist's projected directory. Feist went ahead and copied Rural's alphabetically organized listings, and Rural sued for copyright infringement. In producing the directory, the Court held, Rural had expended sufficient efforts to make the directory useful but insufficient creativity to make it original. As far as the opinion reveals, the Court was moved solely by its adherence to a vision of authorship originality. The opinion wears its values on its sleeve; its rhetoric proceeds from unreconstructed faith in the gospel of romantic authorship.

As a matter of information policy, the Court may have been right to cut back on available grounds of legal protection for data compilations. There is a point, legal scholars say, where too many property rights owned by too many parties creates a legal "smog," or an "anticommons."[57] When this situation is reached, rethinking and rebundling of property rights may be necessary.

Observed in this light, *Feist* might be seen in part as an attempt to avoid a "tragedy of the anticommons," an attempt to make sure that the threshold for copyright ownership was not set so low that all sorts of infringement claims would arise, resulting in the underuse of facts and data from public domain sources.

Whether the U.S. Congress should give databases greater legal protection became a controversial issue. The concern of many opponents was that extending copyright protection to compilations that do not reflect original or creative work would lead to inappropriate and intrusive limits on the flow of scientific information or raise the costs of using such information to a level that would impede scientific progress.[58] Later scientists and engineers could not combine data legitimately accessed from one commercial database with data extracted from other databases to make a complex new database for addressing hard problems without obtaining additional licenses and permissions. This remains perhaps the single most critical problem for scientific and technical research, legal scholars say.[59]

## Electronic Journals as Databases

Electronic databases of DNA sequences, protein structures, or galaxy images permeate the Web, but the Web also opens the way to weaving electronic journals and scientific libraries into a single interconnected database. Already a hyperlink can take a subscriber from one article to related articles in the same journal, other journals, and resources such as electronic databases. By offering authors' raw data or the software used in the analysis, some of the journals even allow readers to double-check an author's work.

As journals become increasingly interconnected, researchers will find themselves hyperlinking from one cited or related article to the next, regardless of who the original publisher is. If the browsing is done in a single publisher's database, it could be covered by a single subscription to the database. But if the hyperlinks connect articles or databases of different publishers, then it will result in "buying by the glass rather than the bottle."[60] One can imagine a variety of licensing schemes in which multiple publishers or holdouts might exercise their ownership and place limits on what researchers can do in acquiring and using the hyperlinked journals and databases.

## Cross-Licensing Schemes

But particularly when intellectual products are multicomponent systems, when broad protection on components led to blockages, they were resolved, in some cases, by the development of (sometimes elaborate) cross-licensing schemes. The staggering complexity of the scholarly journal landscape may motivate publishers to attempt to minimize litigation and other transactional costs by voluntarily entering into cross-licensing arrangements that are tantamount to scholarly publishing pools of intellectual properties.

In fact, there are signs that cross-licensing schemes are emerging in scientific publishing to solve some problems. Scientists and publishers increasingly view titles as merely part of hyperlinked content databases made up of constellations of journals. User profit and nonprofit organizations unveiled a scheme in 1999 designed to, in effect, cross-link journal articles through their reference lists, making it easy for researchers to locate and obtain the text of a referenced article through the Internet.[61] The publishers had consulted their legal advisers and concluded that they would not run afoul of antitrust laws, which prohibit collusion between competitors, as long as they do not try to exclude anyone. The lead organizers would work with the International Digital Object Identifier (DOI) Foundation to devise "tags" that can be used to find and track the journal articles. "We are trying to get away from single journals and think more in terms of developing knowledge environments that integrate a number of relevant sources," said Oxford University Press.[62]

## CONCLUSION

In the early 1990s, the potential of electronic networks attracted attention in a variety of national and international forums. These discussions emphasized types of technology that enabled new modes of production for intellectual works that were beyond automation and portended a transformation where authors became far more collaborative and more iterative modes of intellectual production for an electronic environment where more discrete blocks of knowledge existed before.

This chapter has sought to demonstrate how the persistence of the notion of authorship    individual originality—continues today and makes it difficult for any new legal synthesis that would focus on iterative works or collaborative modes of intellectual production. The law continues to prove ungenerous to multiauthor intellectual products, and such works become marginalized or invisible within the prevailing ideological framework of authorship.

Thoughtful action to reshape traditional protection would advance the transformational potential of today's digital technologies and electronic networks. Initiatives in this area are particularly appropriate in intellectual communities in light of the growing urgency of sound policy and the clear benefits to be generated for scientific and technological progress by international collaboration in electronic networks. Will the intellectual property system be likely to address these issues head on? It continues to be frustrating for intellectual workers to realize that the system rarely does that. But still these concerns must be addressed for the early twenty-first century because "the wrong decisions today could lessen the vitality of our research enterprise, weaken the national system of innovation, and compromise our future technological superiority, which all depend on maintaining an appropriate balance between upstream and downstream uses of data and factual information."[63]

## NOTES

1. James J. Duderstadt, "Plenary Address: An Information Highway to the Future," National NET '91 Conference, Washington, D.C. (March 27, 1991).

2. Jenny Lyn Bader, "Forget Footnotes: Hyperlink." *New York Times*, July 16, 2000.

3. Judy Redfearn, "OECD to Set Up Global Facility on Biodiversity," *Science* 285:5424 (July 2, 1999): 22–23.

4. David E. Rosenbaum, "Database Legislation Spurs Fierce Lobbying," *New York Times,* June 5, 2000, A14.

5. 111 S.Ct. 1282 (1991).

6. J. H. Reichman and Paul F. Uhlir, "Database Protection at the Crossroads: Recent Developments and Their Impact on Science and Technology," *Berkeley Technology Law Journal* 14 (1999): 837.

7. Peter Jaszi, "Toward a Theory of Copyright: The Metamorphoses of 'Authorship,'" *Duke Law Journal* 2 (1991): 455–502; Peter Jaszi, "On the Author Effect: Contemporary Copyright and Collective Creativity," in *The Construction of Authorship,* ed. Martha Woodmansee and Peter Jaszi (Durham, N.C.: Duke University Press, 1994), 29–56.

8. Keith Aoki, "Neocolonialism, Anticommons Property, and Biopiracy in the (Not-So-Brave) New World Order of International Intellectual Property Protection," *Indiana Journal of Global Legal Studies* 6 (1998): nn. 84–86, <http://www.law.indiana.edu/glsj/vol6/no1/aoki.html>.

9. Nicholas Wade, "Background Paper," in *The Science Business: Twentieth Century Fund Report on the Commercialization of Scientific Research* (New York: Priority Press, 1984), 30–31.

10. Carole Ganz-Brown, "Patent Policies to Fine Tune Commercialization of Government-Sponsored University Research," *Science and Public Policy* 26:6 (December 1999): 403–14.

11. John Barton, "Reforming the Patent System," *Science* 287:5460 (March 17, 2000): 1933–34.

12. 1980 Computer Service Copyright Act, enacted December 12, 1980, PL 96-517. See also Ann Branscombe, *Who Owns Information* (New York: Basic Books, 1994), 142.

13. 797 F.2d 1222 (3d Cir. 1986).

14. Seth Shulman, "Software Patents Tangle the Web," *Technology Review* 103:2 (March/April 2000): 68–79, <http://www.technologyreview.com/magazine/mar00/shulman.asp>.

15. Julie E. Cohen and Mark A. Lemley, "Patent Scope and Innovation in the Software Industry," *California Law Review* 89 (January 2001): 1–58, <http://papers.ssrn.com/paper.taf?ABSTRACT ID=209668>; 149 F.3d 1368 (Fed. Cir. 1998).

16. Final Act Embodying the Results of the Uruguay Round of the Multilateral Negotiations, April 15, 1994, Annex 1C, Legal Instruments—Results of the Uruguay Round, vol. 31; 33 I.L.M. 81 (1994), <http://www.wto.org/wto/intellec/1-ipcon.htm>.

17. Directive 96/9/EC of the European Parliament and of the Council, March 11, 1996, <http://www2.echo.lu/legal/en/ipr/database/database.html>.

18. WIPO Diplomatic Conference on Certain Copyright and Neighboring Rights Questions, Geneva, December 2–20, 1996, <http://www.uspto.gov/web/offices/dcom/olia/diplconf/>.

19. James Boyle, *Shamans, Software, and Spleens: Law and the Construction of the Information Society* (Cambridge, Mass.: Harvard University Press, 1996), x–xi.

20. Robert Mazzoleni and Richard R. Nelson, "The Benefits and Costs of Strong Patent Protection: A Contribution to the Current Debate," *Research Policy* 27 (1998): 273–84.

21. Gary Taubes, "Computational Molecular Biology: Software Matchmakers Help Make Sense of Sequences," *Science* 273:5375 (August 2, 1996): 588–90.

22. Aris Persidis, "Bioinformatics," *Nature Biotechnology* 17:8 (August 1999): 828–30.

23. Sylvia J. Spengler, "Bioinformatics in the Information Age," *Science* 287:5456 (February 18, 2000): 1221–23.

24. John Barton, "Reforming the Patent System," *Science* 287:5460 (March 17, 2000): 1933–34.

25. U.S. Patent 5,933819, August 3, 1999.

26. 383 U.S. 519 (1966).

27. Fed. Cases 342, No. 4901 (C.C.D. Mass. 1841).

28. 62 U.S.L.W. 4169.

29. Carole Ganz-Brown, "Electronic Information Markets: An Idea Whose Time Has Come," *Journal of World Intellectual Property* 1:3 (May 1998): 465–93.

30. *Westinghouse v. Boyden Power-Brade Co.,* 170 U.S. 537, 562 (1898).

31. Pamela Samuelson, "Encoding the Law into Digital Libraries," *Communications of the ACM* 41:4 (1998): 13–18.

32. The case *A&M Records Inc. v. Napster Inc.,* 99-5183, is being considered in tandem with a similar suit filed by a group of music composers, *Leiber v. Napster,* 00-0074; <http://thomas.loc.gov/cgi-bin/query/z?c105:H.R.2281.ENR> has the full text of the Digital Millennium Copyright Act (DMCA) H.R. 2281; Scott Carlson, "Metallica Sues Universities and Napster, Charging That Students Engage in Music Piracy" *Chronicle of Higher Education,* April 28, 2000, A50.

33. Shane Ham and Robert D. Atkinson, *Napster and Online Piracy: The Need to Revisit the Digital Millennium Copyright Act* (Washington, D.C.: Progressive Policy Institute, 2000), 1–2, <http://www.dlcppi.org/texts/tech/napster1.htm>.

34. P.L. 105-304; Jeri Clausing, "Report Proposes Update of Copyright Act," *New York Times,* May 22, 2000, C-6.

35. Roger Parloff, "Newbies vs. Netwits," *Law.com,* September 12, 2000, <http://www.law.com/>.

36. *MPAA v. 2600* (S.D.N.Y., August 8, 2000).

37. Opinion, <http://eon.law.harvard.edu/openlaw/DVD/NY/opinion.pdf>; final judgment, <http://eon.law.harvard.edu/openlaw/DVD/NY/finaljudgment.pdf>.

38 Jane C. Ginsburg, "International Copyright: From a 'Bundle' of National Copyright Laws to a Supranational Code?," *Journal of the Copyright Society of the USA* 47 (2000): 265–91.

39. Jenny Lyn Bader, "Forget Footnotes, Hyperlink," *New York Times,* July 16, 2000, Week in Review Desk.

40. Martin H. Sampson, "Hyperlink at Your Own Risk," *Law Journal Extra,* June 24, 1997, Outside Counsel, <http://www.phillipsnizer.com/artnew18.htm>.

41. *eBay Inc. v. Bidder's Edge Inc.* (N.D. Calif., No. 0-99 21200, filed 12/10/99).

42. Brenda Sandburg, "Judge Halts E-Bay's Unwanted Hits," *law.com California,* May 26, 2000, <http://www.callaw.com/opinions/stories/edt0526b.html>.

43. *UMF Recordings Inc. v. MP3.com Inc.* (S.D.N.Y., No. 00-0472).

44. Lessley Anderson, "Judge Explains His Ruling against MP3," *Industry Standard,* May 4, 2000, 07:45 PM PST, <http://www.thestandard.com/article/display/0,1151,14807,00.html>.

45. Michael Learmonth, "The Price of Digital Music," *Industry Standard,* June 12, 2000, <http://www.thestandard.com/article/display/0,1151,15920,00.html>.

46. Alec Foege, "Record Labels Are Hearing an Angry Song," *New York Times,* June 11, 2000.

47. Steven Bachrach, R. Stephen Berry, Martin Blume, Thomas von Foerster, Alexander Fowler, Paul Ginsparg, Stephen Heller, Neil Kestner, Andrew Odlyzko, Ann Okerson, Ron Wigington, and Anne Moffat, "Who Should Own Scientific Papers?" *Science* 281:5383 (September 4, 1998): 1459–60.

48. The patent system has no work-for-hire doctrine. However, in the United States by the 1930s, the patent system initiated in 1790 was under attack on the grounds that its original purpose had been rendered obsolete: Corporate enterprise had undoubtedly displaced the solo inventor as the primary performer of inventive activity. Industrial organizations obviously had not eliminated originality, however, but simply transferred it from the individual scientist, now largely an employable factor in research and development to the corporation.

49. 490 U.S. 730 (1989).

50. 751 F. Supp. 474 (S.D.N.Y. 1990).

51. Dan Carnevale and Jeffrey R. Young, "Who Owns On-Line Courses?: Colleges and Professors Start to Sort It Out," *Chronicle of Higher Education,* December 17, 1999, A45, Information Technology Section.

52. Scott Carlson, "When Professors Create Software, Do They Own It, or Do Their Colleges," *Chronicle of Higher Education,* July 21, 2000, A29, Information Technology Section.

53. 945 F.2d 500 (1991).

54. 147 F.3d 195 (2d Cir. 1998).

55. Faye Buckalew, "Joint Authorship in the Second Circuit," *Brooklyn Law Review* 64 (Summer 1998): n. 217.

56. Nature Opinion, "Debates over Credit for the Annotation of Genomes," *Nature* 405:6788 (June 15, 2000): 719.

57. Michael A. Heller and Rebecca S. Eisenberg, "Can Patents Deter Innovation?: The Anticommons in Biomedical Research," *Science* 280:5364 (May 1, 1998): 698–701.

58. William Gardner and Joseph Rosenbaum, "Database Protection and Access to Information," *Science* 286:5445 (November 26, 1999): 1658.

59. Reichman and Uhlir, "Database Protection," 808.

60. Gary Taubes, "Science Journals Go Wired," *Science* 271:5250 (February 9, 1996): 764.

61. Eliot Marshall, "Journals Launch Private Reference Network," *Science* 286:5444 (November 19, 1999): 1459.

62. "The Writing Is on the Web for Science Journals in Print," *Nature* 397:6716 (January 21, 1999): 195–200.

63. Reichman and Uhlir, "Database Protection," 808.

# Contributors

**Edward L. Ayers** is the Hugh P. Kelly Professor of History at the University of Virginia. His publications include *The Promise of the New South: Life after Reconstruction* (1992), which was a finalist for both the National Book Award and the Pulitzer Prize, and the coedited *Oxford Book of the American South* (1997). His most recent publication, *The Valley of the Shadow: Two Communities in the American Civil War—The Coming of War* (2000), includes a set of three CD-ROMs and a related World Wide Web site, <http://valley. vcdh.virginia.edu>.

**William Sims Bainbridge** is the senior science advisor of the Directorate for Social, Behavioral, and Economic Sciences at the National Science Foundation in Arlington, Virginia. He is the author of fourteen books, including *Social Research Methods and Statistics* (1992) and *Survey Research: A Computer-Assisted Introduction* (1989) and more than a hundred articles in the sociology of religion, space flight, and computing. He was president of the Social Science Computing Association in 1994.

**Randy Bass** is the executive director of Georgetown University's Center for New Designs in Learning and Scholarship (CNDLS) and the director of the American Studies Crossroads Project, an international project on technology and education sponsored by the American Studies Association. In conjunction with the Crossroads Project, he serves as the supervising editor of *Engines of Inquiry: A Practical Guide for Using Technology to Teach American Studies* and is the executive producer of the companion video, *Engines of Inquiry: A Video Tour of Learning and Technology in American Culture Studies.*

**Orville Vernon Burton** is a professor of history and sociology at the University of Illinois at Urbana-Champaign, where he is a University Distinguished Teacher/Scholar. He also heads the initiative for humanities and social sciences at the National Center for Supercomputing Applications. He was selected nationwide as the 1999 U.S. Research and Doctoral University Professor of the Year (presented by the Carnegie Foundation for the Advancement of Teaching and by the Council for Advancement and Support of Education). He was a Pew National Fellow Carnegie Scholar for 2000–2001. He is the author of *In My Father's Home Are Many Mansions: Family and Community in Edgefield, South Carolina* (1985) and other books. He was an early member of the Social Science Computing Association.

**William Evans** is an associate professor in the department of communication at Georgia State University, where he also serves as the director of the Digital Arts and Entertainment Laboratory. He is the coeditor of *Communication and Culture: Language, Performance, Technology, and Media* (1990) and has published numerous articles in such journals as *Journalism and Mass Communication Quarterly, Critical Studies in Mass Communication, Social Science Computer Review,* and *Skeptical Inquirer.* His research interests include computer-supported content analysis, new media, and science and health communication.

**Carole Ganz-Brown** is a senior international analyst at the National Science Foundation in Arlington, Virginia, where she is responsible for electronic network systems and for intellectual property rights policy analysis associated with Internet management and related electronic information and data. In addition to an undergraduate degree in chemistry, a graduate degree in computer and information science, and a doctorate in logic and the philosophy of science, she earned a law degree and is a member of the New York Bar as well as registered to practice before the U.S. Patent and Trademark Office. Her articles have appeared in a number of publications, including most recently the *IEEE Transactions on Information Technology in Biomedicine.*

**Cheris Kramarae** is a visiting professor at the Center for the Study of Women in Society at the University of Oregon, where she is editing the *Routledge International Encyclopedia of Women.* She was previously affiliated with the University of Illinois at Urbana-Champaign, where she was Jubilee Professor of Liberal Arts and Science and a professor of speech communication, sociology, linguistics, and women's studies, and has held visiting appointments at universities in England, France, Germany, the Netherlands, South

Africa, and India. She is the author, editor, or coeditor of ten books and many articles on women and language, language and power, critiques of information technology, and feminist scholarship.

**Daniel J. Myers** is assistant professor of sociology at the University of Notre Dame and faculty fellow of the Joan B. Kroc Institute for International Peace Studies. His research includes studies published in the *American Sociological Review*, the *American Journal of Sociology*, and the *Journal of Conflict Resolution* dealing with collective violence, formal models of collective action, game theory, the diffusion of social phenomena, and media coverage of protest and violence. His book *Toward a More Perfect Union: The Governance of Metropolitan America* (with Ralph W. Conant) reassessing urban development and planning in the United States over the past fifty years is scheduled for publication in 2002.

**Wendy Plotkin** is the project coordinator for "In the Vicinity of Hull-House and the Maxwell Street Market: Chicago, 1889–1935," a historical project of the University of Illinois at Chicago that will mount a major Web site consisting of more than 3,000 period photographs, 200 text documents, contemporary maps and postcards, and interpretive essays. She is the cofounder of H-Net and its first discussion list, H-Urban, and has published reviews of electronic editions and books about the Internet in the *Journal of American History*, the *Journal of the American Planning Association*, and *Public History*. Her doctoral dissertation, "Deeds of Mistrust: Race, Housing, and Restrictive Covenants in Chicago, 1900–1953," is being revised for publication.

**Roy Rosenzweig** is College of Arts and Sciences Distinguished Professor of History at George Mason University, where he also directs the Center for History and New Media. He is the author or coauthor of a number of print and digital publications, including *"Who Built America?"* (2000) and the accompanying CD-ROM covering the years 1914–46.

**H. Jeanie Taylor** is the director of the Office for University Women at the University of Minnesota. She previously served as the deputy director of the Center for Advanced Study at the University of Illinois at Urbana-Champaign, where she and Cheris Kramarae facilitated the Women, Information Technology, and Scholarship (WITS) working colloquium from 1991 to 1995 and coedited, with Maureen Eben, *Women, Information Technology, and Scholarship* (1993). Her current scholarly work looks at the everyday practice of life stories in the context of the interdisciplinary scholarly community at the Bunting Institute, Radcliffe College.

# Index

The University of Illinois Press
is a founding member of the
Association of American University Presses.

———————————————————————

Composed in 10.5/13 Minion
with Citizen display
by Celia Shapland
for the University of Illinois Press
Manufactured by Thomson-Shore, Inc.

University of Illinois Press
1325 South Oak Street
Champaign, IL 61820-6903
www.press.uillinois.edu